OPEN LOOK™
GRAPHICAL USER INTERFACE
FUNCTIONAL SPECIFICATION

Sun Microsystems, Inc.

Addison-Wesley Publishing Company, Inc.
Reading, Massachusetts ▪ Menlo Park, California ▪ New York
Don Mills, Ontario ▪ Wokingham, England ▪ Amsterdam
Bonn ▪ Sydney ▪ Singapore ▪ Tokyo ▪ Madrid ▪ San Juan

The OPEN LOOK Graphical User Interface was developed by Sun Microsystems, Inc. for its users and licensees. Sun acknowledges the pioneering efforts of Xerox in researching and developing the concept of visual or graphical user interfaces for the computer industry. Sun holds a nonexclusive license from Xerox to the Xerox Graphical User Interface, which license also covers Sun's licensees.

UNIX is a registered trademark of AT&T.
OPEN LOOK is a trademark of AT&T.
The Sun logo is a registered trademark of Sun Microsystems, Inc.
Sun—4 is a trademark of Sun Microsystems, Inc.
Patent pending.

Library of Congress Cataloging-in-Publication Data
OPEN LOOK graphical user interface functional specification/Sun Microsystems, Inc.
     p.   cm.
   ISBN 0-201-52365-5
    1. User interfaces (Computer systems) 2. Windows (Computer programs) 3. OPEN LOOK (Computer program) I. Sun Microsystems.
   QA76.9.U83064 1989
   005.4'3—dc20   89-38189
                CIP

Sponsoring Editor: Carole McClendon
Cover Design: Hannus Design Associates
Text Design: Joyce C. Weston
Set in 11-point Helvetica Light by Inprint, Inc.

CDEFGHIJ-MU-943210
Third Printing, July 1990

CONTENTS

Part II   Design Elements   33

Part III   Required OPEN LOOK UI Functionality   219

ACKNOWLEDGMENTS

The OPEN LOOK UI was developed by Sun Microsystems in partnership with AT&T. It is based on the pioneering work done on graphical user interfaces at Xerox PARC in the 1970s.

The "simple, consistent, and efficient" paradigm and many of the visual and functional designs for the OPEN LOOK UI are based on the work of Norm Cox and Alan Mandler, members of the OPEN LOOK UI design team headed by Tony Hoeber at Sun.

Janice Winsor wrote and illustrated the *OPEN LOOK Graphical User Interface Functional Specification.* Norm Cox provided the three-dimensional design illustrations in Chapter 9 and wrote and illustrated the information in Appendix B.

Many people at Sun, AT&T, Xerox, and elsewhere contributed over a two-year period to the design, review, implementation, testing, and refinement of the OPEN LOOK UI. Special thanks to Leif Samuelsson for extensive prototyping work and design contributions, to Bev Harrison for administrative support, and to all those who took part in the open industry review process for their suggestions and contributions to the final design.

Sun would particularly like to acknowledge the following people for their contributions:

From AT&T, Don Alecci, Bruce Barnett, Jim Cunningham, Betty Dall, Lee Davenport, George Derby, Jim Farber, Scott Hansen, Ross Hilbert, Steve Humphrey, John M. Jones, Ruth Klein, Sivan Mahadevan, Don McGovern, Marcel Meth, Carol Nelson, Marcia Paisner, Bill Sherman, Sarah Siegel, Valerie Mitchell-Stevens, Rich Smolucha, Don Ursem, and Mike Zanchelli.

From Sun, Lin Brown, Peter Choy, Ralph Derrickson, Pam Deziel, Tony Hoeber, Bill Joy, Jon Kannegaard, Rick Levenson, Karen Lusardi, Greg McLaughlin, Richard Probst, Scott Ritchie, Jeff Rulifson, Leif Samuelsson, Evelyn Spire, Ian Wallis, Janice Winsor, Dianna Yee, and Geri Younggren.

From Xerox, Dave Curbow, David Goldberg, Janie Phillips, and Paulien Strijland.

From Addison-Wesley, Carole McClendon, Joanne Clapp, Steve Stansel, Diane Freed, and Rachel Guichard.

From Inprint, Ed Rose.

ABOUT THIS BOOK

What is the OPEN LOOK User Interface?

The OPEN LOOK™ User Interface (UI) uses windows and menus with common graphic symbols instead of typed system commands to provide an intuitive environment.

With the OPEN LOOK UI, users are presented with a consistent screen layout that can be used across various platforms and operating systems. This common look and feel benefits end users, application programmers, and software vendors.

The OPEN LOOK UI is not a piece of software. Rather, it is a specification for a user interface that builds on the foundation of graphical user interface design pioneered by the Xerox Corporation.

While it is possible for the application developer to implement the OPEN LOOK UI "from scratch," the usual implementation approach is to use a *toolkit* that has been written for a specific windowing platform. The toolkit provides a set of routines that implement the various interface elements as specified in this book. The application developer, in turn, uses the routines provided by the toolkit to create and position the interface elements as needed.

Audience

The primary audience for this book is the potential developer of a toolkit that implements the OPEN LOOK UI.

Another major audience is the application developer who is interested in either porting an existing application to or developing a new application for the OPEN LOOK UI. A related book, the *OPEN LOOK Graphical User Interface Application Style Guidelines,* is addressed more specifically to the application developer.

By providing guidelines for using the elements of the OPEN LOOK UI, this book promotes consistency across applications.

A third audience for this book is the nontechnical reader who is interested in the general design of the interface. Although the primary focus of this book is the detailed functional description necessary for toolkit and application development, it is important to remember that this functionality must make sense from the perspective of the user. To maintain this focus and emphasize its importance, the functional elements are described from the point of view of how you, as a user, communicate with the OPEN LOOK UI.

Trademark Licensing

The name "OPEN LOOK" is a trademark of AT&T. The right to use the OPEN LOOK trademark is subject to a certification procedure. To encourage consistent OPEN LOOK UI implementation across a wide variety of hardware platforms and operating systems, AT&T offers OPEN LOOK trademark licensing for three levels of certification:

☐ Level 1 is a complete user interface, containing all the essential features. This is the minimum features set required for a toolkit to be certified as level 1 compliant. The requirements for Level 1 certification are documented in *The OPEN LOOK Graphical User Interface Trademark Guide,* which is available from AT&T.

☐ Level 2 is a superset of Level 1. It is anticipated that this level will be the most common level of compliance. The complete set of Level 2 features must be provided for an implementation to be certified as Level 2 compliant.

☐ Level 3 is a superset of Level 2. This level is provided for more specialized features and to provide a mechanism for extending the functionality of the OPEN LOOK UI.

See Appendix A, "Certification," for a detailed list of elements required for each level of certification.

This book presents the technical specifications for the OPEN LOOK UI.

How This Book is Organized

Part I, Introduction

This part of the book addresses the nontechnical audience and contains two chapters that provide an introduction and an overview to the OPEN LOOK UI.

Chapter 1, Design Philosophy: The philosophy behind OPEN LOOK UI design decisions.

Chapter 2, Overview: A brief overview of the OPEN LOOK UI, describing the basic elements and how they work.

Part II, Design Elements

This part of the book begins the technical specification and describes the basic elements of the user interface and how they function.

Chapter 3, Workspace, Icons, and Windows: The elements of the workspace, windows, and icons; the types of windows in an OPEN LOOK UI implementation; and the required and optional elements of those windows.

Chapter 4, Controls: Detailed information about each of the controls and how to use them.

Chapter 5, Control Areas: Detailed information about control area layouts.

Chapter 6, Menu Elements: The elements of menus.

Chapter 7, Scrolling: Scrollbars and ways of scrolling without using scrollbars.

Chapter 8, Scrolling Lists: Basic, editable, and multi-level scrolling lists.

Chapter 9, Color and Three-Dimensional Design: Guidelines and specifications for an OPEN LOOK UI implementation on a color display and for a three-dimensional implementation.

Part III, Required OPEN LOOK UI Functionality

This part of the book describes the required menus and workspace properties, the File Manager, the Process Manager, and mouse and keyboard functionality.

Chapter 10, Required OPEN LOOK UI Menus: The menus that an OPEN LOOK UI implementation must provide: Workspace, Window, Pop-up Window, Property Window Settings, Scrollbar, and Edit for text fields.

Chapter 11, Workspace Properties: The default global settings provided in the Workspace Properties window.

Chapter 12, File Manager: The required elements of the OPEN LOOK file management application.

Chapter 13, Process Manager: The required elements of the OPEN LOOK process management application.

Chapter 14, Keyboard and Mouse Specifications: How mouse buttons are used and keyboard operations.

Part IV, Using the OPEN LOOK UI

This part of the book describes how you use the OPEN LOOK UI.

Chapter 15, Using Menus: How you view and choose from menus.

Chapter 16, Selecting and Operating on Windows, Icons, and Panes: How you select and operate on single and multiple windows, icons, and panes.

Chapter 17, Selecting and Operating on Text and Graphics: How you select and operate on text and graphics.

Chapter 18, Using Property Windows: How to apply settings with property windows.

Appendices

This book has four appendices, as described in the following paragraphs.

Appendix A, Certification: Three levels of certification for the OPEN LOOK UI.

Appendix B, Details of Design Elements: Bitmap renditions for pointers, carets, icons, workspace and menu drop shadow patterns in pixels. Engineering drawings for the visual elements of an OPEN LOOK UI implementation specified in points and inches. Tolerances are provided to allow for variation in pixel and display size.

Appendix C, OPEN LOOK UI Help Text: Help text for the basic required OPEN LOOK UI elements.

Appendix D, International Considerations for the OPEN LOOK User Interface: Issues to consider when designing an international implementation of the OPEN LOOK UI.

Glossary: An alphabetical list of terms used in this book with definitions.

Conventions Used in This Book

The following conventions are used in this book:

☐ Terms introduced for the first time are in *italic type* and are defined in the Glossary.
☐ Mouse buttons are referred to by function, not by location on the mouse. For example, "click SELECT" is used, not "click LEFT."
☐ The names of mouse buttons are capitalized. For example, "press SELECT."
☐ Keyboard keys have an initial capital letter. For example, "to validate a text field, press the Tab key."
☐ To perform certain functions, you hold down one key while you press a second key or mouse button. This combination of keystrokes is shown in the following way: "Press Ctrl/MENU."
☐ Keyboard functions are also referred to by function, not by the location or name of a specific key on the keyboard. For example, SELECTCHAR is used to define the function of selecting a single character by pressing both a modifier key and the SELECT mouse button at the same time.
☐ The term "OPEN LOOK UI implementation" refers to toolkits and applications that have been developed to meet this functional specification.

Device Independence

One of the most innovative aspects of the OPEN LOOK UI is that it is the first graphical user interface designed to run on a wide variety of machines. As an open industry standard, the OPEN LOOK UI must accommodate displays of different sizes and resolutions; monochrome, grayscale, and color; and different keyboards and pointing devices.

Consequently, the OPEN LOOK UI is specified in terms of units that are independent of any particular device. The unit used in this specification is the *point*—the basic unit of typographical measurement—equal to approximately 1/72 of an inch (0.352 millimeters). Refer to Appendix B for detailed specifications of each element.

When units refer to the screen display itself, the unit used in this specification is the pixel, an abbreviation for picture element.

International Considerations

The OPEN LOOK UI does not provide specifications for international markets. Instead, Appendix D provides a discussion of issues that should be considered in the process of designing a toolkit that can be used in a multinational market.

This book describes the user interface as localized for an American English audience, and therefore reflects that bias in the following ways:

☐ The orientation of text is from left to right and top to bottom.
☐ Capitalization styles are recommended based on English usage.
☐ Customary American spelling is used.
☐ A sans serif variable width font is specified for the required elements of the user interface.
☐ Some icons and glyphs may be inappropriate for other languages and locations.

Style Guidelines

The examples in this book show some of the ways elements can be used and combined. The OPEN LOOK UI offers the application developer a great deal of flexibility in deciding how the controls are displayed and grouped together. The examples in this book are for purposes of illustration only and are not intended to be guidelines for an OPEN LOOK UI implementation or to contain exact specifications of design elements. Always refer to the detailed specifications in Appendix B for exact details about design elements. The examples used in this book do not represent existing application implementations.

When appropriate, this specification includes some guideline information. For example, guidelines for implementing color and designing icons are included. When guidelines are included, they are specifically identified, so you can easily distinguish between required elements of an OPEN LOOK UI implementation and suggested information.

See the *OPEN LOOK Graphical User Interface Application Style Guidelines* for more information about guidelines on developing applications for the OPEN LOOK UI.

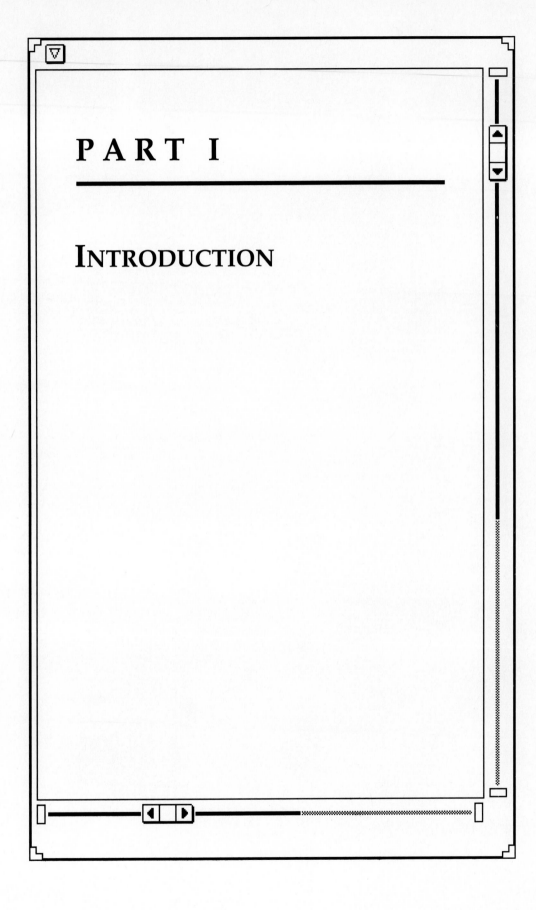

P A R T I

INTRODUCTION

1

DESIGN PHILOSOPHY

This chapter provides an overview of the design philosophy for the OPEN LOOK User Interface.

Basic Design Principles

The intention of the design is to balance the three goals of simplicity, consistency, and efficiency.

☐ When you perform a new task and have no previous model from which to draw experience, the task must be simple to perform. This makes the interface easy to learn and master.

☐ When you perform a new task but have done something similar in the past, the task must be consistent with past experience. In this way, you can transfer learning from old tasks to new.

☐ When you perform a familiar task, the interface must be efficient. Once you have mastered a task, you will want to perform it with minimal effort—the fewest keystrokes and the shortest movements of the mouse pointer.

Table 1-1 shows the goals of the OPEN LOOK UI project and the approach taken to meet them.

Table 1-1   OPEN LOOK UI design goals

Goal	Approach	Benefit
Easy to learn	Base the interface on a small number of simple concepts.	The system is easy to learn initially, and users can get work done right away.
Easy to learn new applications for experienced user	Provide a consistent interface. For example, both the window manager and applications work the same way.	The user can leverage knowledge and learn new applications.
Efficient for experts	Minimize keystrokes and mouse travel.	Increased productivity.
Distinctive user interface	Design a visually uncluttered and consistent look.	The OPEN LOOK UI becomes a signature that people recognize.
Easy migration for other interface users	Harmonize with other user interfaces.	Users can move easily among the major user interfaces with minimal retraining.

The OPEN LOOK UI takes advantage of current bitmap workstation design and operates efficiently in a multi-tasking operating system environment. You can begin an operation in one window and continue working in another without needing to learn the concept of "background processing."

The device independence of the OPEN LOOK UI means that applications developed using the interface will adapt well to new technology as it is developed.

The OPEN LOOK UI design builds on familiar concepts pioneered by Xerox Corporation. Because of the attention paid to functional consistency among user interface designs, you can easily switch between systems without needing to refocus attention on how the interface works.

Visual Style

The visual design of OPEN LOOK UI elements is restrained. The design of each element is clean and simple. It provides a consistent environment that acts as the background against which the application's information is featured. When the interface is uncluttered, the application becomes the center of focus and attention.

The OPEN LOOK UI is based on a standard set of elements. Each element—for example, a font, a button, a symbol, or a menu—is designed with a focus on how it fits into the whole. Borders are used to define different areas of the screen, such as a window, a menu, or a pane. Controls are arranged in groups within these borders.

There are two visual designs for the OPEN LOOK UI:

□ A black-and-white design for use on monochrome displays.
□ A three-dimensional design for use on grayscale and color displays.

Fonts

A sans serif, variable width font is used for the common elements of the OPEN LOOK UI. Consistent use of the same font in all the elements of the interface contributes to the design concept of the interface as a backdrop against which the application is featured. Of course, an application can use whatever fonts the developer chooses in the part of the window that is reserved for the display of application information.

Color

An OPEN LOOK UI implementation can be used on monochrome or color displays. A color implementation can use either black-and-white or three-dimensional design elements. When a color implementation uses black-and-white design elements, the borders are usually black, and color is added to the window background. On systems with a limited number of highly saturated colors, the borders may be in color.

A color implementation provides different sets of colors, called *palettes,* you can use to set colors for various workspace and window elements. The OPEN LOOK UI also provides a way for the application to control the color of its window background independently. There are no restrictions on the way an application can use color in the area of the window controlled exclusively by the application. See Chapter 9 for more information.

International Considerations

The OPEN LOOK UI encourages the development of internationalized implementations and applications to permit localization to specific markets. Issues that should be considered when designing a toolkit for a multinational market are discussed in Appendix D.

Providing a toolkit that supports application development for international or multinational markets requires development work at three levels:

☐ The platform
☐ The programmatic interface
☐ The user interface

The platform is the lowest level. For example, the hardware and operating system determine the character encoding, the interchange protocol, and what characters are permitted for file names. This specification does not define international considerations at this level.

When the programmatic interface level provides the appropriate tools, an application developer can use them to develop an application for multi-national markets. The programmatic interface level must provide the capability for elements such as text, sorting sequence, units, and dates to be *localized,* that is, to meet the unique needs of specific languages and cultures.

The user interface level is closely related to the programmatic interface level, but concerns the specific elements of the OPEN LOOK UI. For example, the direction of text display might require the vertical display of window headers and menus. Icons, glyphs, and color should also be appropriate to the local environment.

2

OVERVIEW

This chapter provides an overview of the OPEN LOOK User Interface by describing how you, a user, interact with an OPEN LOOK UI implementation.

The OPEN LOOK UI contains a rich set of features and capabilities designed to support a wide range of applications, from the simplest utility to the most powerful integrated application. This chapter introduces the basic elements and how they work; it does not attempt to offer a complete description of the interface.

Keep in mind that documenting the appearance and functionality of a graphical user interface is quite different from using it. For example, it may be tedious to describe precisely and completely what happens when you choose an item from a menu. But in practice, it is simple—you just press a mouse button, point at the item you want, and then release the mouse button.

When you first see the OPEN LOOK UI on a computer display, you need to know only the most basic information about how to use the buttons on the mouse to start using it.

The information in this chapter is presented in the following way:

☐ An introduction to the window environment: the work surface *(workspace)* and the pointing device *(mouse),* how you set the insert point where you type input, the Workspace menu, and the File Manager
☐ How application windows and the Window menu look
☐ The kinds of controls you can expect to see in control areas of application windows
☐ How to move through data using OPEN LOOK UI scrollbars
☐ What menus look like and how to use them
☐ The kinds of application windows that pop up to perform transitory functions
☐ How you select and operate on windows and icons
☐ How you select and operate on text and graphics

The Workspace

In the OPEN LOOK UI window environment, the background screen area on which objects such as *windows, icons,* and *menus* are displayed is called the *workspace.* You use the mouse pointer to control these objects and choose your activities. Figure 2-1 shows an example of a workspace.

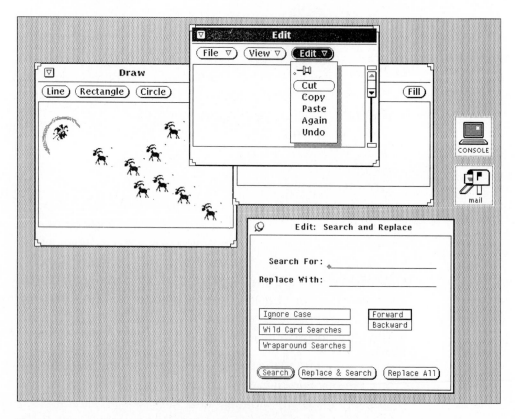

Figure 2-1   A sample workspace in an OPEN LOOK UI implementation.

Windows like Draw and Edit in Figure 2-1 represent graphics and text-editing applications that use the OPEN LOOK UI. Application graphics or text are displayed in *panes* within the window borders and are controlled with a clearly labeled set of *buttons* that describe the function or label the category of choices grouped on the *button menu.*

Icons (the two small squares on the right side of Figure 2-1) are small pictorial representations of application windows. Changing a window to its iconic representation, or closing it, keeps the application out of the way but readily available.

Application windows that pop up to perform transitory functions can be kept on the screen for repeated use by "pinning" them to the workspace with a *pushpin.* The Edit: Search and Replace window in Figure 2-1 is an example of such a *pop-up window* that is pinned to the workspace.

Menus are available both under *menu buttons* in the *control area* and as *pop-up menus* that pop up at the pointer location. Menus can also have pushpins. The Edit menu in Figure 2-1 is an example of a button menu in a control area. It has a pushpin, but the menu is not pinned to the workspace.

Windows and icons can overlap or overlay one another on the workspace. You control the work area of the workspace by opening, moving, resizing, and closing or dismissing the windows of the applications you use.

The OPEN LOOK UI specifies a basic set of standard menus that you use to control windows and icons. In addition, each application window has its own control areas, menus, and pop-up windows that allow you to control the functionality of the application.

Pointers

You access most functions using a pointing device to move the pointer to a specific place on the screen and using the pointing device to perform an action. The mouse is the pointing device described in this book.

The *pointer*—usually an arrow pointing toward the upper left corner of the screen—always shows the location of the mouse on the workspace. An OPEN LOOK UI implementation has standard pointer shapes for specific functions such as copy and move. Each pointer has a *hot spot,* which indicates the active place on the screen. The tip of the arrow is the hot spot. Applications may provide additional pointer shapes.

Using the Mouse Buttons

You control objects on the workspace and in windows by moving the pointer around on the screen and pressing and releasing different mouse buttons. When you want to type text in a window, you move the pointer to the window and click a mouse button to set the place where characters are displayed. This way of directing where you work is called *click-to-type*. A Level 2 implementation has an option that lets you choose where you work by moving the pointer into the window.

This book uses the following terms to describe actions performed with the mouse:

☐ *Press* a mouse button and hold it.
☐ *Release* a mouse button to initiate the action.
☐ *Click* a mouse button by pressing and releasing it before you move the pointer.
☐ *Double-click* a mouse button by clicking twice quickly without moving the pointer.
☐ *Move* the pointer by sliding the mouse with no buttons pressed.
☐ *Drag* the pointer by sliding the mouse with one or more buttons pressed.

An OPEN LOOK UI implementation is designed to be used with a pointing device. The mouse is the most common pointing device. Mouse buttons have three basic functions:

☐ SELECT to select objects or manipulate controls
☐ ADJUST to extend or reduce the number of selected objects
☐ MENU to display and choose from menus

Systems with one- or two-button mice access the three basic mouse functions by using a key from the keyboard in conjunction with one of the mouse buttons, for example, Shift/SELECT. This book refers to mouse buttons by function, not by the location of the button on the mouse.

Figure 2-2 shows the mouse button assignments for one-, two-, and three-button mice. An OPEN LOOK UI implementation allows you to change the mouse button assignments and set other global properties.

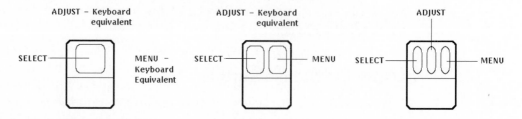

Figure 2-2   Default mouse button function assignments.

Pointer Jumping

Most of the time, you move the pointer with the mouse. However, sometimes an OPEN LOOK UI implementation moves the pointer for you and jumps directly to a specific place on the screen. This is called *pointer jumping*.

For example, when you press the HELP key to display a Help window, the pointer jumps to the pushpin in the header of the Help window so that you can simply click the SELECT mouse button to dismiss the window. The pointer jumps back again when the window is dismissed from the screen.

You can turn off all pointer jumping from the Workspace Properties window.

Workspace Menu

The workspace has a default pop-up menu that you access by pressing the MENU mouse button anywhere on the workspace. The Workspace menu, shown in Figure 2-3, is what you use to start up new applications and set global properties such as window color and the location of mouse button functions.

Figure 2-3   Workspace menu.

Pushpins

Pushpins are used on some menus and all command, property, and help pop-up windows. When a menu or a window has a pushpin, you can pin the menu or window to the screen to keep it available for repeated use.

When you click on an unpinned pushpin, it pops into the hole and the menu or window stays on the screen until you dismiss it by clicking on the pinned pushpin. The pin pops out of the hole and the menu or window is dismissed from the screen.

File Manager

You access all file management functions in an OPEN LOOK UI implementation in a consistent way using the *File Manager* application. The File Manager can be used independently or can be called up from an application window.

Base Windows

The applications you choose from the Workspace menu are displayed on the workspace as *base windows.* Figure 2-4 identifies the visual elements of a simple base window.

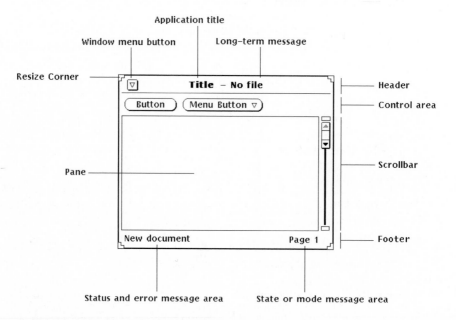

Figure 2-4   A simple base window.

The base window is the framework in which the application contents are displayed. The following lists provide a general indication of which parts of the user interface are specified and which parts are defined by the application developer. The lists are not comprehensive.

The fixed elements of the OPEN LOOK UI include:

☐ The specific graphic design of each of the elements
☐ The fonts used for those elements
☐ The functionality of those elements
☐ The spacing for headers, footers, and scrollbars
☐ The required menus

The application developer defines these elements in the base window:

☐ Application title and any long-term messages in the header
☐ Status and error messages in the footer
☐ Size and locations of panes and control areas
☐ Names and layout of buttons in the control area
☐ Presence or absence of resize corners and scrollbars
☐ Application menus

You can change the area of a window by moving the pointer to one of the four *resize corners*, pressing SELECT, and dragging the resize corner to increase or reduce the total area of the window. Resizing a window changes the window area, but it does not change the scale of the window elements. You can move a window on the workspace by pressing SELECT on the header or footer and dragging the window to the new location.

The *header* is the area at the top of a base window that displays the *Window menu button* and the application title. If Close is the default for the Window menu, you can quickly close a window by clicking SELECT on the Window menu button. When you close a base window, it is displayed on the workspace as an icon. The header can also display long-term messages generated by the application.

The *control area* contains controls such as buttons and menu buttons. The control area and controls are described under "Control Areas and Controls" later in this chapter.

The *pane* is the area of the base window where the application information is displayed and manipulated. An application can have multiple panes within the same base window. When all the application information cannot be displayed at one time, panes have *scrollbars* to allow you to move around in the contents. Scrollbars are covered later in this chapter.

Useful status, error, and state messages from the application are displayed in the *footer* of the base window.

Window Menu

Each window has a Window menu, which you use to set window properties and change window characteristics. When a window is displayed as an icon, it keeps the window menu. You can use the menu to open icons or close windows, expand the size of the window as specified by the application or restore it to its original size, set window properties, move the window to the back of the screen, refresh the window, and quit the application. Figure 2-5 shows the Window menu for base windows.

Figure 2-5 Window menu for base windows.

Pop-up windows have a Window menu with a smaller set of choices.

Control Areas and Controls

The basic controls for an application are displayed in control areas within the base window. The application developer determines the layout and labels for the controls. A control area can contain any of the controls described in this section.

An application can have a single, simple control area at the top of its window or several control areas elsewhere in the window. A complex application can divide its base window into a number of panes, each with its own control area.

You choose your activities in an OPEN LOOK UI implementation using the mouse and a simple set of controls. Figure 2-6 shows examples of all the kinds of controls that can be used in control areas. Most of the time, control areas have button controls. The other controls can be used in any arrangement or combination suitable to the application. Controls always work the same way, regardless of how they are arranged or where they are displayed.

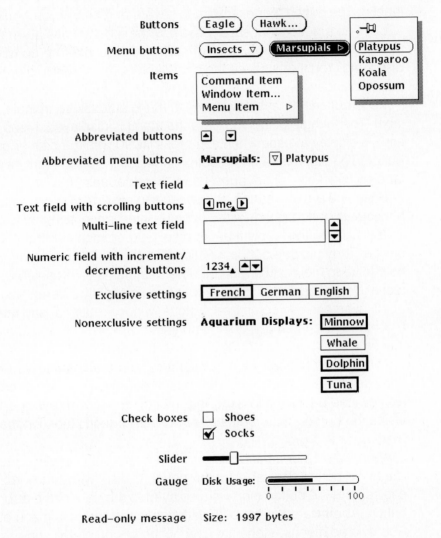

Figure 2-6   Controls in an OPEN LOOK UI implementation.

Controls

Buttons used for single commands have the name of the command as the label on the button. For example, to save a document, you would click SELECT on a button that says "Save." When a button has a *window mark*—three dots—following the label, choosing it causes a pop-up window to be displayed. You then choose the command from the controls provided in the pop-up window.

Menu buttons always have a *menu mark,* an outlined triangle, following the label. The triangle points to where the menu is displayed. Menu buttons always display a menu when you press MENU with the pointer on a menu button. The menu for a menu button labeled "Insects" might have items labeled "Crickets," "Ladybugs," and "Bumblebees."

When you press a button, it *highlights* to provide visual feedback. The Marsupials button in Figure 2-6 is highlighted since its menu is displayed.

Items are button labels that are displayed on menus without the button outline. They provide button functionality on menus and, at the same time, help to keep menus to a manageable size. Items on menus have the same feel and functionality as buttons, but have a slightly different look. Just as an application can use command buttons, window buttons, and menu buttons in a control area, it can use command items, window items, and menu items on menus.

Abbreviated buttons are small square buttons with no text label inside them. They can have a glyph inside the button outline. The most common use for abbreviated buttons is for scrolling. Scrolling buttons have a solid arrowhead inside the border of the button. Abbreviated buttons function the same as buttons.

Abbreviated menu buttons are small square buttons with a menu mark inside the button. The label for the button is displayed to the left, and the choice from the button menu is displayed to the right of the abbreviated menu button. Abbreviated menu buttons function the same as menu buttons. Abbreviated menu buttons are used when it is helpful to show the current choice without displaying a menu.

Text fields are used when the application requires input from the keyboard. For example, you use a text field when you type the name of a document you want to save. When a text field cannot display the entire text string, scrolling buttons are displayed to allow you to scroll the contents of the field. When a text field that can only contain numbers has increment/decrement scrolling buttons, you can click on them to increase or decrease the number displayed in the text field. Text fields can also be displayed with borders and scrollbars to permit multi-line text entry.

Exclusive settings are displayed as touching rectangles. You can make one choice from each group of settings. The chosen setting is shown with a bold border. Exclusive settings are used when the object has a state, and that state can be changed. For example, if you want to change the color of a pen in a drawing application, the pen already has a color setting. You can choose a different pen color from a palette of exclusive setting color choices, but you can use only one pen color at a time. Applications can use a variation of exclusive settings that allows you either to make one choice from each group of settings or to choose none of the settings.

Nonexclusive settings are displayed as separate rectangles. You can choose all, none, or any combination of nonexclusive settings for the same object. Nonexclusive settings are used when you can set many values for one particular object. For example, text attributes such as bold, italic, and underline can all be set for the same word.

Check boxes are another kind of nonexclusive setting. You can choose all, some, or none of the options by toggling the check box to display or suppress the check mark.

Sliders are used to set a numeric value and give a visual indication of the setting. Sliders can have numeric fields and type-in fields. Sliders can be used when an object has a range of possible settings. For example, sliders can be used to adjust the volume of a beep.

Gauges are used to give a visual indication of how full or empty an object is or to show what percentage of a job is complete.

Read-only messages are used to provide useful information that you cannot edit.

Scrolling

When you need to move through the data in an application, you use scrollbars to change the view in the pane. A pane can have both horizontal and vertical scrollbars. Figure 2-7 shows the components of a vertical scrollbar.

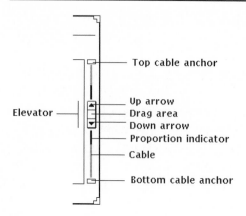

Figure 2-7   Components of a vertical scrollbar.

The *elevator* shows you where you are in the contents that can be viewed in the pane. The dark area of the *cable* (the *proportion indicator*) shows you how much of the total contents is displayed in the pane.

You use the SELECT mouse button to operate the scrollbar. When you scroll upward, you move the view on the data incrementally toward the beginning. When you scroll downward, you move the view on the data incrementally toward the end. You can scroll the contents of a pane in the following ways:

☐ Go to the beginning (click SELECT on the top cable anchor).

☐ Go to the end (click SELECT on the bottom cable anchor).

☐ Display the previous unit at the top of the pane (click SELECT on the up arrow).

☐ Display the next unit at the bottom of the pane (click SELECT on the down arrow).

☐ Display the previous pane of information (click SELECT on the cable above the elevator).

☐ Display the next pane of information (click SELECT on the cable below the elevator).

☐ Move to any arbitrary location (press SELECT in the drag area and drag the elevator).

When you scroll, the elevator moves to reflect the new position of the view into the application data. When the pointer is on the elevator, the pointer automatically moves when the elevator moves. This convenient feature means that you can press or click SELECT to repeat the scrolling action without moving the mouse. When you click on the cable, the pointer automatically moves along the cable to prevent the elevator from colliding with it.

Menus

An OPEN LOOK UI implementation uses menus to provide additional control areas that are hidden from view until you need to use them.

Menus have settings or lists of items that you use to issue commands, display a submenu with additional items, or settings that you use to set parameters. In addition, menus can have a pushpin to keep them on the screen for repeated use.

There are two basic types of menus:

☐ Button menus
☐ Pop-up menus

Each region of the screen in an OPEN LOOK UI implementation that is not a control has a pop-up menu. The pop-up menu that is displayed depends on the location of the pointer. When the pointer is on a menu button and you press MENU, the menu for that button is displayed.

Pop-up menus in an application usually duplicate choices from menus provided in the control area. Pop-up menus save keystrokes, minimize mouse movement, and make the interface more efficient for experienced users. When you use pop-up menus, you do not need to move the pointer away from the work area to issue commands.

The OPEN LOOK UI specifies the items for required pop-up menus. The application developer specifies the choices for all other menus. The required menus are listed below:

☐ Workspace menu
☐ Window menu
☐ Pop-up Window menu
☐ Settings menu for property windows
☐ Scrollbar menu
☐ Edit menu for text fields
☐ Scrolling List menus

The application developer can add choices to the Workspace, Scrollbar, and Edit menus. The Window menus and Settings menu cannot be changed by the application. Figure 2-8 shows examples of menus. The Edit button menu and Edit pop-up menu in the base window are examples of application-defined menus. (Note that this figure shows a configuration that you would never see on the screen, since you have only one pointer and can display only one menu group at a time.)

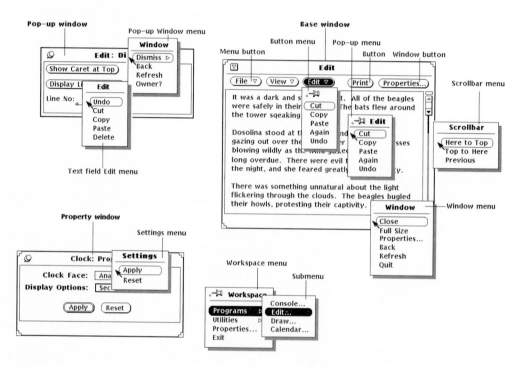

Figure 2-8   Examples of menus in an OPEN LOOK UI implementation.

Using Menus

This section describes the two basic ways you use the MENU mouse button to operate on menus:

☐ Press-drag-release
☐ Click-move-click

The most common way to use a menu is by pressing MENU to display the menu, dragging the pointer to the desired item, and releasing the MENU mouse button to choose the item and dismiss the menu. You must keep the MENU button pressed down to keep the menu on the screen.

Alternatively, you can click MENU once to display the menu and keep it on the screen without holding down the mouse button. You then move the pointer to the desired item, and click either SELECT or MENU again to choose the item and dismiss the menu.

Each menu has a default selection, which offers a quick way to choose an item from a menu. You can view and execute the default selection for a menu button in a control area—using the SELECT mouse button—without displaying the button menu. You can also change the default selection for a menu at any time.

Any menu that has a pushpin can be pinned to the workspace to keep it accessible. The pinned menu becomes a pop-up window and remains on the screen until you dismiss it.

Pop-up Windows

Each application can provide transitory windows called *pop-up windows,* which are displayed to let you fill in information or make choices. A button or menu item that displays a pop-up window always has a window mark following the label.

All pop-up windows except Notices have a pushpin on the left side of the header so that you can pin the window to the workspace to keep it readily available for repeated operations.

Pop-up windows that allow you to set the properties of objects, such as tab settings or fonts in a text editing application, are called *property windows.* Figure 2-9 shows an example of a text property window.

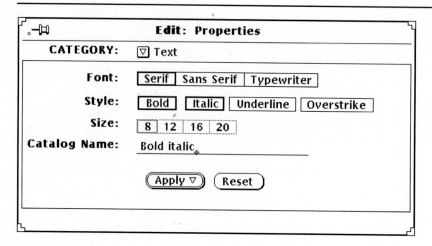

Figure 2-9 An example of a text property window.

Pop-up windows do not close to an icon. Instead, when a command from a pop-up window that affects the selected object or takes action on a function is successfully executed, the pop-up window is dismissed from the screen. For example, when you click on the Apply button to apply properties to a selection, the property window is dismissed from the screen after the properties are applied. You can dismiss a pop-up window without choosing a command by choosing Dismiss from the pop-up Window menu, or using the pushpin to dismiss the window.

Help

You view on-screen help in a Help pop-up window. Move the pointer to the object for which you want help and press the HELP key on the keyboard. A pinned Help window is displayed. The object at the pointer location is displayed in the magnifying glass of the Help window along with explanatory help text. Figure 2-10 shows an example of a Help window.

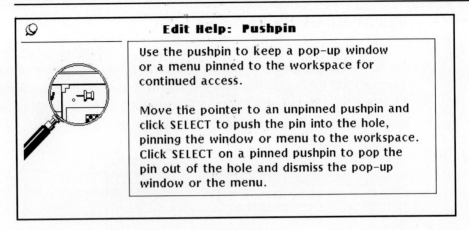

Edit Help: Pushpin

Use the pushpin to keep a pop-up window
or a menu pinned to the workspace for
continued access.

Move the pointer to an unpinned pushpin and
click SELECT to push the pin into the hole,
pinning the window or menu to the workspace.
Click SELECT on a pinned pushpin to pop the
pin out of the hole and dismiss the pop-up
window or the menu.

Figure 2-10   An example of a Help window.

Selecting and Operating on Windows and Icons

The foundation of the OPEN LOOK UI is the *select-then-operate* paradigm.
You first select an object by pointing to it with the pointer, and pressing and
releasing a button on the mouse. Then, using either the mouse or the
keyboard, you choose the operation to be applied to the selected object.

In addition, you can perform certain common operations by *direct manipulation.* For example, selected windows, icons, text, or graphics can be moved
by dragging them to a new location on the screen.

The objects on the workspace (windows and icons) are selected and
manipulated in the same way as objects in an application.

One of the advantages of the OPEN LOOK UI is the ability to control several
windows and icons at once. With the selection paradigm extended to the
workspace, you can select several windows and icons and perform the same
operation on all of them.

The Window Background

The *window background* is any part of a window that is not enclosed by a border or covered by a control, a pushpin, or scrollbar. You use the window background to display the Window menu, select a window, or move a window by dragging. The shaded area in Figure 2-11 is the window background for a base window with a control area, one pane, and a scrollbar.

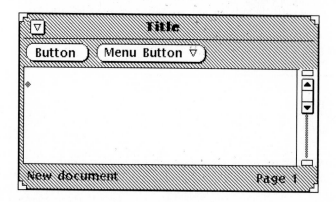

Figure 2-11   The shading shows the background of a base window.

Using the Window Menu

You operate on individual windows and icons at the pointer location by making choices from the *Window menu.* You access the Window menu by pressing or clicking MENU anywhere on the window background (or when the pointer is over any button that has no menu behind it).

To provide a quick way to use the default from the window menu without displaying the menu, the header of each base window has a Window menu button. Clicking SELECT on the Window menu button executes the default item. For example, when the default is Close, clicking SELECT on the Window menu button closes the window to an icon. Pressing or clicking MENU on the Window menu button displays the same Window menu that you access from the window background.

Selecting Windows and Icons

You select a window by moving the pointer to the background and clicking SELECT or ADJUST. Select an icon by moving the pointer anywhere on the icon and clicking SELECT or ADJUST. Since windows can be layered on the workspace and may not be completely visible, clicking SELECT on the window background also brings the window or icon to the front of the screen. Clicking ADJUST selects the window or icon but does not bring it to the front of the screen.

When a window or icon is selected, the border thickens. In Figure 2-12, the Edit window and Console icon are not selected. The Draw window and Mail icon are selected.

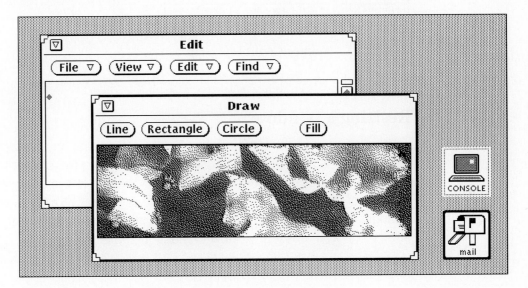

Figure 2-12 Selected and unselected windows and icons.

To select more than one window or icon, click ADJUST on the additional objects you want to select.

Operating on Selected Windows and Icons

You move selected windows and icons directly by pressing SELECT on one of the selected objects and dragging the group to a new location.

You can also operate on groups of selected windows and icons by opening a pop-up window called *Window Controls* from the Workspace menu and using the controls in that window to operate on the selected objects. For example, you can close selected windows and open selected icons in one operation using the Open/Close button in the Window Controls pop-up. Figure 2-13 shows the Window Controls pop-up window.

Figure 2-13   Window Controls pop-up.

Resizing a Window

You can change the dimensions of any window that has resize corners by pressing SELECT on any resize corner and dragging the corner to a new location. The diagonally opposite corner of the window is anchored, and the borders of the window expand or contract as you move the resize corner, changing the area of the window relative to the anchored corner. Figure 2-14 shows how you resize a window to make it smaller.

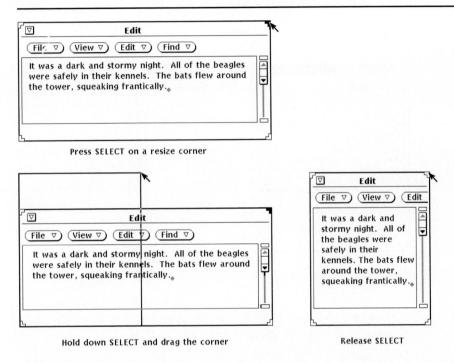

Press SELECT on a resize corner

Hold down SELECT and drag the corner   Release SELECT

Figure 2-14   Resizing a window to make it smaller.

Scaling a Window

A different way to alter the size of a window is to *scale* it. When a window is scaled to a different size, all the elements of the window change to a larger or smaller size, including the font, borders, Window menu button, and controls such as buttons and scrollbars.

You scale a base window by choosing Properties from the Window menu and using the Base Window Scale option from the property window. When you scale a window, all the elements of the window change size proportionally. For example, if you scale a window to a larger size, the upper left corner of the window is anchored in place, and the borders of the window expand to the right and downward. Figure 2-15 shows a window in small scale, with the Window menu displayed and Properties highlighted. You display the Window menu by moving the pointer to the window background and pressing MENU. Then you drag the pointer to highlight Properties.

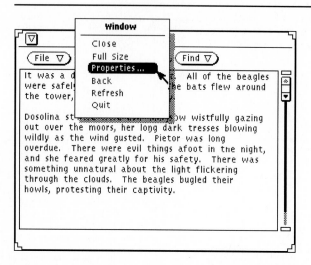

Figure 2-15   Choosing Properties from the Window menu.

When you release MENU, the Window menu is dismissed and the Properties window is displayed, as shown in Figure 2-16.

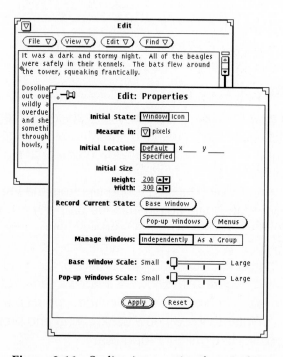

Figure 2-16   Scaling is an option for window properties.

28

You then move the pointer to the slider box for the base window scale setting, press SELECT, and drag the slider box to the next setting, as shown in Figure 2-17.

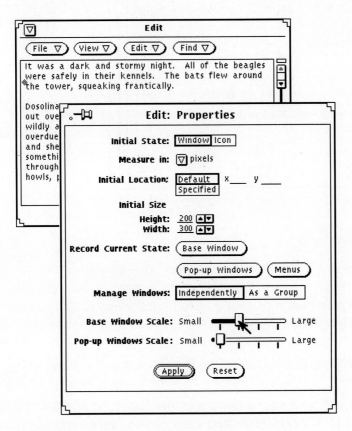

Figure 2-17   Drag the slider box to the next setting.

To apply this setting, click SELECT on the Apply button. The property window is dismissed and the setting is changed. The window is displayed in the larger size, as shown in Figure 2-18.

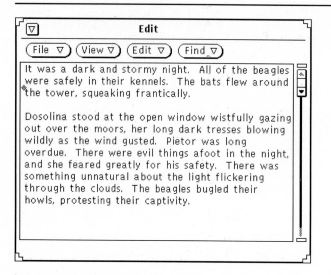

Figure 2-18 Click SELECT on the Apply button to apply the setting and dismiss the property window.

You can scale the base window and pop-up windows for an application independently of each other. Using the Scaling option, you can display the pop-up windows in a smaller size to conserve space on the workspace and choose a larger scaling size for the base window of the application.

Selecting and Operating on Text and Graphics

To select text, move the pointer to the beginning of the text you want to select, press SELECT, and drag the mouse to *wipe through the selection.* As you move the pointer, the text is highlighted. Release SELECT to complete the selection. You can also select text by moving the pointer to the beginning of the text you want to select, clicking SELECT, and then moving the pointer to the end of the text you want to select and clicking ADJUST.

Once text is selected, copy or move it directly by dragging. Alternatively, use the Cut or Copy keys (or their equivalents) on the keyboard to store text on the clipboard. You insert data from the clipboard at a new location using the Paste key.

Select graphic objects by clicking SELECT on the object or clicking ADJUST to toggle the selected state of the object.

Once you have selected graphic objects, you operate on them the same as you do on selected text.

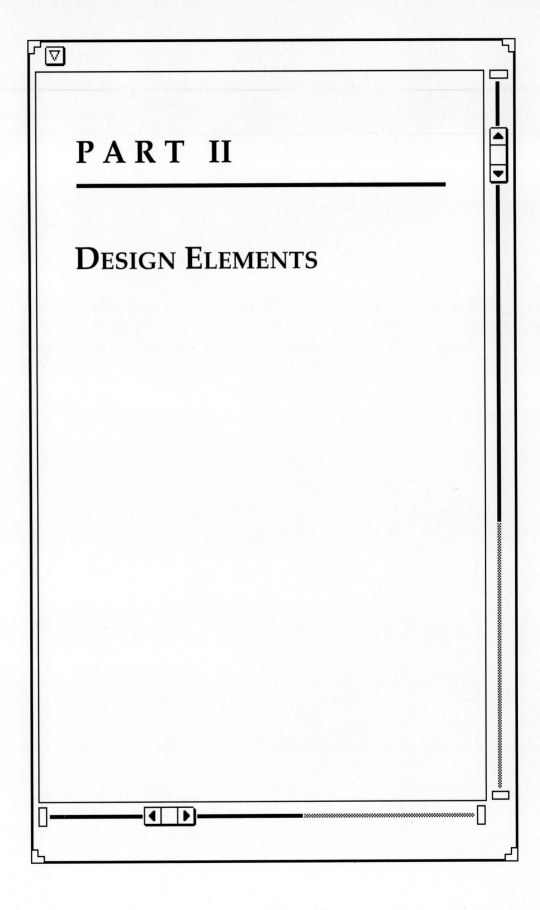

PART II

DESIGN ELEMENTS

3

WORKSPACE, ICONS, AND WINDOWS

This chapter begins the technical specifications section of this book with a description of the workspace, icons, and windows. Refer to Appendix B for detailed graphic representations of the elements described in this chapter.

In an OPEN LOOK User Interface implementation, windows and icons can be selected and manipulated both individually and as a group. Since more than one object can be selected at the same time, the visual distinction between selected and unselected icons and windows is an important part of the user interface.

This chapter describes the visual elements of the workspace, icons, and windows. It shows the distinction between the selected and unselected states for windows and icons. See Chapter 16 for a detailed description of how to select and operate on icons and windows. See Chapter 18 for information about how to use property windows.

The Workspace

Icons and windows are displayed on the workspace, which has a 50 percent pattern, as specified in Appendix B. Color implementations set the workspace color from the Workspace Properties window.

The Workspace Grid

The workspace contains an invisible grid which has a default grid increment of 13 points. When icons are positioned on the workspace, they automatically snap to intersecting points on this grid. You can change the default grid increments or turn the grid off from the Workspace Properties window. See Chapter 11 for more information about the workspace grid.

Reserved Areas

Some OPEN LOOK UI implementations may permit you to define *virtual edges* for the workspace to create a *reserved area* on the workspace that permits the display of icons and special application windows. A certain class of applications can be moved onto the reserved area of the workspace. You define virtual edges from the Workspace Properties window. A 1-point line demarcates the boundary between the workspace and the reserved area of the screen, as shown in Figure 3-1.

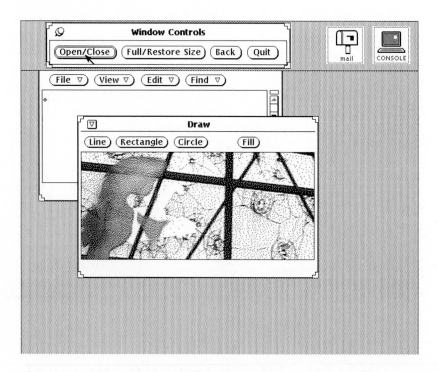

Figure 3-1 The workspace with a reserved area at the top of the screen.

In this example, a virtual edge is defined near the top of the workspace. The Window Controls pop-up is displayed in the reserved area, as are two icons. The Edit window is partially obscured, just as it would be if the window were moved partially off the actual edge of the screen.

When an OPEN LOOK UI implementation provides reserved areas of the screen, you can move icons onto the reserved area. Most windows, however, consider the virtual edge to be the physical edge of the screen, and they disappear under the virtual edge when you drag the window beyond that edge. An application must be able to specify whether or not you can move its window onto the reserved area of the workspace. See Chapter 16 for more information about moving icons and windows.

Default Pointer Shapes

The pointer—usually an arrow pointing up and to the left—shows the location of the mouse on the workspace. The OPEN LOOK UI has standard pointer shapes for specific functions such as copy and move.

When the pointer is an arrow, the tip of the arrow is the hot spot that indicates the active place on the screen. Applications may provide additional pointer shapes.

Table 3-1 shows the default pointers for a Level 1 implementation and tells you when you see them.

When you initiate an activity, the shape of the pointer changes to give you visual feedback while you are performing an operation. Generally, the pointer is displayed when you press a mouse button, when you drag the pointer beyond the damping factor to initiate a move or copy, or when an event cannot be acted upon. When you release the mouse button to complete the action, the appropriate pointer is displayed. The pointer may change to the busy pointer until the operation is complete, and then change again to the basic pointer.

Some OPEN LOOK UI implementations may not be able to support large pointers efficiently. In addition, some languages, such as Kanji, require a larger text area than that provided by the text move and text copy pointers. In these cases, the OPEN LOOK UI implementation uses the standard move and copy pointers in place of the text move and text copy pointers.

Table 3-1   Level 1 default pointers.

 The *basic pointer* is used for such basic functions as selecting objects and manipulating controls. The hot spot is the tip of the arrow.

 When you move an object by dragging, the pointer changes to the *move pointer*. The hot spot is the tip of the arrow.

 When you copy an object by dragging, the pointer changes to the *duplicate pointer*. The hot spot is the tip of the arrow.

 When an application is busy and cannot accept input, the pointer changes to a stopwatch. The hot spot is the middle of the stopwatch.

 While a mouse button is pressed on an area that does not accept that action, or when you drag an object to an inappropriate destination, the *question mark pointer* is displayed.

 When you copy text by dragging, the pointer changes to the *text duplicate pointer*. The at least the first three characters of the text are displayed in 10-point type in the rectangle, and are followed by a More arrow then the selection is more than three characters. The hot spot is the tip of the arrow.

 When you move text by dragging, the pointer changes to the *text move pointer*. The first three characters of the text are displayed in 10-point type in the rectangle, and are followed by a More arrow when the selection is more than three characters. The hot spot is the tip of the arrow.

Table 3-2 shows the additional default pointers for a Level 2 implementation and tells you when you see them.

Table 3-2   Level 2 additional default pointers.

 In a Level 2 implementation, when you initiate panning (moving the entire contents of a pane relative to the pane outline), the pointer is changed to the *panning pointer.* The hot spot is the tip of the arrow.

 In a Level 2 implementation, the basic pointer changes to the *target pointer,* with a halo around the tip of the arrow when the hot spot is on the border of a pane that can be selected.

See Chapter 7 for information about panning. See Chapter 16 for information about selecting panes.

Icons

This book uses the term *icon* specifically to mean a graphic representation of a closed window. Other graphic images used in an OPEN LOOK UI implementation are referred to as *glyphs.* When a base window is closed to an icon, the only change to the application is in its visual representation on the workspace. The application keeps running even when it is closed to an icon. When the icon is opened, it is replaced on the screen by its opened window.

The OPEN LOOK UI specifies a basic icon size (65 by 65 points) and design for bordered and borderless icons. However, an OPEN LOOK UI implementation can use icons of a nonstandard size and configuration. If an OPEN LOOK UI implementation provides an icon editor application, it would be helpful to provide the application developer with the ability to scale an application design to the three sizes most commonly required for different display resolutions:

☐ Low resolution
☐ Medium resolution
☐ High resolution

In addition, such an application could provide a way to scale to the standard glyph size required for display in the File Manager. See "Images for Use with the File Manager" later in this chapter and Chapter 12 for more information about File Manager glyphs.

Any icon can be displayed in an unselected or selected state. In addition, an unselected or selected icon can show the standard *busy pattern* as the icon background. An icon is "busy" when its application cannot accept user input—for example, when a mail application is incorporating new mail. The following sections describe default bordered and borderless icons and nonstandard icons.

Default Icon Elements

Each default icon has three elements:

☐ A border
☐ An optional image
☐ An optional text label

Figure 3-2 shows examples of unselected icons.

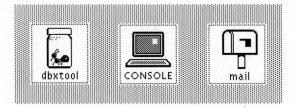

Figure 3-2   Examples of default bordered icons.

To present a uniform appearance, the pictures on each icon should be approximately the same size. The default text label on the icon is the same as the title that is displayed in the header of the opened window.

When an application has more than one base window, the application determines the text that is displayed in the text area of the icon for additional base windows.

Borders

On monochrome displays, unselected icons are enclosed in a 1-point white square border and a 1-point dotted line (alternating dark and white points). The icon size is 65 points square. The top two-thirds of the icon is the symbol image area. The bottom third is the text area. Figure 3-3 shows the border and the image and text areas.

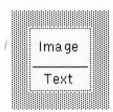

Figure 3-3   The icon border and the image and text areas.

Images

The graphic image for an icon should be a unique design that is easily recognizable whether or not a title is displayed in the icon text area. The image can change to represent a change in state of the application. The examples in this book of a mail application icon show a rural American mail box with a flag. When the flag is down, there are no new mail files in the mail box. When the flag is up and the door to the mailbox is opened, you have new mail messages. Any application can use a graphic mnemonic such as this to show a change in the state of the application while the window is displayed as an icon.

Images for Use with the File Manager

The File Manager displays files as glyphs and has a set of default glyphs that represent folders, data files, and applications. See Chapter 12 for a complete specification of the File Manager.

An application can provide two additional image designs to use for display in the File Manager:

☐ The image area from the default icon that can be displayed in place of the default File Manager application glyph.

☐ An image that fits inside the 32-by-40-point border of the File Manager data file glyph.

Figure 3-4 shows an example of the image area from a mail application on the left, and a smaller version of the same image inside the border of a File Manager data file glyph on the right.

Figure 3-4   Examples of glyphs for use with the File Manager.

You would use the image on the left to open the mail application, and the image on the right to open a data file that contained a message bound to the mail application.

Title

Each icon can have a title that, by default, is the same as the title on the application window. The application can use a shorter title for the icon if needed or choose not to display a title. The application can specify whether or not long-term messages such as file names are displayed in the icon.

State Feedback

Default bordered icons that are selected have a 3-point border. The icon can be in a busy state whether or not the icon is selected. The top two icons in Figure 3-5 show unselected and selected default icons. The bottom two icons show unselected and selected busy icons.

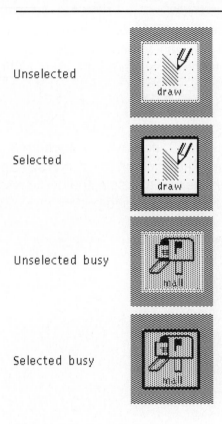

Unselected

Selected

Unselected busy

Selected busy

Figure 3-5   Icon states.

Borderless Icons

On grayscale or color displays, the icon border is not needed, since the background color can be specified as a lightly saturated shade that provides enough contrast for the icon and the text label to be visible against it.

Figure 3-6 shows an example of an icon without a border.

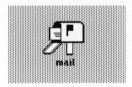

Figure 3-6   An icon without a border.

When an OPEN LOOK UI implementation uses a grayscale or color display, you can choose whether or not you want to display unselected icons with borders. You set this option from the Workspace Properties window, as described in Chapter 11.

State Feedback

When you select a borderless icon, it displays the standard 3-point border. The icon can be in a busy state whether or not the icon is selected. The top two icons in Figure 3-7 show unselected and selected borderless icons. The bottom two icons show unselected and selected busy icons.

Unselected

Selected

Unselected busy

Selected busy

Figure 3-7   Icon states.

Nonstandard Icons

An application can specify an icon of nonstandard size and shape. Nonstandard icons must be in increments of 13 points (the standard 65-point icon uses 5 of these increments) so that they display evenly on the 13-pixel workspace grid. When an application specifies nonstandard icons, it communicates the correct icon size to the window manager so that icons are placed appropriately on the workspace grid.

Figure 3-8 shows an example of an icon for a scheduling application. The icon displays the current month and date in a format larger than 65 points square and contains no label. This icon uses the standard border in a nonstandard size. The selection and busy feedback are the same as for default icons.

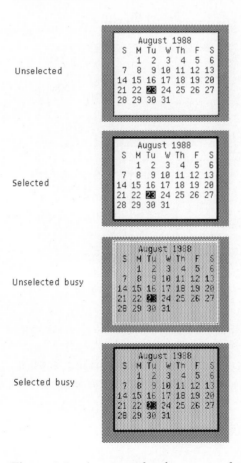

Figure 3-8   An example of a nonstandard icon.

Figure 3-9 shows examples of nonstandard, nonrectangular icons.

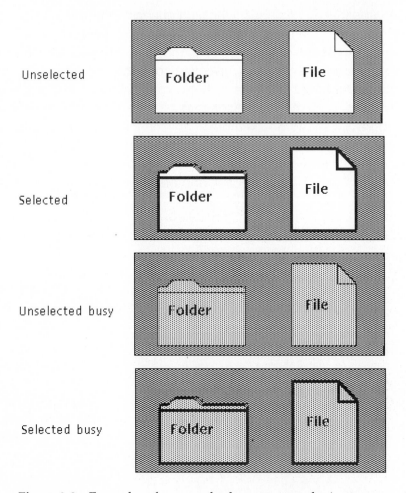

Figure 3-9 Examples of nonstandard, nonrectangular icons.

You can drag File Manager folders and data file glyphs out of the File Manager pane and put them on the workspace. Applications determine how the data file is displayed as an icon on the workspace. A folder glyph can be displayed as a nonrectangular icon that has all the attributes of other icons:

☐ A border
☐ An optional image or text label inside the border

□ The required base Window menu
□ A bold border when you select the icon
□ Standard busy feedback when appropriate

The icon can be opened to display a base window. An opened data file icon is displayed in a base window of the application to which the data file is bound. See Chapter 12 for a description of the File Manager.

Positions

Icons snap to an invisible grid on the workspace. This permits you to position icons immediately adjacent to one another, or show an equal amount of the workspace between icons.

When an application is started or when an open window is closed, the first icon is displayed in the initial default region at the edge of the screen that you specified from the Workspace Properties window. Subsequent icons are positioned 65 points to the right or below the previous icon position so that the borders of icons are immediately adjacent to one another. When you use the Top setting, the first icon is displayed at the upper left corner of the workspace. Subsequent icons are displayed one icon width to the right of the previous icon. When the last icon reaches the top right corner of the screen, the next icon is moved one icon width down from the top of the screen, and a second row is formed following the same placement pattern.

This same pattern is used for each of the other settings. When you use the Bottom setting, the first icon is displayed at the lower left corner. When you use the Left setting, the first icon is displayed at the upper left corner. When you use the Right setting, the first icon is displayed at the upper right corner. The Location setting applies to future placement of icons and does not affect the location of any icons already displayed on the workspace.

You choose the *default icon region* (top, bottom, left, or right) from the Workspace Properties window. The default icon region defines the part of the screen that the icons move to when they are closed.

Icons can be moved anywhere on the workspace that is permitted by the workspace grid, including any reserved areas of the workspace. When you move an icon from its default position, the new position is recorded and is used the next time the base window is opened and then closed again.

Base Windows

An OPEN LOOK UI implementation has two kinds of windows:

☐ Base windows (the application's primary window)
☐ Pop-up windows (transient windows that pop up to accomplish a specific purpose and are dismissed by you or by the application when appropriate)

This section describes base windows. Pop-up windows are described later in this chapter.

The base window is the application's main window. Each base window has required and optional elements. These elements are described in the following sections.

Required Elements for Standard Base Windows

Standard base windows have the following required elements:

☐ The standard base Window menu
☐ A 2-point border
☐ A header, with the name of the application centered
☐ A Window menu button in the upper left corner of the header
☐ At least one of the following two elements:
  ▫ Control area (an unbordered area where controls such as buttons are located)
  ▫ Pane (a bordered rectangle where the application displays text and graphics)

Figure 3-10 shows the required elements of a base window except for the Window menu. The window on the top has a control area but no pane, while the window on the bottom has a pane but no control area.

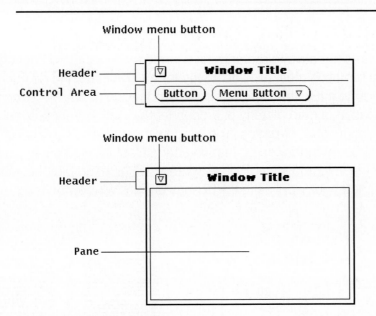

Figure 3-10   Minimum base window layout.

Although the minimum configuration includes either a pane or a control area, a more typical configuration is for a base window to have at least one pane and one control area located above the pane. Figure 3-11 shows a typical base window layout with a control area above a pane.

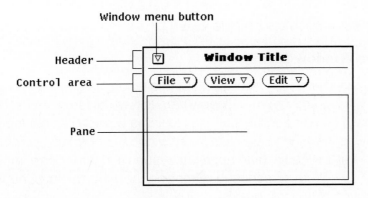

Figure 3-11   Typical base window layout.

Nonstandard Base Windows

As an alternative to rectangular windows with required elements, a Level 2 implementation must provide a way for an application to design a window that does not contain the standard base window elements. For example, a clock application, a map display of a continent, a dial, and a notebook do not need headers, footers, or panes. The window must always have a Window menu, some background area so that you can select it, and some visual feedback to show the selected state. Figure 3-12 shows an example of a clock application and a notebook application with nonstandard window layouts.

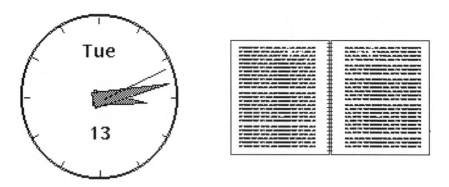

Figure 3-12   Examples of nonstandard base windows.

Each of the required elements of a base window is described in the following sections.

Base Window Menu

Each window in an OPEN LOOK UI implementation has a Window menu. The base window and pop-up window menus have different items. You use the Window menu for actions such as closing a window or opening an icon, displaying the window you use to set window properties, temporarily adjusting the area of a window to an application-specified larger size, moving a window to the back of the screen, and refreshing the window. See Chapter 10 for a description of window menus.

The base window menu always has a Properties item that is used to set specific properties for the window. An OPEN LOOK UI implementation has a basic required set of window properties. The application cannot add settings to this property window. See "Property Windows" later in this chapter for a description of the window properties.

Header

The header of each window has a Window menu button and a title.

Window Menu Buttons

The Window menu button is displayed on the left side of the header in every base window. Clicking SELECT on the Window menu button activates the default item from the Window menu without displaying the menu. An ADJUST click on the Window menu button displays the question mark pointer. Clicking or pressing MENU on the Window menu button displays the Window menu, just as it does anywhere on the window background.

Title

Each base window has a title. By default, the title is the same as the title on the icon. The title and any long-term messages are centered, in sans serif bold type.

Control Areas

A control area is any area within the borders of the base window, excluding the header or footer, where controls are displayed. A control area can be positioned anywhere in the window or within a pane. The standard configuration is for control areas to be above a pane that uses those controls. See Chapter 5 for a detailed description of control areas.

Panes

Panes are *tiled* (not overlapping) within the base window and are outlined with a 1-point border. All text panes in an OPEN LOOK UI implementation support text cut/copy/paste operations from the keyboard, and use the clipboard for these operations.

A Level 2 implementation supports the Clipboard window, which you can access from the Workspace menu. You can use the Clipboard window to view the data that will be inserted by a paste operation.

An application can provide Replace and Append functions on a Copy button menu; these allow you to replace the contents of the clipboard with the current selection or to append the current selection to the existing contents of the clipboard.

The OPEN LOOK UI does not restrict the kinds of panes that an implementation can provide for an application. The two most basic types of panes used by applications are a text pane that has some editing capabilities and a graphics pane. However, applications can combine text and graphics capabilities within the same pane.

Any pane that is used in an OPEN LOOK UI implementation supports basic text or graphics selection and operation functionality, as described in detail in Chapter 17.

You can select a pane when you apply functions to that pane such as resizing or setting application properties. When a pane is selected, it has a 2-point border. See Chapter 16 for a description of selecting panes.

Optional Elements

Base windows have the following optional elements, if needed by the application: resize corners, a scrollbar, and a footer for displaying one-line status and error messages. Long-term messages can be displayed in the header, such as the name of a file that is being edited in a text window.

The optional elements of a base window are shown in Figure 3-13.

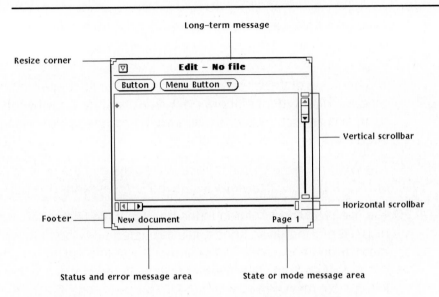

Figure 3-13   Optional elements of a standard base window.

Long-term Messages

When a *long-term message* is displayed in the header, the entire line is centered. The long-term message is not considered part of the application title and is not displayed in any pop-up windows generated by the application. When a window is resized smaller, long-term messages are truncated in the same way other header information is.

The application determines whether long-term messages, such as file names that are displayed in the window header, are also displayed in the icon when the window is closed.

Resize Corners

Resize corners are used to shrink or expand the area of an individual window. They change the window area proportionally; that is, without changing the relative size of the controls, glyphs, or fonts displayed in the window. Although resize corners are optional, the default is for base windows to have them.

The application determines whether the data displayed in the panes in the window are redisplayed to conform to the new area of the pane. See Chapter 16 for a description of resizing windows.

The contents of the window background behave in the following manner when the window is resized:

☐ The contents of the window are "anchored" in the upper left corner of the window. The borders of the window are expanded downward and to the right, and are contracted leftward from the right border and upward from the bottom border.

☐ The Window menu button is always displayed in the header of a base window. The pushpin is always displayed in the header of a pop-up window.

☐ The title is always centered in the header. If the title cannot be completely displayed in the given space, it is truncated from the right and an inactive *more arrow* is displayed at the end of the text to indicate that some information is hidden from view. (Note that this information is not scrollable.) Any information messages are treated in the same way. Figure 3-14 shows the header of a resized window with the title truncated and a more arrow.

Figure 3-14   A resized window with truncated title and a More arrow.

☐ In the window footer, any information or error message in the left message area is truncated from the right and an inactive more arrow is displayed at the end of the text to show that some information is hidden from view. When the left message disappears, the right message is truncated from the right.

Controls in control areas need not automatically be rearranged so that they are visible after the window is resized. For example, some buttons may be only partially visible or may fall outside the new window boundaries. The application determines whether or not buttons in the control area are rearranged after you resize a window. The application also determines how the area of panes in a multi-pane window is reallocated.

Scrollbars

Scrollbars allow you to move through the application data and change the view in the pane when the information you work with does not fit within the borders of the pane. Scrollbars can be displayed vertically and/or horizontally. See Chapter 7 for a description of scrollbars.

Footers

The application uses the footer area of the base window to display one-line information and error messages. The footer has two message areas, right and left. Status and error messages on the left of the footer are left-justified. State messages, such as mode or page, on the right of the footer are right-justified.

An OPEN LOOK UI implementation provides the following ways of displaying messages in a base window:

□ *Normal messages* such as prompts and status information are displayed in the footer, header, control area, or pane without flashing or beeping.

□ *Important messages* are displayed in the footer. An "important" message always flashes several times and beeps. You can turn off the beep from the Workspace Properties window.

In a Level 2 implementation, the application can use the Help pop-up window to display more information about a specific error message that is displayed in the left message area. When you move the pointer onto the left side of the footer and press the HELP key, a Help window is displayed that contains the more detailed explanation of the error message. The application can also use the Help window to display help text for status or state messages that are displayed on the right side of the footer. See "Help" later in this chapter for more information about the Help pop-up window.

In a Level 2 implementation, if an application requires more space for messages, it can replace the message area in the footer with a scrollable text pane of two or more lines. Message logs can be implemented as pop-up windows with a scrollable text pane.

Minimum Window Sizes

When you resize a base window to reduce or *shrink* the area of the window, it cannot shrink beyond a minimum window size, according to the following rules:

☐ Headers, footers, and control areas keep the same height.

☐ The header must always be wide enough to display the Window menu button. The title need not be displayed if the width of the header is too small to accommodate any truncated title information.

☐ The width of the vertical scrollbar area or the height of the horizontal scrollbar always remains the same.

☐ Scrollbars cannot shrink smaller than the height of the *minimum scrollbar.*

☐ Panes cannot shrink smaller than 16 points in any direction.

☐ Panes with scrollbars cannot shrink smaller than the height of the minimum scrollbar. See Chapter 7 for a description of minimum scrollbars. The minimum dimension of a pane without a scrollbar is 16 points square.

Figure 3-15 show some examples of minimum window sizes for different pane configurations of a window that has a control area and a footer.

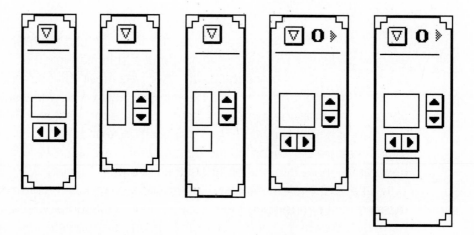

Figure 3-15   An example of minimum window sizes for base windows.

When you resize a pop-up window, the width of the header is always large enough to display the unpinned pushpin, as shown in Figure 3-16.

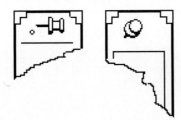

Figure 3-16   Minimum width for pop-up windows.

Multiple Base Windows

Although most applications have only one base window, more complex applications may have several. Each base window is equal to any other base window in the same application. It can be operated on independently and it has its own icon. The application determines the title that is displayed in the icon for each base window.

An application can also use multiple base windows, where one base window is designated as a "control base window," and other base windows, which close to independent icons, are subsidiary to the control base window. An example of this kind of application is a spreadsheet application in which each spreadsheet is a base window. A control base window contains a separate set of controls that act on the individual spreadsheet windows.

When an application uses multiple base windows in the way described in the preceding paragraphs, selecting Quit from the Window menu of the control base window quits all the base windows. Selecting Quit from the Window menu of a subsidiary base window (a spreadsheet window in this example) quits only that window.

Window Background and Foreground

An OPEN LOOK UI implementation makes a functional distinction between the background and the foreground of a window. You use the background to access the Window menu, to select a window, and to move it by dragging.

The window background is any part of the window that is not enclosed by a border or covered by a control such as a button, a setting, a text field, or a scrollbar. Labels for controls and read-only messages in the header or in a control area or pane are part of the window background.

The various elements of the window such as resize corners, the Window menu button, scrollbars, controls, and panes are foreground objects and are displayed against the window background.

The shaded area in Figure 3-17 is the background of a window with a control area and a pane.

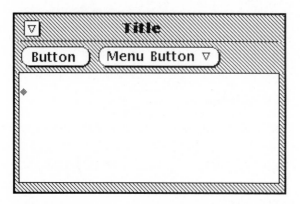

Figure 3-17   The shaded area is the background of a window with a control area and a pane.

The shaded area in Figure 3-18 is the background of a window with a control area, a footer, and a pane with a vertical scrollbar.

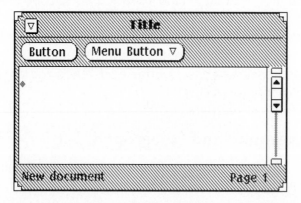

Figure 3-18   The shaded area is the background of a window with a footer and vertical scrollbar.

When possible, the OPEN LOOK UI implementation should consider the region between the right side of the scrollbar and the border of the window as part of the scrollbar area. Some implementations will consider that region part of the window background.

The shaded area in Figure 3-19 is the background of a window with a control area, a footer, and a pane with a horizontal scrollbar.

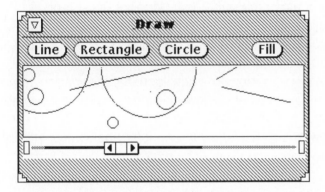

Figure 3-19   The shaded area is the background of a window with a footer and horizontal scrollbar.

The shaded area in Figure 3-20 is the background of a header and a control area that contains abbreviated buttons, settings, and a text field. Note that the category labels for the settings and the text field are part of the window background, but the controls themselves are in the foreground.

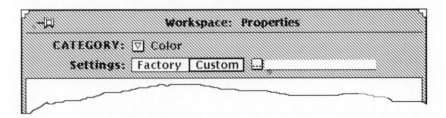

Figure 3-20   The shaded area is the background of a window with settings and a text field.

Base Window Positions at Startup

When you start up base windows, the OPEN LOOK UI default specifies that they are positioned on the screen in the following way: The first base window is positioned in the upper left corner of the screen. Subsequent base windows are positioned along the diagonal from the upper left to the lower right corner of the screen. When the lower right corner is reached, subsequent base windows start again at the upper left corner of the screen.

The application can define different defaults for base window positions at startup, and you can change those default window startup positions from the Workspace Properties window.

When you move a window to a new location, the window remembers that location. When you close a window and then reopen it, the window returns to its last location.

Base window positions at startup and icon positions at startup are defined separately.

State Feedback

Each window can be displayed in three states:

☐ Unselected
☐ Selected
☐ Busy

Unselected windows show the specified 2-point border.

Selected Windows

When you select a window, the border thickens. Figure 3-21 shows an unselected window with a selected window overlapping it. See Chapter 16 for information about selecting windows.

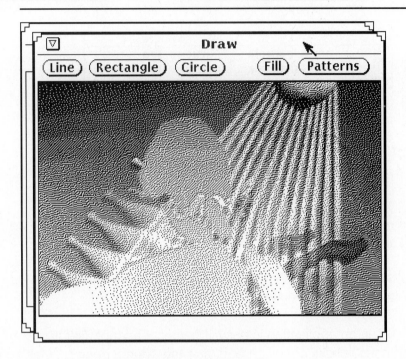

Figure 3-21   Selected window feedback.

Busy Windows

When the application is busy and cannot accept any user input, such as when a mail application is incorporating new mail, the header displays the standard busy pattern. The Window menu button is not busy, and you can access all Window menu functions from it. The standard busy pattern is specified in Appendix B. The standard busy pattern is always gray, even in color implementations. Figure 3-22 shows the header of a busy base window and a busy pop-up window.

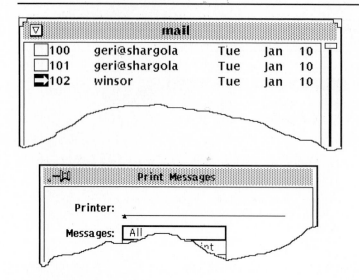

Figure 3-22   Busy windows.

When an application is busy, it does not accept user input. Any keystrokes or mouse clicks are discarded, and the system beeps. When you move the pointer over a busy window, the busy pointer is displayed.

Input Area

An *input area* is the region on the screen that accepts input from the keyboard. When an input area displays the characters you type, you set the place where characters are displayed by clicking SELECT or ADJUST to set the *insert point*. These areas include text panes, single-line text fields commonly found in control areas, and pop-up windows. The insert point is marked by a *caret*—a solid triangle at the text baseline—to show the exact place where characters typed from the keyboard are inserted into the text area.

Active Caret

You can set the initial insert point by positioning the pointer at the exact location where you want the caret and clicking SELECT or ADJUST. When you release the mouse button, the header of the window is *highlighted* and the active caret is displayed, as shown in Figure 3-23.

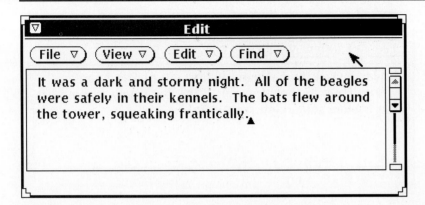

Figure 3-23   A window with an active input area and an active caret.

The window is not automatically brought to the front of the screen. The OPEN LOOK UI implementation determines whether or not the active caret blinks. When possible, it is recommended that the active caret blink. When an implementation supports a blinking caret, suppressing the blink is not a required user-settable option.

A Level 2 implementation has an option that always brings a window to the front of the screen when you click SELECT anywhere in the window to set the input area, but not when you click ADJUST. You set this option from the Workspace Properties window. See Chapter 11 for information about how to set this option.

Inactive Caret

When a window has an active caret and you change the input area to a different window, the active caret changes to an inactive caret and is displayed as a dimmed diamond, as shown in Figure 3-24. The header of the window is not highlighted.

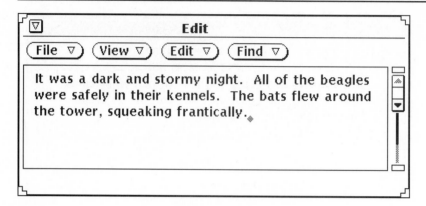

Figure 3-24 A window with an inactive caret.

When the window contains read-only information, the header of the window is not highlighted, and any caret in that window is displayed as inactive.

Activating an Inactive Caret

When a window has an inactive caret, you can change the inactive caret to an active caret by clicking SELECT anywhere on the window background. The window is selected and the border thickens when you press SELECT. When you release SELECT, the window is brought to the front of the screen, the header highlights, and the inactive caret becomes active. Clicking ADJUST on the window background does not restore the insert point. An ADJUST click toggles the state of the window, selecting it if unselected and deselecting it if selected.

Move Pointer Option

A Level 2 implementation has an option that allows you to change the input area without clicking SELECT. The Move Pointer option allows you to move the pointer into the window to change the input area to that window and activate the inactive caret. You set this option from the Workspace Properties window. You set the insert point to a different place in the window by moving the pointer and clicking SELECT as described above.

When you set the Move Pointer option from the Workspace Properties window, the header of a window that has the active input area does not highlight. Instead, it displays 2-point lines at the top and bottom of the header, as shown in Figure 3-25. The different input area feedback allows you to tell at a glance that the Move Pointer option is set.

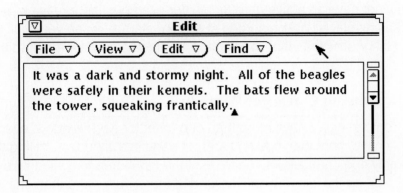

Figure 3-25   The header highlights in a different way when you set the input area by moving the pointer into the window.

There is always a 1-point white line between the window border and the 2-point line at the top of the header. When the window border thickens to show selection, this 1-point white space is maintained. There is always a corresponding 1-point white line below the 2-point line at the bottom of the header, as shown in Figure 3-26.

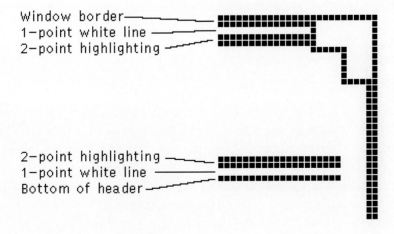

Figure 3-26   Detail of Move Pointer input area feedback.

Number of Active Carets

You can have only one active caret at a time. There are times when you may not have an active caret at all. For example, there may not be any input areas displayed on the screen at system startup, when you click SELECT to set the input area to the workspace, or when a window that had the input area is closed to an icon.

Number of Carets per Window

You can never have more than one caret for each window, even though you may have more than one text area or pane in a window. Limiting the window to only one caret allows you to reset the input area to a window by clicking SELECT on the window background. If there were more than one inactive caret, the window manager would be unable to determine which caret to activate.

When an application permits you to split panes, you may see multiple carets in a window. However, there is actually only one caret with multiple views of it displayed in a window.

Input Area Without a Caret

Most of the time you set the input area to type text. In some cases the keystrokes are used to activate a control or to select an item in a scrolling list. When a window accepts keyboard input but does not have a caret, the header of the window with the input area still highlights, as shown in Figure 3-27.

Figure 3-27   Keyboard input area feedback.

When there is no active insert point, the OPEN LOOK UI implementation beeps when characters are typed.

Input Area on the Workspace

You can set the input area to the workspace so that you can use keyboard functions or accelerators on the Workspace menu or in the Workspace Properties window. You do this by clicking SELECT on the workspace background. When you set the workspace as the input area, there is no visual feedback from the workspace itself.

System Restoring a Previous Input Area

An OPEN LOOK UI implementation always records the location of the last caret that was made inactive. This information is used by the system in the following cases.

□ When you dismiss or close a window with the input area, the input area is automatically restored to the previous window. If the previous one is not available because it was in the window that you dismissed or closed, the input area goes to the workspace.

□ In a Level 2 implementation, the window manager uses this information when you use the TOGGLEINPUT navigation accelerator to change the input area to the most recently used window.

A Level 2 implementation also records the sequence of input areas, and uses this information when you use the NEXTWINDOW or PREVWINDOW keys to change the input area from window to window.

Pop-up Windows

You invoke pop-up windows from an application by using a button or an item on a menu that has a window mark. You also invoke pop-up windows when you request Help. Pop-up Notices are automatically displayed by the application to inform you about certain conditions.

Pop-up windows are displayed to accomplish a specific purpose and are usually dismissed, either by you or by the application, when they have accomplished that purpose. They are never displayed as icons.

Kinds of Pop-up Windows

The various kinds of pop-up windows are listed below and are described in the following sections:

□ *Command windows* give operands and set parameters needed for a command.
□ *Property windows* set more persistent properties associated with an object, an application, or a window.
□ *Help windows* display help text for the object under the pointer.
□ *Notices* are special pop-up windows that are used to confirm requests for actions that cannot be undone and to display messages and conditions that must be brought to your attention.

Pop-up Window Ownership

Pop-up windows are owned by the originating base window and operate on that base window's application. You use pop-up windows to enter commands, change properties, or access help for that application. For example, an Edit: Load command window can only be used to load information into the Edit window that invoked the pop-up.

Multiple Invocations of a Pop-up Window

You cannot display multiple versions of the same pop-up window from an application. If you choose the control (window button or menu command) that displays a pop-up window, the opened window is moved to the front of the screen.

Pop-up Windows That Block Input to the Application

The application can specify that an individual pop-up window blocks all input to the rest of the application. Notices, for example, always block input to the application until you respond by clicking on a button in the Notice. When a Notice is displayed, each window for that application displays the standard busy pattern in the header.

Command windows and property windows, when specified as blocking pop-up windows, can also block input to the application. When a blocking pop-up window is displayed, the header of each opened window in that application, except for the pop-up window itself, displays the standard busy pattern.

Help windows never block input to the application.

The Pop-up Window Menu

Each pop-up window has a pop-up Window menu that you access from the pop-up window background. The choices on the pop-up Window menu vary slightly from the base Window menu. See Chapter 10.

You do not "close" a pop-up window, since that term is reserved for changing a window to its iconic representation. Instead, you "dismiss" pop-up windows. The label on the first button on the pop-up Window menu is Dismiss. Property windows use a slight variation from this convention. When you have made changes to the property window but have not yet applied them, the Dismiss label is changed to Cancel. For more information, see Chapter 10.

Grouping Pop-up Windows

When you close a base window, the pop-up windows associated with that base window are also dismissed. When the base window is opened, the pop-up windows are also opened if they were open when you closed the base window.

In a Level 2 implementation, one of the window properties is a Manage Windows setting that you can use to group all pop-up windows for an application with their base window so that you can move all the windows to the front or back of the screen as a group. The Manage Windows setting also determines whether or not dragging a base window also drags its associated pop-up windows. See "Level 2 Window Properties" later in this chapter for more information about grouping windows.

You can dismiss pop-up windows individually or in groups from the pop-up Window menu using the Dismiss submenu buttons labeled This Window and All Pop-ups.

Pointer Jumping

Most of the time you control the movement of the pointer on the screen. However, in some cases an OPEN LOOK UI implementation moves the pointer independently of the mouse and jumps it directly to a specific place on the screen. *Pointer jumping,* as it is called, makes the user interface efficient by minimizing unnecessary mouse movement. The pointer jumps to pop-up windows in the following ways:

☐ In Notices, the pointer jumps to the default button.
☐ In command windows, the pointer jumps to the default button or to the pushpin when there is no default button.
☐ In property windows, the pointer jumps to the Apply button.
☐ In help windows, the pointer jumps to the pushpin.

You can disable all pointer jumping from the Workspace Properties window. As long as you do not move the pointer off the button, the pointer jumps back to its previous location when the pop-up window is dismissed.

When you move the pointer from the initial control in the pop-up window, the pointer does not jump back. It remains at its last location when the pop-up window is dismissed.

When an application is invoked, or when you open an application from an icon, the pointer does not jump to any pop-up windows that are initially displayed.

An application can suppress pointer jumping for situations in which it is inappropriate. As an example, it makes little sense to jump the pointer to a read-only window in a graphics application that magnifies the pixels in a drawing and has no other controls. In this instance, the application can specify that the pointer does not jump to that specific pop-up window when it is invoked. In addition, an application can specify that certain pop-up windows do not accept keyboard input and, therefore, cannot become the input area.

Restoring the Insert Point

When the pointer jumps to a pop-up window that has an input area, the application moves the insert point to the pop-up window. When there is more than one possible place for the insert point, the insert point is moved to the first field the first time the window is invoked, or to the last field that was accessed.

When the pop-up window with the insert point is dismissed, the previous insert point is restored in one of the following ways:

☐ The insert point is restored to the most recently active caret.
☐ If the most recently active caret is not shown because it has been scrolled off the screen, the header of the window with the active input area highlights. The first character you type in the pane with the active caret scrolls the text with the caret so that it is repositioned at the first line in the pane.
☐ If the most recently active caret is in a window that has been closed, the input area is set to the workspace.

Command Windows

A command window allows you to set parameters for a command. Command windows always have all the required elements of a base window except for the Window menu button. Command windows can use any or all of

the optional elements of a base window. The default is for command windows
not to have resize corners. However, an application with many command
windows may need to specify them for command windows.

Pushpins

All command windows have one additional element: a pushpin on the left
side of the header that can be used to keep the command window displayed
after a command has been executed.

A pushpin has two states: pinned and unpinned. Clicking SELECT on the
pushpin toggles between the two states. The application specifies the default
state for the pushpin. Each time you display a pop-up window, it uses the
application-specified pushpin state.

Unpinned Windows

When a command window is unpinned, the command is executed and the
window is dismissed when you choose a command that affects the selected
object or takes action on a function. When a command window is pinned,
clicking SELECT on a button in the command window executes the command.
However, the command window remains on the screen, available for repeated
use, until you dismiss it by unpinning the pushpin or choosing Dismiss from
the Window menu.

Figure 3-28 shows an unpinned command window. In this example, clicking
SELECT on the Load button loads the file and dismisses the command window
from the screen. When the command cannot be executed, the pop-up
window is not automatically dismissed. It remains displayed so that you can
issue another command.

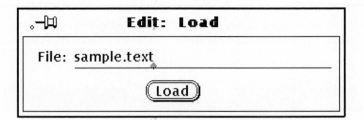

Figure 3-28 A sample unpinned command window.

If you do not want to load a file, you can dismiss the window by choosing Dismiss from the Window menu or by first clicking SELECT on the pushpin to pin the window and then clicking SELECT on the pushpin to unpin it and dismiss the window.

Pinned Windows

Clicking SELECT on the pushpin pins the window to the workspace, as shown in Figure 3-29. It remains available for repeated use.

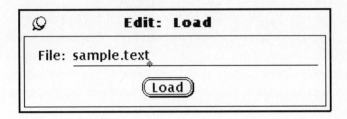

Figure 3-29   A sample pinned command window.

After the window is pinned, clicking SELECT on the Load button loads the file but does not remove the command window from the screen. Clicking SELECT on the pushpin unpins the window and dismisses it. As with any other window, you can dismiss the command window whether it is pinned or unpinned by choosing Dismiss from the Window menu.

Default Controls

A default control is specified for each command window to determine where the pointer jumps when the window is displayed, and what action is performed when you use the DEFAULTACTION key from the keyboard.

When a command window has one button, the application designates that button as the default for that command window. When a command window has more than one button, the application designates one button as the default. When a command window has no buttons, but contains other controls or read-only information, the OPEN LOOK UI implementation designates the pushpin as the default.

Buttons are centered at the bottom of the pane of a command window. See the *OPEN LOOK Graphical User Interface Application Style Guidelines* for guidelines on designing command windows.

Locations

The application determines where the command windows pop up. If you move a command window, it pops up in the new location the next time it is displayed. The locations of pop-up windows are remembered during a single invocation of an application. When you quit the application, the next time the application is invoked, all application-defined default positions for base and pop-up windows are used.

In a Level 2 implementation, one of the window properties allows you to record the current state and location of base windows, pop-up windows, and menus. Use the Pop-up Windows button to record the existing configuration and state of pop-up windows for an application. You can open or close pop-up windows, move them to specific locations on the screen, click SELECT on the Pop-up Windows button, and then click SELECT on the Apply button to preserve that configuration. See "Property Windows" in this chapter for more information.

State of Parameters

When you dismiss a command window without executing a command, any changes that have been made in the window are retained. The next time the window is opened, that information is displayed. For example, in Figure 3-28, if a different file name is typed in the File field, but you do not click SELECT on the Load button, the field is not reset or cleared when the window is dis-missed.

The state of the pushpin is not remembered. Each time a pop-up window is displayed, the application uses the default pushpin state.

Titles

The command window is titled according to the following conventions: The title of the application is followed by a colon and the function of the window. For example, the title of a graphics window that displays fill patterns is Draw: Patterns. If the window is too narrow to display the application title and function, the application name and the colon are dropped. In this case, the title of the window is "Patterns."

Property Windows

A property window is a pop-up window that allows you to set properties for the currently selected object or objects. These objects can be windows or icons on the workspace, panes in a window, or text and graphics.

You set properties by following these steps:

1 Select the object.

2 Choose the Properties item on a menu, by using the Properties button in a control area, or pressing the Properties key on the keyboard. The property window is displayed.

3 Change the settings in the property window.

4 Click SELECT on the Apply button in the property window to apply those settings. The property window is dismissed unless it is pinned.

See Chapter 18 for information about how to apply properties.

Property windows have all the required elements of a command window. They always have a control area within a pane, and they may have the optional elements of a base window.

Required Property Window Buttons

In addition to the usual required elements, property windows have the following required buttons centered at the bottom of the window, as shown in Figure 3-30:

☐ An Apply button that you use to apply the settings in the property window to the selection. Apply is always the default and is the only button in a property window that dismisses the unpinned window when its command is executed. When the property window is displayed, the pointer jumps to the Apply button.

☐ A Reset button that you use to reset the settings in the property window to the values for the original selection.

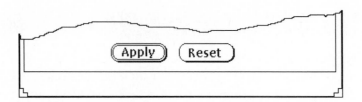

Figure 3-30   Required property window buttons.

Optional Property Window Buttons

When the application allows you to specify a new group of settings as the default, it can add a Set Default button to the bottom of the property window, as shown in Figure 3-31.

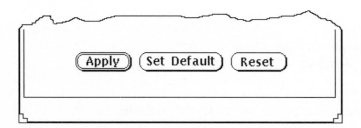

Figure 3-31   Set Default button for property windows.

You specify a new group of default settings by changing the settings in the property window and then clicking SELECT on the Set Default button to register those settings as the new defaults.

Applying Properties to Two Selections

Property windows that support two selections of the same type within the same application change the Apply button to a menu button. The Apply menu has the following two items:

☐ Original Selection (the default)
☐ New Selection (inactive unless there is an original selection)

When you make a second selection of the same type within the same application, the highlighting on the original selection is dimmed and the New Selection item on the Apply menu is activated, as shown in Figure 3-32. For more information, see "Two Active Selections" later in this chapter and Chapter 18.

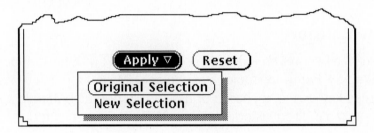

Figure 3-32   Apply menu for property windows.

Settings Pop-up Menu

As a convenience, pressing MENU anywhere in the pane displays a Settings pop-up menu. The items on the Settings menu must always provide the same functionality as the buttons and button menus at the bottom of the property window. Figure 3-33 shows the Settings menu with both required and optional items. See Chapter 10 for a complete description of the Settings menu.

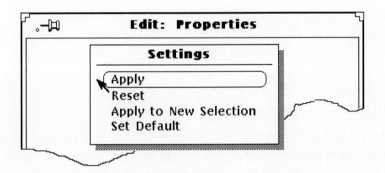

Figure 3-33   Property window pop-up Settings menu.

Titles

The property window displays the application title followed by a colon and the word Properties. However, when a property window sets only one kind of property, that property is displayed in the header following the title of the application.

Single Category

Figure 3-34 shows an example of a simple text property window with only one category. In this example, first you select text, then you press the Properties key on the keyboard or use the Properties button in a control area to display the property window. The settings for the selected text are reflected in the property window.

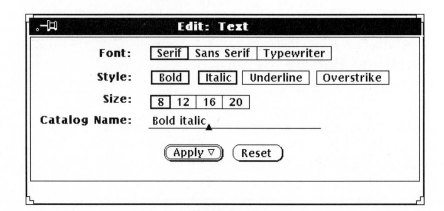

Figure 3-34   A sample text property window.

Multiple Categories

When there is more than one category for a property window, the property window has a control area above the pane. The application uses that control area to display a list of the classes of properties that you can display in the property window pane. The examples in this book show the label "CATEGORY." However, an application can use a label that is appropriate to the information displayed in the property window. For example, an application could change the "CATEGORY" label to "DISPLAY."

When there is a limited set of categories, the choices may be presented as exclusive or nonexclusive settings, as shown in Figure 3-35. Clicking SELECT on a different setting displays the options for that setting in the pane.

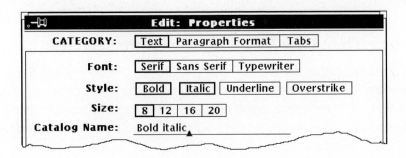

Figure 3-35 A sample property window with a CATEGORY label and exclusive settings in the control area.

When a property window has a number of different categories that can be displayed within the pane of the property window, the choices may be presented on an abbreviated menu button, as shown in Figure 3-36.

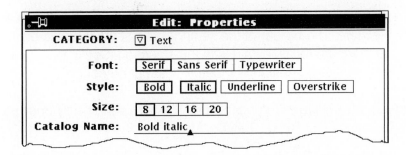

Figure 3-36 A sample property window with a control area.

The control area of this property window contains a Category: abbreviated menu button. The current category is displayed to the right of the menu button. You change the contents of the pane to display another category by pressing MENU on the abbreviated menu button, choosing a different category from the menu, and releasing MENU. When you choose a different category, the labels and settings in the pane change to reflect the choices you can make from the new category. Clicking SELECT on the abbreviated menu button returns the current category to the default setting.

Changing categories does not apply any changes to settings in categories that are not visible in the pane.

More Than One Value for the Same Selection

If the selection consists of a single object, the controls in the property window reflect the state of the object by accurately reporting on all of the settings. For example, when all the words in a selected sentence have the same font, style, size, and catalog name, each setting is shown in the text property window.

However, when there is more than one setting within the selection—for example, when a word in a selected sentence is in italics but the rest of the sentence is in the regular font—the property window shows you that information using the following conventions:

☐ The setting reflects the value of the first object in the selection. For text, this is the first character in reading order. For graphics, it is the first object selected.

☐ The setting of the current control in the property window is in an indeterminate state. The border of the setting (but not the label) is dimmed to show that there are multiple values in the selection. See Chapter 4 for information about the visual design of indeterminate state controls.

Figure 3-37 shows the borders for the Size settings dimmed.

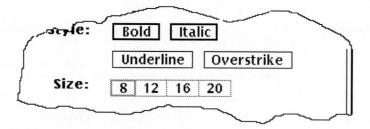

Figure 3-37   A sample property window with an indeterminate setting.

Settings that are in this indeterminate state are not applied to selected objects when you click on the Apply button. Clicking SELECT on a setting or editing a text field returns the feedback to normal, and the setting is then applied when you click SELECT on the Apply button. In this way, you can selectively change one or more settings across a range of objects.

Change Bars

A Level 2 implementation supports change bars in property windows. The application can display a *change bar* on the left side of the pane to show which settings have been modified. Change bars make it easy for you to determine whether any settings have been changed.

Suppose that you click SELECT on the "12" in the example in Figure 3-37. The dimmed border is replaced by a specific setting, and a change bar is displayed on the left side of the pane, as shown in Figure 3-38.

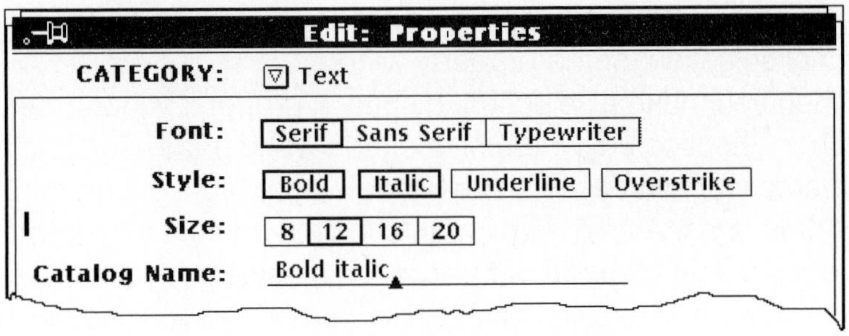

Figure 3-38   Property window with a change bar.

When you make a change in a text field and the contents of the text field have not been validated, the application can display a dimmed change bar to the left of the text field until the contents have been validated. When the contents have been validated, the change bar is displayed as a solid vertical line.

When you change the display in the property window from one category to another and have changed properties that have not yet been applied, a change bar is displayed to the left of the Category label to show that you have changed settings in other categories and that those changes have not yet been applied.

As an additional visual indication that changes to other categories have not been applied, the Apply label in the property window and on the Settings menu changes to Apply All as soon as you change from one category with new settings to a different category.

When you apply settings to a pinned property window, the change bars are removed from the property window.

Dismissing Property Windows

When a property window is dismissed before you apply the changes to the selection, the changes are discarded and a Notice is not displayed. The Window menu button displays the word Cancel rather than Dismiss.

Two Active Selections

Property windows support two active selections at the same time so that you can make other selections anywhere on the workspace without losing the original selection for the property window.

When you make a selection, display a property window, and then make another selection anywhere else on the workspace—including a selection of the same type within the same window—the highlighting on the original selection dims. A color implementation may display the dimmed selection either as a lighter shade of the specified selection color or as gray. The property window is still active, and you can apply properties from the property window to the original selection at any time.

The example in Figure 3-39 shows a dimmed original selection that results from the following steps:

1 Select "windshield viper," in the Edit window.
2 Use the Properties button on a menu to display the Edit: Properties window.
3 Move the pointer to the text field in the Edit: Properties window and select "Bold Italic."
4 The highlighting on "windshield viper" dims to show that it is not the primary selection.
5 You can type a different catalog name and apply that setting to the text with the dimmed highlighting using the Original Selection item from the Apply button menu.

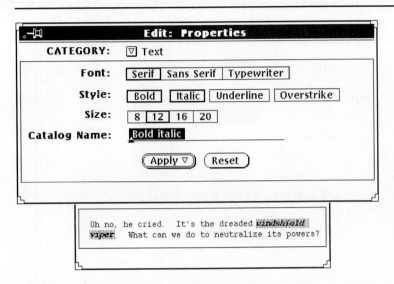

Figure 3-39 A property window with selected text and a window with a dimmed selection in the pane.

When you make a selection of the same kind in the same window, the New Selection item on the Apply button menu is activated, and you can apply properties to either selection. Use the Original Selection item to apply properties to the original dimmed selection. Use the New Selection item to apply properties to the new highlighted selection. Chapter 18 contains a complete a description of selecting and applying changes with property windows.

Level 1 Window Properties

You set window properties by using the Window menu Properties button to display a property window. The basic minimum set of Level 1 window properties is listed below:

□ Initial state (icon or window)
□ Initial location
□ Initial size
□ Record Current category with a Base Window State button
□ Window color (when appropriate)

Figure 3-40 shows the minimum Level 1 set of window properties.

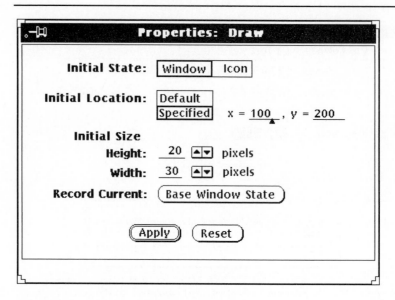

Figure 3-40   Level 1 window properties.

You use this property window to specify whether the application is displayed as a window or an icon at startup, the initial location of the base window, and the initial size of the window. When you apply these settings, they apply to subsequent invocations of the application and do not change the current location, state, or size.

The initial location is specified for subsequent invocations of this application by typing in x and y coordinates—x = 0, and y = 0—at the upper left corner of the screen. Alternatively, clicking SELECT on the Base Window State button fills in the current x and y coordinates of the window and the current size of the window. You can use these values or edit the field to modify them. When you set the initial location to Default, the x and y numeric fields are not displayed.

This example shows the initial size specified by number of pixels in height and width.

Level 2 Window Properties

A Level 2 implementation has the Level 1 required properties and the following minimum set of additional properties:

☐ Measure in: abbreviated menu button providing units of measurement for defining window size and location
☐ Base window scale
☐ Pop-up window scale
☐ Manage Windows settings
☐ Record Current State buttons

The property window shown in Figure 3-41 has Color settings, the required Level 1 properties, and the minimum Level 2 properties.

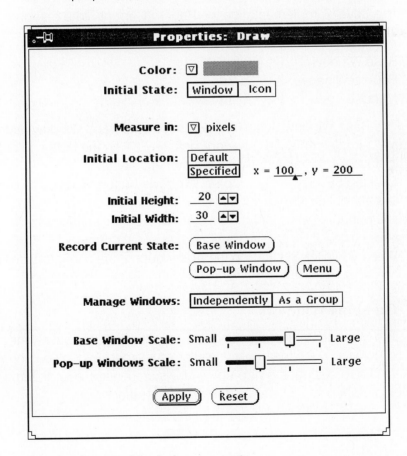

Figure 3-41   Level 2 window properties.

85

The Measure in: Category

The Measure in: category has an abbreviated menu button that displays the units in which you can specify window size and location. Typical units of measurement provided on this menu are:

☐ Pixels
☐ Millimeters
☐ Inches

When you click SELECT on the Apply button, the configurations are recorded and used the next time you start up the application.

The Record Current State Button

In a Level 2 implementation the Record Current State category has three buttons:

☐ Base Window
☐ Pop-up Window
☐ Menu

The Base Window button is the same as the Base Window State button in a Level 1 implementation. You can click SELECT on the button to enter the current location and location in the numeric fields.

Clicking SELECT on the Pop-up Windows button records the current position and state of the pop-up windows for the application. Clicking SELECT on the Menu button records the current state and default settings for all application menus.

When you click SELECT on the Apply button, the configurations are recorded and used the next time you start up the application.

Grouping Windows

The Manage Windows setting lets you operate on a base window and its pop-up windows either individually or as a group. When you choose the As a Group setting, the pop-up windows are always associated with the base window when you initiate the following operations from it:

☐ Clicking SELECT on the background of the base window brings the base window and all of its opened pop-up windows to the front of the screen. The pop-up windows are layered in front of the base window.

☐ Choosing Back from the Window menu of the base window moves the base window and all of its opened pop-up windows to the back of the screen. The pop-up windows are layered in front of the base window.

☐ Moving the pointer to the background of the base window, pressing SELECT, and dragging the base window moves the base window and all of its opened pop-up windows, keeping the pop-up windows in the same positions relative to the base window. None of the windows in the group can be moved completely off the screen.

To provide maximum flexibility in moving and layering pop-up windows, when As a Group is set you can still operate individually on any pop-up window in the group by initiating operations from the pop-up window instead of from the base window, as follows:

☐ Clicking SELECT on a pop-up window brings only that window to the front of the screen.
☐ Choosing Back from the pop-up Window menu moves only that window to the back of the screen.
☐ Moving the pointer to the background of a pop-up window, pressing SELECT, and dragging the pop-up window moves only that window.

Scaling Windows

The Scale settings allow you to set the scale of the base window and pop-up windows for any application independently. When you change the scale of a window, the upper left corner of the window is anchored at its previous location, and the window expands from that point unless the new scaling size would move the right and bottom border of the window off the screen. In that instance, the window origin is adjusted so that as much of the window as possible is displayed on the screen. A window's origin can never be adjusted so that the upper left corner of the window moves off the screen.

The scaling sizes that are provided depend on the individual OPEN LOOK UI implementation and can be displayed on the property window as exclusive settings when the number is limited. The minimum requirement is to provide two scaling sizes. When a slider is used and the number of sizes is limited, the slider moves smoothly when you drag it, but it jumps to the closest tick mark when you release SELECT.

Help

An OPEN LOOK UI implementation supports on-screen context-sensitive help both for elements of the interface and for applications. Help text for required elements of the OPEN LOOK UI is provided in Appendix C. The Window menu button displays help text for that element. In addition, it displays help text about selecting and operating on windows and panes.

Each application has its own Help window. There is no limit to the number of Help windows that you can display at the same time: You can display one Help window for each application that is displayed on the workspace. The application provides help text for all application elements, within the borders of windows and panes. A general description of the application (provided by the application developer) is displayed when the pointer is on the window background and you press the HELP key.

The name of the object under the pointer is displayed in the header of the Help window, the object under the pointer is displayed in the magnifying glass, and the help text for that object is displayed in the pane of the Help window.

An OPEN LOOK UI implementation must provide a way for the application to add help text to the standard help for scrollbars if that functionality is expanded by the application developer.

The Help Window

The Help window has the standard elements of a control pop-up window header, and has a pane but no control area. In addition, the portion of the screen at the pointer location is displayed in the magnifying glass to the left of the help text. The Help window is always displayed with the pushpin pinned, and the pointer jumps to the pushpin.

The pane of a Help window is large enough to display 50 characters and 10 lines of help text. The help text is centered vertically in the pane.

A sample Help window is shown in Figure 3-42.

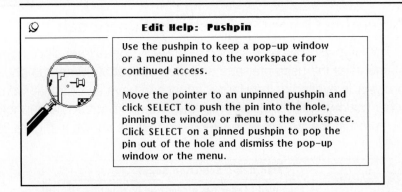

Figure 3-42   A sample Help window.

When help text has more than 10 lines, Help windows have a scrollbar and resize corners, as shown in Figure 3-43.

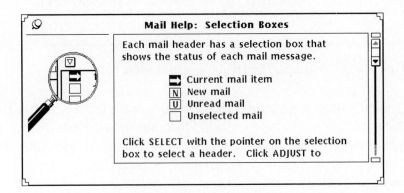

Figure 3-43   A sample Help window with a scrollbar.

Application help text can have the following elements:

☐ Text attributes such as bold and italics
☐ Glyphs (as illustrated in Figure 3-43, above)

An OPEN LOOK UI implementation supports automatic word wrapping of text in Help windows. An application can turn off automatic word wrapping and specify a different length for lines of text help.

Accessing Other On-Line Help Functionality

The Help window is designed to provide context-sensitive help for visual elements of the user interface and the application. When an on-line help browser is available, the Help window can have an optional *More button* or other buttons with labels appropriate to the expanded help functionality, centered at the bottom of the Help window, as shown in Figure 3-44.

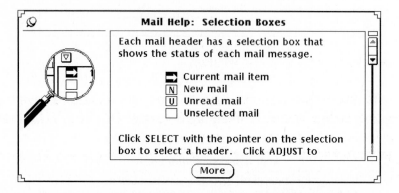

Figure 3-44   A sample Help window with a More button.

What happens when you click SELECT on the More button is determined by the application and the expanded help facility available on your system. The application might use the More button to display on-line documentation in the pane of the Help window. Alternatively, it could display a menu of other help items or a new window.

The More button can also be used in the Help window that displays information about the Window menu button to allow you to access help text from the application.

Conversely, an application can use a More button in the Help window that displays general information about the application to allow you to access help text about how to select and operate on windows and panes.

Using Help

Not every keyboard has a key labeled "Help," but an OPEN LOOK UI implementation requires that a key on the keyboard be specified as the HELP key. You set the key used to access Help from the Workspace Properties window.

You access help text in the following way:

1 Move the pointer to the object for which you want help.

2 Press the HELP key. A Help window is displayed. The pointer jumps to the pushpin in the Help window.

3 Click SELECT on the pushpin to dismiss the Help window. The Help window is dismissed, and the pointer jumps back to its last location.

Alternatively, you can move the pointer to another object in the same application and press the HELP key again. The new help text is displayed in the pane of the same Help window. As with all pop-up windows, once you move the pointer from its original position in the pop-up window, the pointer does not jump back when you dismiss the window.

The OPEN LOOK UI implementation determines whether or not output to the screen is frozen when a menu is displayed. When you use the HELP key while a menu is displayed, if the output to the screen is frozen, the menu is dismissed, the Help window is displayed showing help text for the object that was under the pointer (either the menu background or a specific control) when the menu was displayed, and the pointer jumps to the Help window.

If the output to the screen is not frozen, the Help window is displayed and the pointer remains on the menu. Pointer jumping is automatically suppressed in this situation so that you can read the help text and activate the control immediately if it is the one you want to use.

The OPEN LOOK UI does not specify how help text strings are referenced, how objects are linked to the help text, or where the messages are stored.

Notices

Notices are used to confirm major operations that cannot be undone and to report serious warnings and errors. Notices differ from other pop-up windows in the following ways:

□ Notices are initiated by the application.

□ Notices consist of a few sentences that describe the situation and tell you how to proceed.

□ Notices limit the choices you can make to a few buttons.

□ Notices cannot be moved.

□ A default button is always specified.

□ Notices do not have headers and footers.

☐ Notices are displayed in a font that is one scaling size larger than the window font to attract attention. When the window is in the largest font, the Notice uses that font.

☐ Notices block input to the originating application, not to the entire screen.

☐ When a Notice is displayed, the OPEN LOOK UI implementation flushes the buffer queue, discarding keystrokes and mouse clicks for the application. Flushing the buffer queue prevents you from inadvertently dismissing a Notice by typing or mousing ahead.

The Notice Window

The Notice window has the following required elements:

☐ A 2-point border with a pane positioned 2 points from the Notice border.
☐ At least one button.

When the OPEN LOOK UI implementation can support nonrectangular shapes, the Notice has an optional three-dimensional triangular shadow pointing to the place on the screen that originated the Notice, as shown in Figure 3-45.

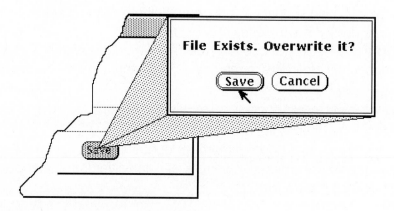

Figure 3-45   A sample Notice.

Notice Use and Placement

The Notice window pops up from the place of origin of the Notice function to give you a visual reminder of the action that originated the Notice. The pointer jumps to the default button but is not constrained to the buttons. The header of the base window and any open pop-up windows of the application that generated the Notice display the standard busy pattern. When you click SELECT on one of the buttons, the Notice is dismissed and the pointer jumps back to its last location.

You can move the pointer out of the Notice and perform operations in other windows. However, if you do this, when you return to the Notice and choose an option, the pointer will not jump back.

Buttons in a Notice are centered under the text within the pane. The application specifies where the text lines are broken. When the application does not specify where to break the lines, the OPEN LOOK UI implementation, by default, breaks the text to keep the area of the Notice as close to square as possible to avoid creating long skinny rectangles.

Notices always pop up toward the center of the screen. In the example shown in Figure 3-45, the originating window is in the lower left corner of the screen. Figure 3-46 shows the same Notice when the originating window is positioned in the upper right corner of the screen.

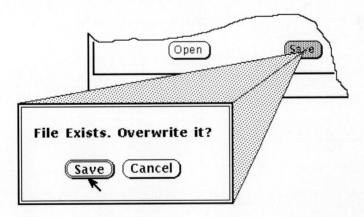

Figure 3-46   The Notice window is always displayed toward the center of the screen.

When the Notice originates from a pop-up menu that has been removed, the menu is redisplayed when the implementation can support that function.

On a small screen, the implementation automatically adjusts the Notice window and its associated shadow so that the buttons always remain on the screen. Figure 3-47 shows the progression of steps an implementation takes to make sure the useful part of the Notice always remains visible. In the top example, the space between the Notice window and the originating button has been shortened. In the second example, the shadow is displayed only from one side of the window. In the third example, the originating button is under the Notice, and no shadow is displayed. In the extreme case (not shown), the borders of the Notice window are moved off the screen.

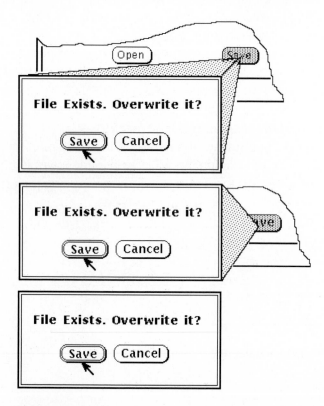

Figure 3-47 The Notice shadow is automatically adjusted to keep the Notice window on the screen.

The *OPEN LOOK Graphical User Interface Application Style Guidelines* provides suggestions for Notice messages and layout.

4

CONTROLS

The OPEN LOOK User Interface provides a simple and consistent set of application controls. There are two basic designs for each element of the OPEN LOOK UI:

☐ A black-and-white design for use on monochrome and low-resolution color systems.
☐ A three-dimensional design for use on grayscale and medium to high-resolution color systems.

The controls in this chapter specify the black-and-white design and show examples of three-dimensional controls. See Chapter 9 for more information about controls in a color implementation and for details of the three-dimensional design.

This chapter describes the following controls, the visual feedback for each control, and how you use them.

☐ Button controls (command, window, and menu buttons)
☐ Items on menus (command, window, and menu items)
☐ Settings (exclusive and nonexclusive)
☐ Check boxes
☐ Sliders and gauges
☐ Text and numeric fields
☐ Read-only messages

These controls can be used in control areas and panes in all windows. Settings and menu items are the only controls used in menus. See Chapter 6 for more information about controls in menus.

A table summarizing control usage is provided at the end of the chapter. See Chapters 5 and 6 for examples of how these controls are used.

Visual Feedback

Each control has a consistent visual feedback convention that shows the following conditions when appropriate for the control:

☐ The selection or setting feedback is used to show that you have pressed SELECT with the pointer on a control. An ADJUST click momentarily displays the question mark pointer. When appropriate, the visual feedback for pressing MENU is described. When MENU is not an appropriate input, the menu click is ignored and the question mark pointer is momentarily displayed.

☐ The *default ring* is used on buttons in pop-up windows and on menu items and settings to show the individual control that is the default choice.

☐ The *inactive* state is used to show that a command cannot be executed or is not currently available.

☐ The *indeterminate* state is used only in property windows to show that a selection has more than one value for an individual setting.

☐ The *busy* state is used on button controls and menu items to show that a button is executing an application command and cannot accept further input until the process is complete.

The following sections describe each control and the visual feedback for each state.

Button Controls

Button controls are the most common kind of control. There are two kinds of button controls:

☐ Buttons
☐ Menu buttons

Buttons are used for single commands. The label on the button describes the function that is executed.

Menu buttons are used to group commands into logical sets on a menu that is kept out of the way until it is needed. The label on the menu button is the title of the group of commands on the menu and submenus, not one of the commands.

Figure 4-1 shows a button and a menu button.

Figure 4-1   A button and a menu button.

In a three-dimensional implementation, the outlines of buttons are light on the top and dark on the bottom to create a three-dimensional effect, as shown in Figure 4-2.

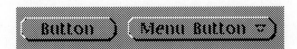

Figure 4-2   A button and a menu button in a three-dimensional implementation.

This section describes the elements that are common to buttons and menu buttons. Differences between the button controls are described in the following sections.

Button controls can be displayed both horizontally (the default) and vertically. When buttons are arrayed horizontally, the button label is centered in the button. When buttons are arrayed vertically, button labels are left-justified. As a guideline, button labels are one word where possible, and each word has an initial capital letter (in languages that support capitalization).

Application developers can use a glyph or a pattern in button controls instead of a button label. As a guideline, to keep the base window uncluttered, it is strongly recommended that buttons in the control area of a base window not contain glyphs.

Visual Feedback for Button Controls

Each button control consistently uses visual feedback conventions to show the conditions described below:

☐ When the pointer is on a button and you press SELECT, the button highlights. An ADJUST or MENU click momentarily displays the question mark pointer.

☐ When the pointer is on a menu button and you press MENU, the menu button highlights and the button menu is displayed. An ADJUST click momentarily displays the question mark pointer.

☐ When the pointer is on a menu button and you press SELECT, the default setting from the first menu under the menu button is displayed in place of the menu button. (See Chapter 5 for examples of this feedback.)

☐ When a button or menu button is the default, a ring is displayed inside the button outline.

☐ When a button is inactive, the button outline and label are dimmed.

☐ When a button is busy, the button background shows the standard busy pattern. The standard busy pattern is always gray, even in color implementations.

Buttons do not have an indeterminate state.
Figure 4-3 shows examples of the visual feedback for button controls.

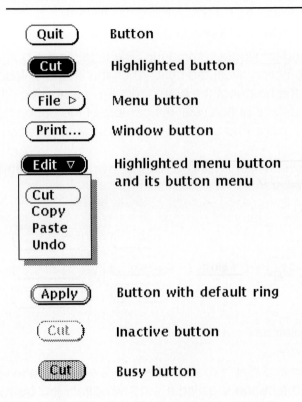

Figure 4-3 Visual feedback for button controls.

In a three-dimensional implementation, when you press SELECT, the dark shadow below and to the right of the highlighted button is replaced by white, and the white above and to the left of the button is replaced by a dark shadow, giving the illusion that the button is being pushed into the control area. The color in the border of the button is darkened to give an additional feeling of depth. Figure 4-4 shows a button with the dark and light reversed. Since this example uses a 50 percent gray pattern to show the effect, no darkening is shown in this example.

Figure 4-4 The button on the left shows highlighting for a three-dimensional implementation.

Buttons

Buttons are used for single commands. The label on the button relates to the name of the function executed by it. When the image or label that is displayed within the border of the button requires more space than is specified by the default button size, the corners of the button retain the same shape, and the height of the button is adjusted. The application specifies the width for buttons.

Figure 4-5 shows horizontal and vertical arrays of buttons and examples of buttons that are taller than the default size.

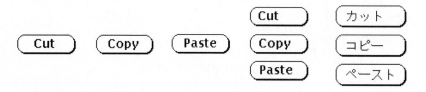

Figure 4-5 Horizontal and vertical button arrays.

When the command that is executed displays either a base window or a pop-up window, the button is called a *window button.* The button label always has a *window mark* (...) following it.

Figure 4-6 shows horizontal and vertical window buttons.

Figure 4-6 Horizontal and vertical window buttons.

When a window that originated from a window button is already displayed on the workspace, clicking SELECT again on that button does not display a new window. Instead, the current pop-up window is brought to the front of the screen.

Menu Buttons

Menu buttons are used to group commands in logical sets. The label on the menu button is the title for the group of commands on the menu and sub-menus. Menu buttons always have a visual element that is provided by the OPEN LOOK UI implementation called a *menu mark*. The menu mark is a hollow triangle glyph that points down when the menu is positioned below the button and to the right when the menu appears to the right of the button. Figure 4-7 shows both horizontal and vertical button arrays. The dotted line shows the menu position for the highlighted buttons. See Chapter 15 for more information about menu positions.

Figure 4-7   Horizontal and vertical menu button arrays.

When buttons are arrayed vertically, the menu mark is right-justified, as shown in Figure 4-8.

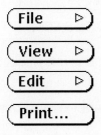

Figure 4-8   Alignment of menu mark in vertical button arrays.

The button menu is like a control area that is kept out of the way until you need to use it. When menu buttons are displayed in control areas, the application developer can choose whether the button menu appears centered beneath the button for horizontal arrays, or to the right of the button for vertical arrays.

Menu Items

When button controls are displayed on menus, they keep their labels and/or glyphs but do not display the button borders. These borderless button labels are called menu items. Menu items have the same "feel" as buttons, but have a slightly different look. You can choose whether or not to display the submenu for items that have a menu mark, depending on how you drag the pointer onto or within the item. See Chapter 6 for more information about menu items.

Abbreviated Button Controls

Button controls can be displayed in a small form without a title. *Abbreviated button controls* function in the same way as other button controls, and use the same visual feedback conventions. This section describes abbreviated buttons and abbreviated menu buttons.

Abbreviated Buttons

Abbreviated buttons have the following elements:

- ☐ A 1-point square border with a drop shadow
- ☐ An optional bold, right-justified label followed by a colon positioned to the left of the abbreviated menu button
- ☐ A Level 2 implementation supports an optional glyph within the border of the abbreviated button

Figure 4-9 shows some typical examples of abbreviated buttons that are used for scrolling.

▲ ▼

◀ ▶

Figure 4-9   Abbreviated scrolling buttons.

Abbreviated buttons in a three-dimensional implementation show the same light border at the top and left, and a dark shadow to the right and below the button. Highlighting reverses the dark and light parts of the border.

Abbreviated Menu Buttons

Abbreviated menu buttons are used when the application developer wants to show the current choice from the button menu without displaying the menu. Abbreviated menu buttons are used most frequently in command and property windows.

An abbreviated menu button has the following elements:

☐ A 1-point square border with a drop shadow
☐ A menu mark within the border of the button that points to where the menu will be displayed
☐ An optional bold, right-justified label followed by a colon positioned to the left of the abbreviated menu button
☐ An optional current item in the regular font positioned to the right of the abbreviated menu button. This setting shows the current item from the abbreviated button menu. Alternatively, the abbreviated menu button can have an optional text field positioned to the right of the abbreviated menu button that contains the current item.

The menu for an abbreviated menu button is the same as any button menu and can contain any combination of items and settings.

Figure 4-10 shows three examples of abbreviated menu buttons.

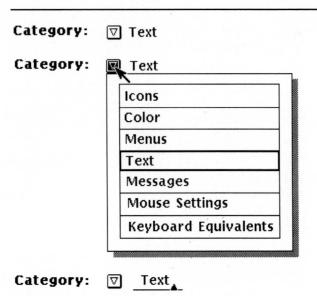

Figure 4-10   Examples of abbreviated menu buttons.

The first example in Figure 4-10, shows an abbreviated menu button for a property window with the current item displayed to the right.

The second example shows how the abbreviated menu button looks when you press MENU to display the button menu. The left side of an abbreviated button menu is aligned with the left side of the menu button, and the top of the menu is aligned with the bottom menu button line.

An OPEN LOOK UI implementation also supports a text field to the right of the abbreviated menu button that shows the current item from the menu. This variation is used when you can add items to the menu. In the third example, the current value is presented as a text field. When the application validates the text field, the contents of the text field are added to the choices on the menu.

When you move the pointer onto the abbreviated menu button and press SELECT, the default item on the menu is displayed to the right of the button. Releasing SELECT chooses the default item.

Exclusive Settings

Exclusive settings are lists of choices from which only one item can be selected. Exclusive settings have the following elements:

☐ A 2-point rectangular or square border around the current setting
☐ A 1-point rectangular or square border around settings that are not current
☐ An optional bold, right-justified label followed by a colon positioned to the left of the settings
☐ A glyph or text label within the border of each setting. Text labels are in the regular font and are centered within the border. When exclusive settings are arranged vertically, the label is left-justified within the border.

Figure 4-11 shows examples of exclusive text and pattern settings. Green and the solid black pattern are the chosen settings. Note that patterns or colors displayed as exclusive settings have 3 points of white space between the border and the pattern to keep the current setting visible.

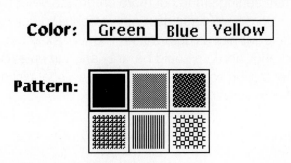

Figure 4-11   Exclusive settings.

In a three-dimensional implementation, settings have the same sort of visual outline as buttons, with a white line to the top and left, and a dark shadow to the bottom and right of the setting. To show exact patterns and prevent muting of colors in a palette, the application must be able to specify that settings or classes of settings can be highlighted without any darkening within the border of the setting.

Figure 4-12 shows an example of three-dimensional settings with Green as the chosen setting.

Figure 4-12 Exclusive settings in a three-dimensional implementation.

Setting Feedback

To change a setting, move the pointer to another setting and click SELECT. The bold border on the previous setting is moved to the new setting. An ADJUST or MENU click momentarily displays the question mark pointer.

The OPEN LOOK UI implementation may need to adjust the bold border that shows a chosen setting, depending on the resolution of the display. For example, on a medium-resolution display, a 2-pixel border provides enough visual feedback. However, on a high-resolution display, a 3-pixel border is required.

To make the current setting stand out more on grayscale or high-resolution screens, the interior borders of settings, both vertical and horizontal, can be lighter than the outline without using a dotted line. For example, on a gray-scale screen, the interior borders could be gray and the outer borders black. Medium- and low-resolution screens do not make a visual distinction between the interior and exterior border.

Default Settings

When exclusive settings are used on menus and while you are pressing the default modifier key and MENU, the default setting has a 3-point dark-light-dark border. In the example on the left in Figure 4-13, Small is the default setting. In the example on the right, the solid pattern is the default setting.

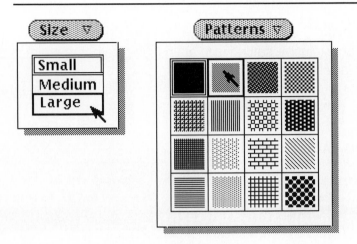

Figure 4-13 Exclusive setting defaults.

When the chosen setting is also the default setting, the solid border overlaps the open border so an open border is not shown, and the border is 3 points.

Indeterminate State

In property windows, when a selection contains more than one value for an exclusive setting, the 2-point border is indeterminate. The visual feedback to show an indeterminate setting is to dim the borders. The first object in the selection determines the bold border for the setting that is shown as dimmed. In the example shown in Figure 4-14, selected objects might be green and yellow. The current setting border for the Green setting is dimmed to show that the first selected object is green, and that other objects are not the same color.

Figure 4-14 An indeterminate exclusive setting.

See Chapter 3 for more information about indeterminate settings in property windows.

Inactive State

When an exclusive setting is in an inactive state, the entire category is dimmed, as shown in Figure 4-15.

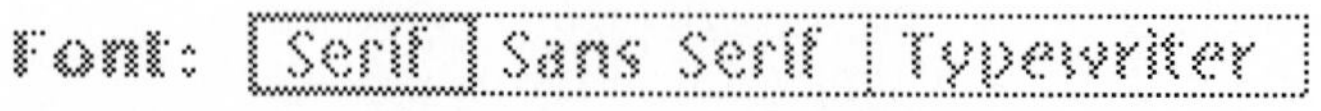

Font: [Serif] Sans Serif | Typewriter |

Figure 4-15   An inactive exclusive setting.

Variation on Exclusive Settings

There are times when an application may permit you to choose none of the options from a list of exclusive settings. To support this, an OPEN LOOK UI implementation provides a variation of exclusive settings. When you click SELECT on a current setting, it toggles to a deselected state. This allows you to choose none of the settings.

For example, using this variation of exclusive settings allows a graphics application to provide a palette for a fill pattern without needing to include a setting for "None." Figure 4-16 shows how you choose none of the patterns of an exclusive setting in a pop-up window.

Move the pointer to the setting with the bold border.

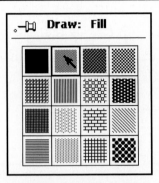

Click SELECT to toggle the setting, choosing none of the Fill patterns

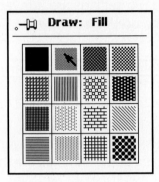

Figure 4-16   Exclusive setting variation.

Nonexclusive Settings

Nonexclusive settings are used to set multiple values for the same object. Nonexclusive settings have the following elements:

☐ An optional bold, right-justified label followed by a colon positioned to the left of the settings
☐ Separate 1-point rectangular or square borders
☐ A 2-point rectangular or square border around a setting that is current
☐ A glyph or text label within the border of each setting. Text labels are in the regular font and are centered within the rectangle. When nonexclusive settings are arranged horizontally, the label is left-justified.

In a color or grayscale implementation, nonexclusive settings have the same visual design and highlighting feedback as exclusive settings.

Nonexclusive settings can be used to show a single choice that can be either "on" or "off." Figure 4-17 shows a single nonexclusive setting without a label for a graphics application in which you can choose whether or not to constrain objects to a grid in the drawing area.

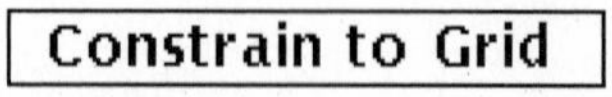

| Constrain to Grid |

Figure 4-17   A single nonexclusive setting.

When nonexclusive settings are arrayed horizontally, each setting label is centered within the border, as shown in Figure 4-18.

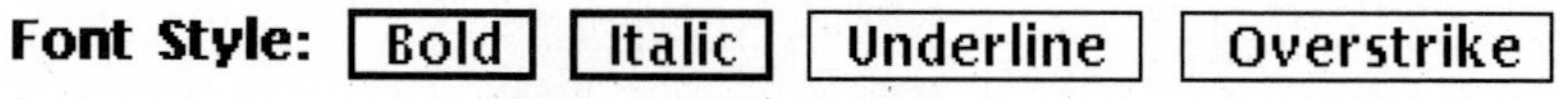

Font Style: | Bold | | Italic | | Underline | | Overstrike |

Figure 4-18   Nonexclusive settings arrayed horizontally.

When nonexclusive settings are arrayed vertically, the settings are displayed in rectangles of the same size with left-justified setting names, as shown in Figure 4-19.

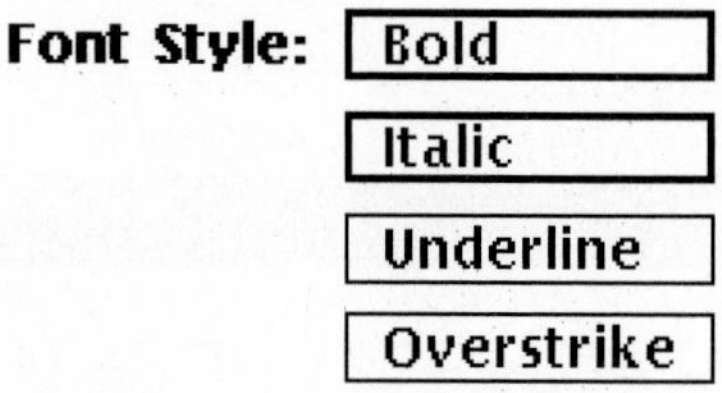

Font Style: | Bold |
| Italic |
| Underline |
| Overstrike |

Figure 4-19   Nonexclusive settings arrayed vertically.

Nonexclusive settings can also be grouped in other combinations. The application developer determines whether the settings are displayed in rectangles of the same size with left-justified setting names or arranged in some other layout. Figure 4-20 shows examples of different layouts of exclusive settings.

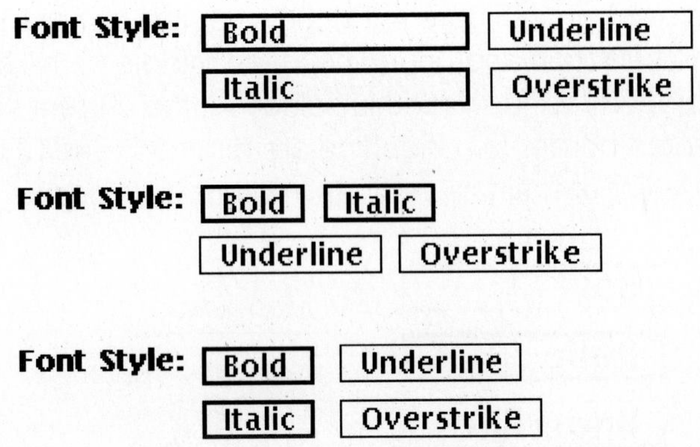

Font Style: | Bold | | Underline |
| Italic | | Overstrike |

Font Style: | Bold | | Italic |
| Underline | | Overstrike |

Font Style: | Bold | | Underline |
| Italic | | Overstrike |

Figure 4-20 Nonexclusive settings arrayed in columns.

Setting Feedback

Settings that are active have a two-point bold border. Move the pointer to one of the rectangles and click SELECT to toggle the setting. In the example shown in Figure 4-20, Bold and Italic are the chosen font style settings. An ADJUST or MENU click momentarily displays the question mark pointer.

Default Setting

When nonexclusive settings are used on menus, there is only one default, even though you can choose more than one setting. The default setting is the same as that for exclusive settings: It has a dark-light-dark border.

Indeterminate State

The border for the setting (or settings) in an indeterminate state is dimmed. For example, suppose you have selected text that is in an italic font, but only some of the text is bold and underlined. The OPEN LOOK UI implementation considers both the current setting and the indeterminate state. When the first item in the selection is the current setting, and there are additional settings within the selection, one indeterminate setting may have a bold border and another one may have a 1-point border.

In the example shown in Figure 4-21, the selected text has bold at the beginning of the selection and underline in the middle of the selection. When you display a property window for this selection, the current setting for Bold and the unselected border for Underline are dimmed. See Chapter 3 for more information about indeterminate settings in property windows.

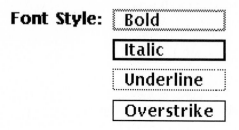

Figure 4-21 Indeterminate state nonexclusive settings.

Inactive State

The entire setting is dimmed, including the label, the borders, and the text.

Check Boxes

Check boxes are a kind of nonexclusive setting provided for lists of items that have a yes/no or on/off response when a label is not required. Check boxes cannot be used in menus.

Check boxes have the following elements:

☐ A square 1-point border when the check box setting is "off" or "no"
☐ A check mark in the check box when the setting is "on" or "yes"

Figure 4-22 shows a check box in the "off" and "on" states.

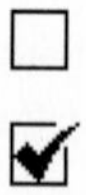

Figure 4-22 Check boxes.

Figure 4-23 shows an example of check boxes in a text property window.

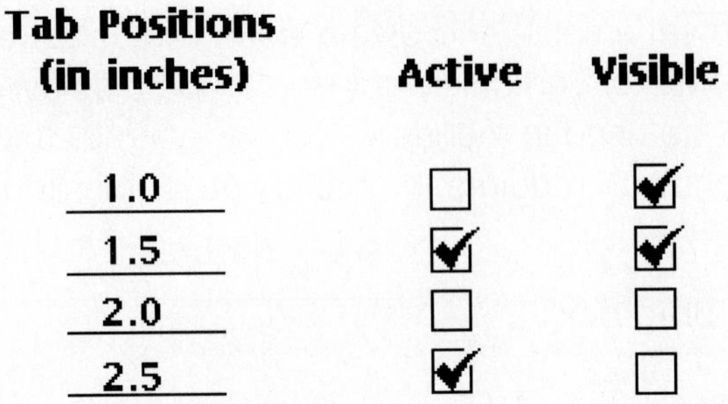

**Tab Positions
(in inches)**   **Active**   **Visible**

1.0	☐	☑
1.5	☑	☑
2.0	☐	☐
2.5	☑	☐

Figure 4-23   A matrix of check boxes.

Setting Feedback

Move the pointer to a check box and click SELECT to toggle the state of the check box. An ADJUST or MENU click momentarily displays the question mark pointer.

Default Setting

Check boxes cannot be used in menus; they therefore lack default settings.

Indeterminate State

The entire check box is dimmed, since check boxes are used in conjunction with other controls that can show an indeterminate state.

Inactive State

The entire check box is dimmed.

Sliders

Sliders are used to set a value and give a visual indication about a setting. Sliders can be horizontal or vertical, and they can be displayed in a variety of ways. Sliders cannot be used in menus.

A Level 1 implementation requires the basic horizontal slider with the following elements:

□ A slider bar with a drag box
□ An optional label
□ Optional maximum/minimum value labels (either text or numeric)
□ An optional read-only current value field
□ An optional type-in field

The examples in this section show the placement, usage, and descriptions for default placement of slider controls. The OPEN LOOK UI implementation can provide additional display variations.

Figure 4-24 shows examples of Level 1 horizontal sliders.

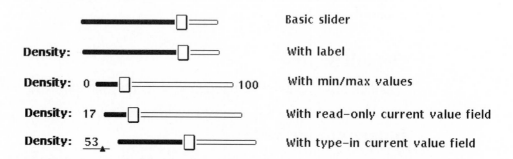

Figure 4-24 Level 1 horizontal sliders.

Figure 4-25 shows a three-dimensional slider.

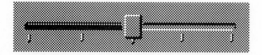

Figure 4-25 A three-dimensional slider.

114

A Level 2 implementation requires the following additional elements for horizontal sliders, as shown in Figure 4-26:

☐ Optional end boxes with a 1-point border at either end of the slider that you can use to go to the beginning or end of the scale
☐ Optional tick marks
☐ Optional tick mark maximum/minimum value labels

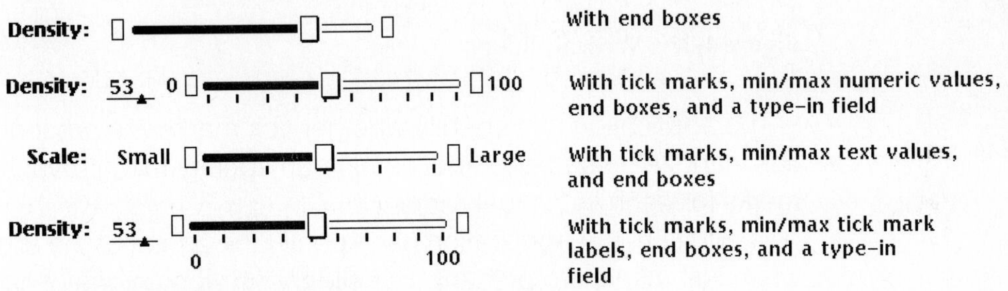

Figure 4-26   Level 2 horizontal slider elements.

A Level 2 implementation supports vertical sliders with the following elements, as shown in Figure 4-27:

☐ An optional label
☐ Optional minimum/maximum value labels (either text or numeric)
☐ An optional read-only current value field
☐ An optional type-in field
☐ Optional end boxes
☐ Optional tick marks
☐ Optional tick mark minimum/maximum value labels

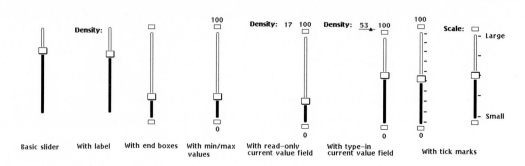

Figure 4-27   Vertical sliders.

The application can specify whether tick marks are present or not. When tick marks are used, the application can specify the interval between tick marks for each individual slider.

In addition, the application can specify the action of the slider drag box when tick marks are present. The slider can work in one of two ways:

☐ The drag box snaps to the nearest tick mark when you release SELECT.
☐ You can position the drag box at any point along the slider, and the tick marks provide visual feedback.

Setting Feedback

The drag box and end boxes highlight when you press SELECT. An ADJUST or MENU click momentarily displays the question mark pointer.

Default Setting

Sliders cannot be used on menus; they therefore lack default settings.

Indeterminate State

The slider is dimmed; the label is not.

Inactive State

The label and the entire slider are dimmed.

Using Sliders

You can change the value of the slider in the following ways, depending on the functionality implemented by an application:

☐ Move the pointer to the slider drag box and press SELECT. The drag box highlights, and the pointer stays in the drag box. Drag the pointer to change the setting, and then release SELECT.

☐ Click SELECT on the slider bar to the left or right of the slider drag box to change the setting by one increment. The drag box pushes the pointer ahead of it as the settings change, if necessary, to allow repeated clicks.

☐ Click SELECT in the open rectangle at either end of the slider to change the setting to either the minimum or the maximum. The rectangle is highlighted while you press SELECT.

☐ Type the value in the field. When you press Return, the drag box on the slider moves to correspond with the typed value. If you type a number beyond either end of the numeric range, when the field is validated, the slider drag box moves to the maximum or minimum, and the value in the numeric field automatically changes to reflect the correct number.

The slider responds to typed input in a text or numeric field only when you validate the data by pressing the validation character (typically Tab or Return) specified by the application.

Gauges

The OPEN LOOK UI specifies read-only gauges that an application can use to provide useful information. Gauges can be used to show status information such as percent of disk used or buffer storage capacity. Gauges cannot be used in menus.

Read-only gauges have the following elements:

☐ A 1-point outline
☐ A dark area in the center of the outline
☐ Optional tick marks below a horizontal gauge or to the right of a vertical gauge

□ Optional numbers or labels at the first and last tick mark
□ An optional right-justified bold label followed by a colon to the left of the gauge

Gauges can be displayed horizontally or vertically. Figure 4-28 shows examples of horizontal and vertical gauges.

Figure 4-28 Gauges.

Gauges show no selection or setting feedback, have no default setting, and have no indeterminate or busy state.

Gauges can have an inactive state when the information shown by the gauge is not current or has not been updated.

In a three-dimensional implementation, gauges look much like sliders.

Text Fields

Type-in text or numeric fields are used to type information from the keyboard. Text fields are never used on menus. Text fields can be displayed anywhere in a control area or a pane, and may follow other controls such as nonexclusive settings or sliders.

Text fields have the following elements:

□ A right-justified bold label followed by a colon to the left of the text field
□ A 1-point underline defining the length of the field for single-line text fields
□ A 1-point rectangular or square border defining the area of the field for multi-line text fields. Multi-line text fields can be a fixed size or scrollable. A scrollable multi-line text field has a scrollbar.

☐ Optional increment/decrement buttons to the right of a single-line numeric text field
☐ Scrolling buttons at the beginning and end of a single-line text field when the text does not fit in the field
☐ Level 2 implementations have a pop-up Edit menu that is displayed when you press MENU in the type-in area. See Chapter 10 for more information about the text field Edit menu.

Figure 4-29 shows an example of a basic text field with a label and a line.

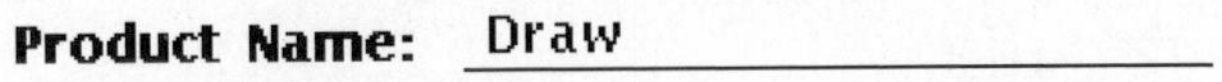

Product Name: <u>Draw</u>

Figure 4-29   A basic text field.

In a three-dimensional implementation, a text field is a 2-point dark line with a 1-point white line directly above it, as shown in Figure 4-30.

Product Name: <u>Draw</u>

Figure 4-30   A basic text field in a three-dimensional implementation.

The editing capabilities of text fields are the same as they are for text panes. You move the pointer to the text field and click SELECT to set the insert point. The header of the window highlights.

The caret for text fields is the standard text caret—a solid black triangle when the field has the active insert point and a gray diamond when it is inactive. The caret overlaps the line and does not break it. See Chapter 3 for illustrations of the standard text carets.

Scrolling in Text Fields

Text fields have an application-specified fixed length. However, when you can type more characters than the length of the field permits and the field contains more text than it can show, *scrolling buttons*—abbreviated buttons with a triangular arrowhead—are displayed at the beginning and/or the end of the line within the text field to show that there are more characters in the direction shown by the arrow. The scrolling buttons are displayed interactively only when the text string is longer than the display field.

Text fields should generally be long enough that scrolling buttons are not needed for normal operation.

Figure 4-31 illustrates how the scrolling buttons function. Note that if "ABCDEF" is a value expected in normal operation, the application should define a field long enough to contain those characters without requiring the scrolling buttons.

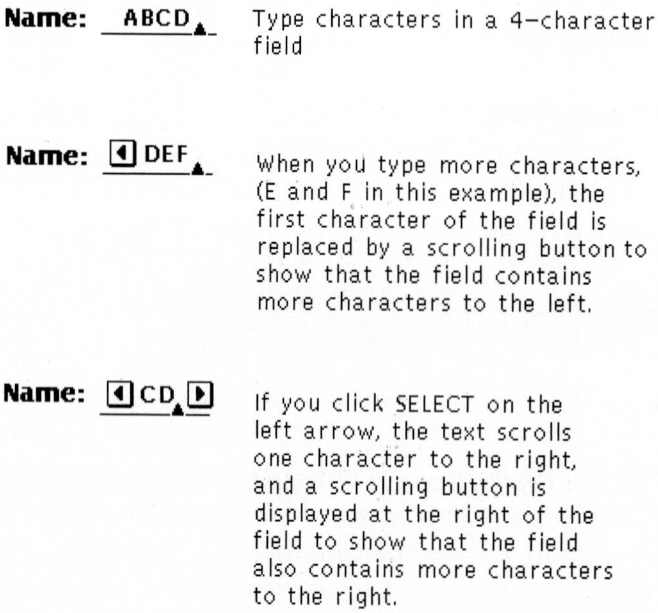

Name: ABCD ▲ Type characters in a 4-character field

Name: ◀ DEF ▲ When you type more characters, (E and F in this example), the first character of the field is replaced by a scrolling button to show that the field contains more characters to the left.

Name: ◀ CD ▲ ▶ If you click SELECT on the left arrow, the text scrolls one character to the right, and a scrolling button is displayed at the right of the field to show that the field also contains more characters to the right.

Figure 4-31 A text field with horizontal scrolling buttons.

When you press SELECT on one of the scrolling arrows, it displays the standard highlighting feedback. When you release SELECT, the text in the field scrolls one "a" character width.

When a text field with scrolling buttons contains proportionally spaced characters, the text field always displays complete characters. The new text is aligned with the end of the text field, and white space is added as padding at the beginning of the line to adjust the spacing.

A Level 2 implementation provides automatic scrolling when a text field cannot display the entire text string. When you use wipe-through selection in a text field and the pointer reaches the beginning or end of the text that is displayed in the field, the contents of the field automatically scroll until the beginning or end of the text is displayed. The pointer is not constrained during this operation.

Numeric Text Fields

Text fields that allow only numeric values may have increment/decrement buttons to the right of the field, as shown in Figure 4-32, to permit a quick way to increment or decrement the value in the field. For example, assuming that the numbers are sequential, click SELECT on the up arrow to change the number in the field to 14. Then click SELECT on the down arrow to return the number to 13. Click SELECT again on the down arrow to change the number to 12.

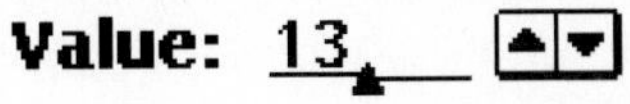

Value: 13 [▲|▼]

Figure 4-32   A numeric text field with increment/decrement buttons.

An OPEN LOOK UI implementation must provide a way for applications to specify non-numeric characters for use with hexadecimal numeric systems and to specify delimiters, brackets, braces, and parentheses as acceptable input for numeric fields.

Multi-Line Text Fields

A Level 2 implementation provides multi-line text fields. Multi-line text fields can be limited to a fixed size, or they can be scrollable, depending on the requirements of the application.

An application might specify a fixed-size multi-line text field for entering information into a database that can handle only a fixed number of characters for each field.

When there is no restriction on the number of characters that can be typed in a multi-line text field, the application defines the size of the multi-line text field border and displays a scrollbar to the right of the border, as shown in Figure 4-33.

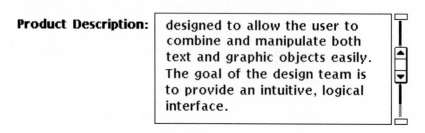

Figure 4-33 A multi-line text field with a scrollbar.

Text Field Example

Figure 4-34 shows an example of a numeric field, a single-line text field, and a nonscrollable multi-line text field.

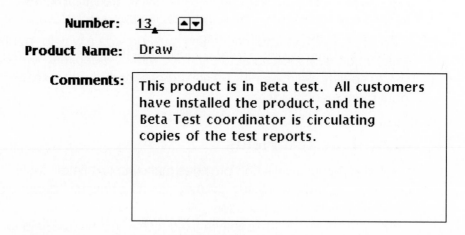

Figure 4-34 An example of text fields.

Validating Text Fields

The application determines whether or not to *validate* a given text field. Validation commonly includes checking the information in the field to be sure that it contains data that the application can use. For example, if you type numeric characters in a field that accepts only alphabetic characters, when the field is validated, the application informs you that alphabetic input is required. Validation from the application can occur on a per-field or per-form (when all changes are applied) basis. Per-field validation occurs when you press Tab or Return, or when the insert point is set to another text field.

All numeric fields, including those for sliders, provide immediate error checking for invalid characters. When you type an illegal character, the system beeps and displays the message "Not a number" in the footer.

In a Level 2 implementation, when you make a change in a text field and have not validated the contents of that field, an application can display a dimmed change bar to the left of the text field until the contents have been validated.

Setting Feedback

The active caret is set when you press SELECT or ADJUST. An ADJUST click extends or reduces the selection. In a Level 1 implementation, a MENU click momentarily displays the question mark pointer.

In a Level 2 implementation, pressing MENU displays the text field Edit menu. See Chapter 10 for a description of the Edit menu.

Default Settings

Text fields cannot be used in menus; they therefore lack default settings.

Indeterminate State

The text line or text rectangle is dimmed to show an indeterminate state text field. The label is not dimmed.

Inactive State

The label and the text line or text rectangle are dimmed for text fields.

Messages

An OPEN LOOK UI implementation supports the display of read-only
messages in panes or control areas. Read-only messages can consist of a
text string or a glyph. For example, the information about file size, modification, access, and type in the example shown in Figure 4-35 are read-only
messages that provide information about a file.

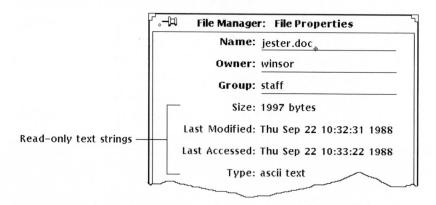

Figure 4-35   Text messages in a property window.

When read-only messages are displayed on the window background or in a
pane, they do not interfere with the normal functioning of that area of the
window. For example, the application title in the header is a read-only
message. You can click SELECT anywhere on the header, whether the pointer
is on the title or not, to select the window. When you press MENU with the
pointer on a read-only message, the menu appropriate to that area of the
window is displayed.

Summary Table

Table 4-1 is a summary checklist of control features and where they are used. Chapters 5 and 6 describe how the controls in this chapter are used in control areas and menus.

Table 4-1   Summary of controls and where they are used.

Features	Control Area	Menu	Pane	Window Header
Button controls	✓	☐	✓	✓ *
Menu items	☐	✓	☐	☐
Exclusive settings	✓	✓	✓	☐
Nonexclusive settings	✓	✓	✓	☐
Check boxes	✓	☐	✓	☐
Sliders	✓	☐	✓	☐
Gauges	✓	☐	✓	☐
Text fields	✓	☐	✓	☐
Read-only messages	✓	☐	✓	✓

*Window menu button only.

5

CONTROL AREAS

A control area is an unbordered region of a window where application controls such as buttons and settings are displayed. A control area can be anywhere in a base window, pop-up window, or in a pane within a base or pop-up window.

Positions of Control Areas Around Panes

An OPEN LOOK UI implementation supports any configuration of control areas around and within panes. Controls can be arranged horizontally or vertically.

Button controls are the most common objects in a control area around a pane. Usually there is one control area at the top of a window and a pane beneath it, as shown in Figure 5-1.

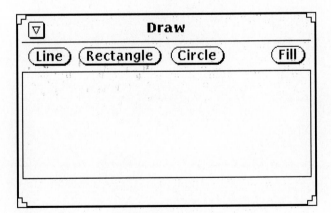

Figure 5-1   A control area above a pane.

The control area can be on one side or the other of the pane, as shown in Figure 5-2.

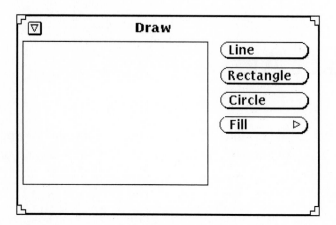

Figure 5-2 A control area to the right of a pane.

Controls can be used to govern more than one pane. Controls do not need to be grouped on the same side of the pane. Figure 5-3 shows controls at the top, right side, and bottom of a pane.

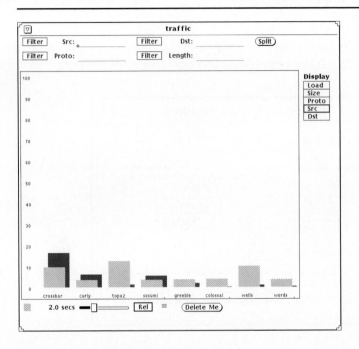

Figure 5-3 Control areas around a pane.

Control Areas Within Panes

The entire window can be a pane containing a control area. Such a configuration is most likely to occur in command windows that pop up to perform specific functions. When the entire window is a control area, the controls are displayed within a pane. This minimizes the window background area and shows the controls more clearly in a color implementation.

Control areas within panes usually contain varied combinations of the following controls:

☐ Buttons and menu buttons
☐ Exclusive and nonexclusive settings
☐ Check boxes
☐ Sliders
☐ Text and numeric fields

The following examples show various combinations of controls in command window panes. Figure 5-4 shows an example of a command window with text fields, buttons, and exclusive and nonexclusive settings.

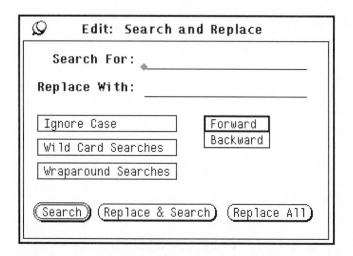

Figure 5-4   A control area pane in a command window.

The application developer determines the layout of controls within a pane. Figure 5-5 shows an example of check boxes and sliders within a pane.

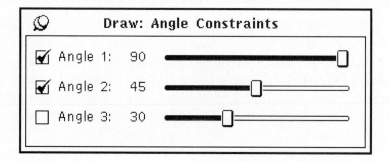

Figure 5-5   A control area pane with check boxes and sliders.

Figure 5-6 shows an example of a command window with exclusive and nonexclusive settings, a numeric field, a slider, and a button.

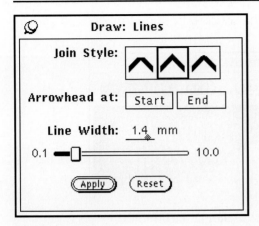

Figure 5-6 A control area pane with exclusive and nonexclusive settings, a type-in text field, and a slider.

Using Window Buttons in a Control Area

The following examples show the steps and visual feedback when you use a window button. To use a window button in a control area, first move the pointer onto it, as shown in Figure 5-7.

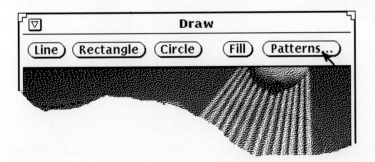

Figure 5-7 Move the pointer onto a window button in the control area.

Then press SELECT. The window button highlights as shown in Figure 5-8.

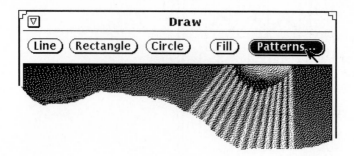

Figure 5-8   Press SELECT to highlight the button.

To activate the button, release SELECT. The button displays the standard busy pattern while it is executing the command, as shown in Figure 5-9. The busy pattern may be displayed momentarily. If you do not want to activate the button, move the pointer off the button and release SELECT.

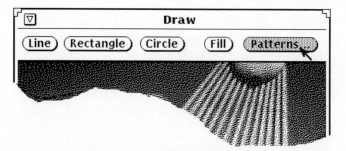

Figure 5-9   Release SELECT to activate the command that displays the pop-up window.

When the command is complete, the button returns to its normal appearance. In this example, the Patterns pop-up window is displayed and the pointer jumps to the pushpin, as shown in Figure 5-10. See Chapter 3 for information about pointer jumping.

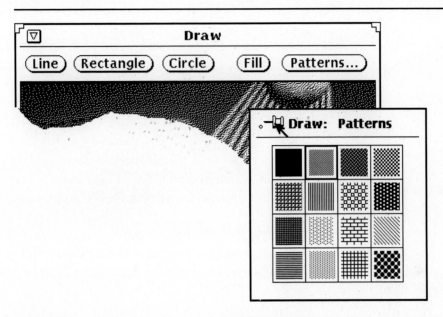

Figure 5-10 When the window is displayed, the button returns to its regular appearance.

Using Command Buttons in a Control Area

Using command buttons in a control area is similar to using window buttons in a control area. You move the pointer onto the button. Pressing SELECT highlights the button. Releasing SELECT activates the command. The busy pattern may be momentarily displayed, and then the button returns to its normal appearance.

If the command cannot be executed, an error message is displayed in the footer of the window from which you initiated the command. When an unsuccessful command is initiated from a pop-up window, it is not dismissed, regardless of the state of the pushpin.

Using Menu Buttons in a Control Area

You can use menu buttons in a control area in two ways:

☐ Press SELECT to view the default from the button menu in the control area. Release SELECT to execute the default.

☐ Press MENU to display the menu for the menu button. To dismiss the menu, move the pointer off it and release MENU. To execute a command, press MENU, drag the pointer onto an item in the menu, and release MENU.

The following sections describe how to use menu buttons in a control area to display menu defaults and how to choose from menu buttons in a control area. For a detailed description of viewing and choosing from menus see Chapter 15.

Menu Defaults for Menu Buttons

The default control for a button menu is the one that is automatically used when you click SELECT on a menu button in a control area or on a stay-up menu. Menu defaults provide a quick and convenient way to activate a function, while still providing the flexibility of making a different choice or quickly changing the default setting. The visual designs for control default settings are described in Chapter 4. See Chapter 6 for more information about menu defaults and Chapter 15 for information about how to change the menu default.

Viewing Menu Button Defaults in a Control Area

When menu buttons are displayed in a control area, you can view the default for the menu immediately under the menu button without displaying the menu.

You do this by moving the pointer to a menu button in the control area and pressing SELECT. The default choice for the menu immediately under the menu button is displayed in the area occupied by the menu button. Releasing SELECT executes the default and returns the menu button to its normal state. Moving the pointer off the button before releasing SELECT returns the menu button to its normal state without executing the default.

134

Note that this view shows the default on the menu that is immediately under the menu button. When this default is, itself, an item that displays a menu, the view does not show the bottom level default that is executed when SELECT is released. Showing the default for only one level of menu prevents possible ambiguity if several bottom-level menus have similar choices.

The following examples show how defaults are displayed for each kind of control.

When the text string for the default item is short enough to fit within the border of the menu button, it is displayed in its entirety. When the text is too long, it is truncated to fit within the menu button outline. A nonscrollable more arrow is displayed to show that the text has been truncated, as shown in Figure 5-11.

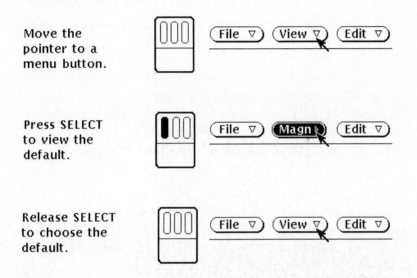

Move the pointer to a menu button.

Press SELECT to view the default.

Release SELECT to choose the default.

Figure 5-11   Viewing a text item default.

When the default is an exclusive setting, the outline of the menu button changes to a rectangle, and the current choice is shown selected (with a bold border), as shown in Figure 5-12. If the default is smaller than the button, the rectangle is the same size as the button, and the default is centered within that rectangle. If the default is larger than the button, it is displayed from the upper left corner and shows as much as possible of the default in the button area.

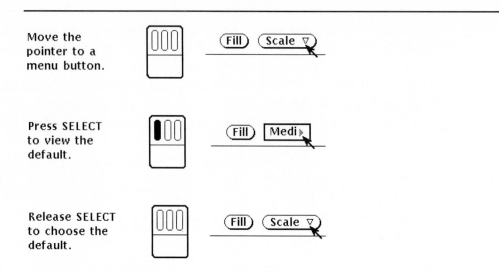

Figure 5-12   Viewing an exclusive setting default.

When the default is a nonexclusive setting, the outline of the menu button changes to a rectangular or square border, and the current value is toggled to show the state that is selected if the mouse button is released. If the current value is on (bold border), the default shows it in the off state (1-point border), and vice versa. Figure 5-13 shows the current value with a 1-point border.

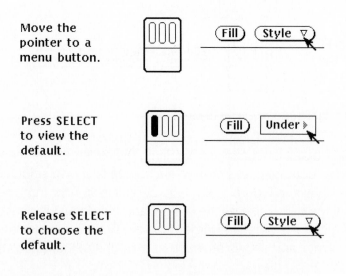

Figure 5-13   Viewing a nonexclusive setting default.

An image or pattern from a menu of exclusive settings is displayed as a bold rectangle the same size as the button. A portion of the pattern starting from the upper left corner is displayed within the border, as shown in Figure 5-14.

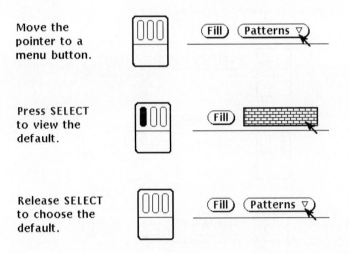

Figure 5-14 Viewing a pattern exclusive setting default.

When the default is a pushpin, it is shown in the button outline, pinned, as shown in Figure 5-15.

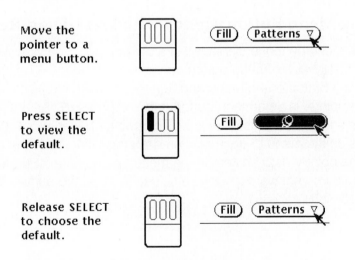

Figure 5-15 Viewing a pushpin default.

Inactive Default Settings

When a default setting on the button menu is inactive, the default is shown dimmed when you press SELECT. When you release SELECT, the system beeps to let you know that the default setting is unavailable. Figure 5-16 shows an example of viewing an inactive default item.

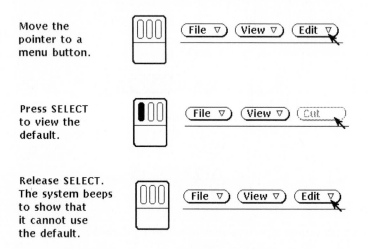

Move the
pointer to a
menu button.

Press SELECT
to view the
default.

Release SELECT.
The system beeps
to show that
it cannot use
the default.

Figure 5-16   Viewing an inactive default item.

Viewing Menu Button Menus with Press-Drag-Release

When a menu button is displayed in a control area, you view its menu by pressing MENU on the menu button, as shown in Figure 5-17. Drag the pointer off the menu button or the menu and release MENU to dismiss the menu. When the pointer is on a menu button and you press MENU, the button highlights and the menu is displayed. The pointer never jumps into the menu; it remains on the menu button until you drag the pointer into the menu.

Drag the pointer onto an item in the menu and release MENU to make a choice. If you do not want to make a selection, drag the pointer off the menu and release MENU.

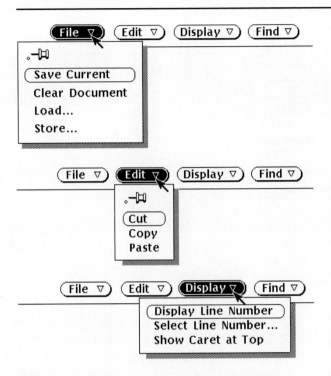

Figure 5-17 Viewing button menus (horizontal).

Viewing Stay-up Menus

When you click MENU on a menu button, the menu is displayed and remains on the screen until the next mouse click is received. Just as a pinned menu becomes a command window, a *stay-up menu* becomes a transitory control area. The difference between a pinned menu and a stay-up menu is that the stay-up menu is dismissed as soon as you choose a control. A pinned menu remains displayed until you dismiss it. All the controls in a stay-up menu function like controls in a pinned menu. The originating button displays the standard busy pattern, as shown in Figure 5-18.

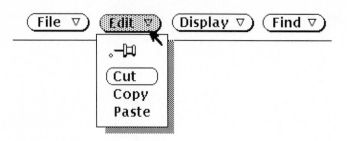

Figure 5-18   A menu button displays the standard busy pattern when the menu is displayed in stay-up mode.

Viewing menu button defaults with SELECT works exactly the same way it does in control areas. Clicking MENU with the pointer on an item with a menu mark without moving the pointer beyond the damping factor displays the submenu in stay-up mode. Pressing MENU without moving the pointer displays the submenu in press-drag-release mode.

Clicking SELECT or MENU anywhere off the stay-up menu items dismisses the menu from the screen and does nothing else. For example, if you click SELECT on a button in the control area with a stay-up menu displayed on the screen, the menu is dismissed. You must click SELECT again on the button in the control area to choose that function. An ADJUST click momentarily displays the question mark pointer.

See Chapter 15 for more information about viewing menus and submenus and choosing from them.

6

Menu Elements

Menus enable you to make choices from a small, fixed set of options. When an application requires the display of a large number of choices, the application should use a *scrolling list*. See Chapter 8 for scrolling list specifications.

This chapter explains the required and optional elements used in menus. See Chapter 15 for information about how you view and choose from menus, and for the specifications for the placement of menus.

Menu Types

An OPEN LOOK UI implementation provides two basic types of menus:

☐ Button menus, which are displayed from menu buttons.
☐ Pop-up menus, which pop up at the pointer location and control the region under the pointer.

Menu Groups and Submenus

This section defines the terms used to describe menus. When a menu has an item that displays an additional menu, the additional menu is called a *submenu*. Any menu and its submenus are called a *menu group*.

There is no restriction on the number of submenus that can be included in a menu group.

Required Menu Elements

Each menu has the following elements:

☐ Menu outline
☐ Drop shadow
☐ Items and/or settings
☐ One default choice per menu
☐ Pop-up menus always have a title

The specifications for menu titles are provided under "Menu Titles" later in this chapter.

The only optional menu element is the pushpin. Pushpins on menus are described under "The Optional Pushpin" later in this chapter.

Border and Drop Shadow

Menu borders are rectangles with a drop shadow, as shown in Figure 6-1.

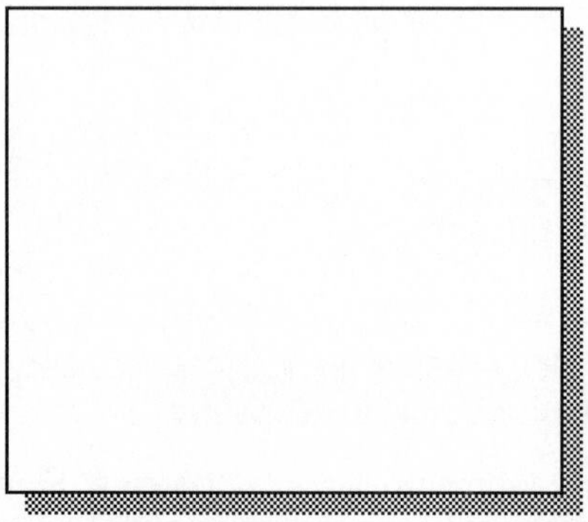

Figure 6-1   A sample menu border and drop shadow.

The border is a 1-point rectangle. The drop shadow is 6 points wide, and starts at the seventh point from the upper right and lower left corners of the menu outline.

On monochrome systems, the drop shadow is 75 percent gray. The shadow is always visible. When possible in an OPEN LOOK UI implementation, the shadow is transparent, allowing the information behind the drop shadow to show through.

In a color implementation, the drop shadow is a darkening of the color under the drop shadow. The drop shadow can be an overlay of a 75 percent stippled pattern over the color background, increased in saturation, or grayed.

When the shadow cannot be implemented as transparent, the opaque shadow obscures the information behind it.

Controls

Each menu has at least one control. The application developer chooses the appropriate control to provide efficient interaction with the application. A menu can have the following controls:

☐ Items
☐ Exclusive settings
☐ Nonexclusive settings

These controls can be used on menus in any combination. The functionality of settings is described in Chapter 4. The following sections describe these controls and show examples of how they can be used in menus and submenus.

Items on Menus

Items on menus are similar to buttons, as described in Chapter 4, and they provide the same functionality as command, window, and menu buttons:

☐ A *command item* is like a command button. You use it to execute the command named in the item.
☐ A *window item* is like a window button. When the item is followed by a window mark, a window is displayed.
☐ A *menu item* is like a menu button. You use it to display a submenu.

Items on menus are displayed vertically, and the width of the menu is always enough to accommodate the longest text item, whether that is an item or a setting on the menu, or the title of a pop-up menu. Window marks follow the item label. Menu marks are always right-justified and are aligned following the longest text item on the menu. Figure 6-2 shows an example of a button menu with all three types of items.

Figure 6-2 A menu with three kinds of items.

Programs and Utilities are menu items. The menu mark points to the right to show that the submenus will be displayed to the right of the item. Properties is an item with a window mark; choosing it displays a property window. Exit is a command item; choosing it exits the workspace.

The Programs item has a default ring to show that it is the default item on the menu. See "Menu Defaults" later in this chapter for more information about menu defaults, and Chapter 15 for information about changing a menu default.

Highlighting Feedback. When you drag the pointer onto a menu item, an oval with the same dimensions as the default ring highlights, as shown in Figure 6-3.

Figure 6-3 A menu with a highlighted item.

The highlighting follows the pointer as you drag it from item to item. As soon as you drag the pointer onto any menu item, the default ring is no longer displayed on the menu. Releasing MENU when an item is highlighted activates the item. See Chapter 15 for more information about choosing from menus.

Displaying Submenus. In an item with a menu mark, the submenu is displayed when you drag the pointer to the right, beyond the drag-right distance that you specify from the Workspace Properties window. The default drag-right distance is 5 pixels. See Chapter 11 for more information about setting the drag-right distance. Figure 6-4 shows the submenu for a menu item.

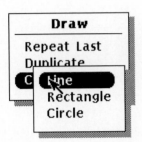

Figure 6-4   A submenu for a menu item.

The default item on the submenu is aligned horizontally with the originating item, and the position of the pointer determines the vertical alignment of the submenu. See Chapter 15 for the specification of menu and submenu positions.

Grouping Menu Items. An OPEN LOOK UI implementation must provide a way for an application to increase the amount of white space between controls to allow controls with similar functions to be grouped. Figure 6-5 shows an example of a menu that has items grouped.

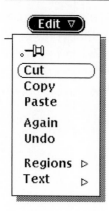

Figure 6-5   A menu with white space between groups of items.

Multi-Column Menus. Menus can have more than one column of items. A multi-column menu may have a 1-point vertical line between each of the columns, as shown in Figure 6-6.

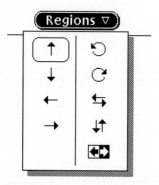

Figure 6-6   A menu with two columns of items.

Exclusive Settings

Figure 6-7 shows an example of exclusive settings on a menu for a Modes menu button in a drawing application. In this example, exclusive settings are arranged in a square grid.

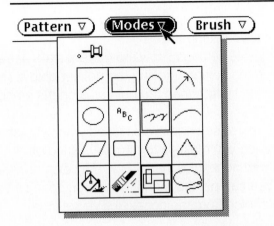

Figure 6-7   Example of exclusive settings on a menu.

When exclusive settings are used on menus, the current setting has a bold border when the pointer is not on a setting. When you drag the pointer onto a setting, the bold border follows the pointer and the default ring is not displayed.

Nonexclusive Settings

Figure 6-8 shows an example of a menu that has items and a submenu that has nonexclusive settings. In the example, the chosen settings on the submenu are Bold and Italic. Underline and Overstrike are not chosen.

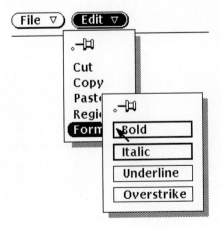

Figure 6-8   An example of nonexclusive settings on a submenu.

When they are displayed in groups, nonexclusive settings are formatted in the same way as exclusive settings.

Menus with nonexclusive settings show the current state of each setting unless the pointer is on the setting. Moving the pointer onto a setting toggles the setting to its opposite state. When the pointer is on the menu, no default ring is displayed.

A menu with nonexclusive settings is dismissed when you choose one setting, even if the choice you make is to turn the setting off. An application that provides menus with nonexclusive settings may also provide a pushpin on the menu so that you can pin the menu to the workspace if you want to make more than one choice from the nonexclusive settings.

Mixing Controls on Menus

A Level 2 implementation allows an application to mix items and exclusive and nonexclusive settings on the same menu. Figure 6-9 shows an example of a menu that has both an item with a window mark and exclusive settings.

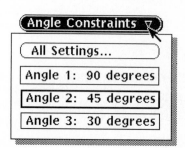

Figure 6-9   An example of mixed controls on a menu.

Menu Titles

Pop-up menus always have titles. Menus or submenus that originate from menu buttons or menu items do not have titles, since the name of the menu button or item that you press to display the menu or submenu acts as the title for the submenu.

A menu with a title is always wide enough to display the menu title. The title is centered, in bold type, and has a 1-point line beneath it, as shown in Figure 6-10.

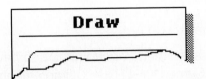

Figure 6-10 An example of a menu title.

Menu Defaults

Each menu or submenu has only one default (even when nonexclusive settings permit more than one choice from a menu). When the application does not specify a default, an OPEN LOOK UI implementation uses the first item on the menu as the default. When a menu has a pushpin, the pushpin is the first item on the menu. If the default is removed from a menu by an application, the application is responsible for setting a new default. When the application does not reset the default, the first item on the menu becomes the default. Chapter 4 shows the visual designs for exclusive and nonexclusive setting defaults.

Default settings are displayed only when the pointer is not on a menu control. They are never displayed on submenus unless you press the SETMENUDEFAULT modifier key to display or set the menu default.

An OPEN LOOK UI implementation searches for menu defaults from the originating menu down through the levels of submenus (from left to right) and executes the default at the end of the search chain.

How Menu Defaults Affect Other Windows

The default for each menu, including window and scrollbar menus, is set individually for each menu in each invocation of an application, even if you have several windows open that are running the *same* application. The default setting is not saved across invocations of that application.

Level 2 implementations allow you to save the application configuration for window properties, including the current default settings, for all menus. In this way, you can customize the menu defaults for an application. See Chapter 3 for more information about window properties.

The Optional Pushpin

Any OPEN LOOK UI implementation menu or submenu can have a pushpin at the top left side of the menu. Some OPEN LOOK UI implementations, based on earlier versions of the *OPEN LOOK Graphical User Interface Functional Specification* have pushpins positioned at the top right side of the menu.

The application developer determines which menus have pushpins. When a menu has a pushpin, you can use it to keep a frequently used menu pinned to the workspace.

The pushpin can be set as the menu default either by the application or by you. When the pushpin is the default, the unpinned pushpin has a circle around the pinhole. Figure 6-11 shows a pushpin with a default ring.

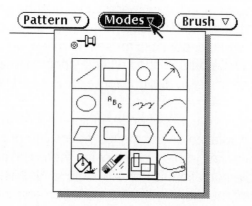

Figure 6-11   The pushpin as the default on a menu.

See Chapter 15 for a description of how to pin a menu to the workspace.

Figure 6-12 shows a menu group in which both the button menu and the submenu have pushpins. In this example, you can pin each menu separately.

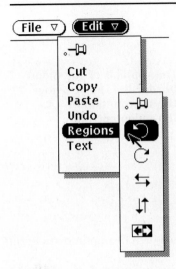

Figure 6-12   A menu and a submenu that both have pushpins.

When any menu in a menu group that has a pushpin is pinned to the workspace, other menus in the group are dismissed. In the example shown in Figure 6-12, if you pin the Regions submenu, the Edit menu is dismissed.

Button Menu Placement

When a menu is displayed from a menu button with the menu mark pointing downward, the menu is always centered beneath the originating button. The top of the menu is 1 point below the bottom line of the button, as shown in Figure 6-13.

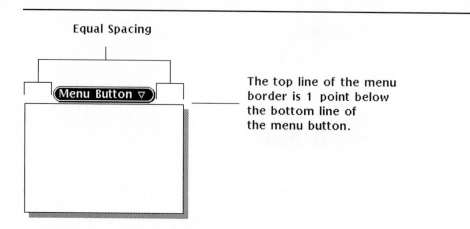

Figure 6-13   Menu alignment for buttons when the menu mark points down.

When a menu is displayed from an abbreviated menu button, the top of the menu is 1 point below the bottom line of the button and the left edge of the menu aligns with the left edge of the button, as shown in Figure 6-14.

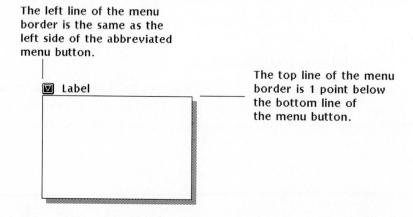

Figure 6-14   Menu alignment for abbreviated buttons when the menu mark points down.

When a menu button has the menu mark pointing to the right, the menu is displayed with the default item aligned with the originating menu button. The line for the left side of the menu is 1 point to the right of the menu button, as shown in Figure 6-15.

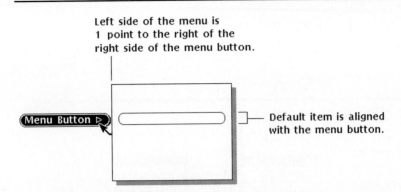

Figure 6-15 Menu alignment for buttons when the menu mark points to the right.

When an abbreviated menu button has the menu mark pointing to the right, the menu is displayed following the same rules for menu buttons: The default item aligns with the originating button and the left side of the menu is 1 point to the right of the abbreviated menu button, as shown in Figure 6-16.

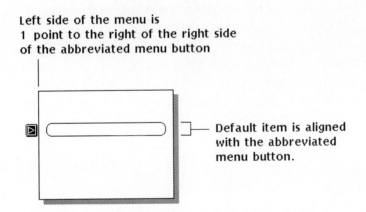

Figure 6-16 Menu alignment for abbreviated buttons when the menu mark points to the right.

When you have a window at the bottom of the screen, and the menu does not fit between the bottom of the menu button and the bottom of the screen, the menu is repositioned so that the menu is always completely on the screen, as shown in Figure 6-17.

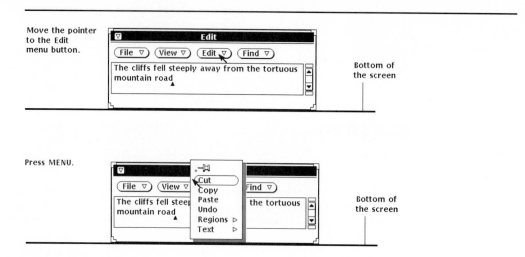

Figure 6-17   Alignment for menus at the bottom of the screen.

The menu is centered on the originating menu button, as usual. The bottom of the drop shadow aligns with the bottom of the screen. The pointer moves as needed so that it is positioned a few points to the left of the default item on the button menu.

When the menu or submenu bumps against the right side of the screen, the pointer moves as needed so that it is positioned a few points on the left side of the default item on the button menu. The menu is pushed to the left so that the right side of the drop shadow aligns with the right side of the screen.

See Chapter 15 for menu placement specifications.

7

SCROLLING

This chapter describes the appearance and functionality of scrollbars and specifies two ways to scroll without using a scrollbar.

Scrollbars

Scrollbars let you change the view of the data displayed in a pane, and move directly to the beginning or end of the information available in a pane; they let you split panes and remove split panes.

Scrollbars are displayed next to a pane when the pane can contain scrollable information. The default position for vertical scrollbars is on the right side of the pane.

Some implementations may provide an option that you set from the Workspace Properties window to display vertical scrollbars at the left side of panes.

Horizontal scrollbars are always positioned at the bottom of a pane, and a pane can have both horizontal and vertical scrollbars. Horizontal and vertical scrollbars work in exactly the same way.

Figure 7-1 shows the components of a vertical scrollbar: the elevator (the arrow buttons and the drag area), the cable, and the top and bottom cable anchors.

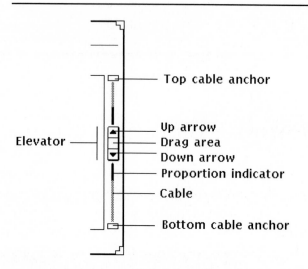

Figure 7-1   Vertical scrollbar components.

Figure 7-2 shows a horizontal scrollbar. In a horizontal scrollbar, the orientation is left and right, rather than top and bottom. The directional components of a horizontal scrollbar are, therefore, called left and right cable anchors, and left and right arrows.

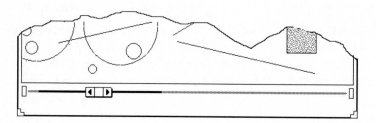

Figure 7-2   A horizontal scrollbar.

When scrollbars are displayed horizontally, there is no dividing line between the scrollbar and the footer. The shaded area in Figure 7-3 shows the distinction between the scrollbar area and the footer.

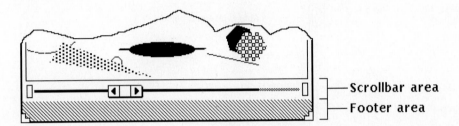

Figure 7-3   The shading shows the footer area.

When a pane has a scrollbar, the following rules apply:

☐ A complete scrollbar is displayed whenever possible.
☐ When the pane is too small to show a scrollbar and a cable, the cable is not displayed.
☐ When the pane is too small to show the cable anchors and the elevator, an abbreviated scrollbar is displayed. The abbreviated scrollbar has cable anchors and scrolling arrows but has no drag area.
☐ In Level 2 implementations, when the pane is too small to show the cable anchors of the abbreviated scrollbar, the minimum scrollbar is displayed.

Figure 7-4 shows an example of each of these scrollbars.

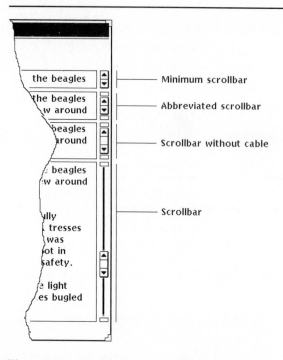

Figure 7-4   Four ways scrollbars are displayed.

Each of these scrollbars can be displayed horizontally as well as vertically. Note that the minimum size of a text area with a scrollbar in a Level 1 implementation is the size of an abbreviated scrollbar.

In a Level 2 implementation, the minimum size of a text area with a scrollbar is the size of the minimum scrollbar. See Chapter 3 for a discussion of minimum window sizes.

Scrollbar Cable

The length of the scrollbar cable represents the total size of the data from the application that can be viewed incrementally in the pane.

Scrollbar Cable Proportion Indicator

The scrollbar cable proportion indicator is the dark area of the cable that shows the portion of the total application data that is visible in the pane. The proportion indicator is always attached to the elevator. Figure 7-5 shows some configurations for the proportion indicator.

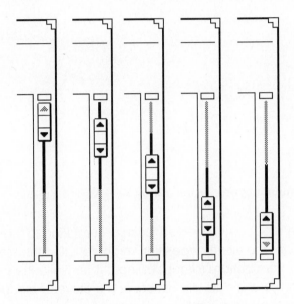

Figure 7-5   Scrollbar cable proportion indicator.

When the elevator is at the top of the pane, the proportion indicator is displayed below the elevator. When the elevator is in the middle of the pane, the proportion indicator extends above and below the elevator. When the elevator is at the bottom of the pane, the proportion indicator is displayed above the elevator.

When all of the contents are visible in the pane, the entire cable is dark.

If the proportion indicator is smaller than the elevator, a 3-point long dark area is shown either at the top or bottom of the elevator to indicate that only a small portion of the data is visible in the pane, as shown in Figure 7-6.

Figure 7-6   The minimum proportion indicator.

When the data block being viewed is large in relation to the viewing pane, the computation for the elevator position might result in the elevator being positioned at the very bottom (or top) of the cable, while the view is not at the end (or beginning) of the data. In this case, the elevator is repositioned 2 points from the end of the cable.

Elevator Positions

Just as the proportion indicator shows the part of the data visible in the pane, the location of the elevator shows the position of the pane in the total data represented by the cable. For example, the five scrollbars in Figure 7-5 show the elevator moving sequentially through the contents, from the beginning (at the left) to the end (at the right) of the data.

Scrollbar Operation

Use the SELECT mouse button to manipulate the scrollbar. The pane can be considered a window into the data; moving the scrollbar elevator moves the view of the data. Clicking on the down arrow in a text application shows the next line of text at the bottom of the pane (pushing the first line of text off the top of the pane). An ADJUST click momentarily displays the question mark pointer. Clicking or pressing MENU anywhere in the scrollbar area displays the Scrollbar menu.

Normalization

The application developer determines whether scrolled objects are adjusted so they are always fully displayed (*normalized*). For example, when you scroll text in a pane, it moves line by line so that the full height of the characters is displayed.

Drag Area

Press SELECT, and drag in the drag area of the elevator to move the view in the pane forward or backward in the application data. The drag area highlights, and the pointer rides the drag area. The mouse can be moved anywhere, but the pointer remains constrained to the drag area until you release SELECT.

In a Level 2 implementation, the contents of the pane are updated as you drag the elevator. When you release SELECT, the drag area returns to normal.

An OPEN LOOK UI implementation permits you to move rapidly to a relative position in a large file. If you scroll so quickly that the view in the pane cannot keep up with the position in the data, you do not need to wait for all the data to scroll through the pane. The scrolling display can jump ahead to the new point in the data.

Up and Down Arrows

When the up or down arrow cannot be used to scroll up or down because you are at the beginning or the end of the data that can be scrolled, the arrow is dimmed. When all the data are visible in the pane, both the up and down arrows are dimmed.

When you click SELECT on the up arrow, it highlights, the elevator moves up one unit (displaying one new unit at the top of the pane), and the up arrow returns to normal.

When you click SELECT on the down arrow, it highlights, the elevator moves down one unit (displaying one new unit at the bottom of the pane), and the down arrow returns to normal.

Pressing SELECT repeats the click function. The pointer is locked on the elevator and rides it up or down until you release SELECT. This allows you to keep the mouse in the same position on the pad as you scroll through data in a pane.

If you are using the scrollbar with an absolute pointing device, such as a light pen, you can disable the scrollbar pointer jumping from the Workspace Properties window.

Cable Area

Clicking SELECT below the elevator anywhere in the scrollbar region between the elevator and the bottom cable anchor moves the view on the data downward one pane. The elevator is repositioned downward accordingly.

Clicking SELECT above the elevator moves the view on the data upward one pane. The elevator is repositioned upward accordingly.

Pressing SELECT repeats. The pointer jumps ahead on the cable to stay out of the way of the elevator, if necessary.

Cable Anchors

You move the view to the beginning of the data by clicking SELECT on the top cable anchor. The following actions are performed:

1 The top cable anchor highlights while you press SELECT.
2 The view in the pane is moved to show the beginning of the data.
3 The elevator is moved to the top of the pane, and the proportion indicator is displayed below it.
4 The top cable anchor returns to its normal state.

You move the view to the end of the data by clicking SELECT on the bottom cable anchor. The following actions are performed:

1 The bottom cable anchor highlights while SELECT is pressed.
2 The view in the pane is moved to show the end of the data. The last line of the contents is displayed in the middle of the pane.
3 The elevator is moved to the bottom of the pane, and the proportion indicator is displayed above it.
4 The bottom cable anchor returns to its normal state.

Splitting Panes

In some applications such as text or graphics editors, you may want to view different parts of the contents of a pane at the same time. A new view may be created by dividing a single pane into two or more parts. This process is called "pane splitting." A Level 2 implementation provides pane splitting functionality. An application can specify whether a given pane can be split.

You can split a pane either from the Scrollbar menu or by using the cable anchors. When a pane can be split, the application displays the Split View item on the Scrollbar menu for that pane. The following section, "How to Split a Pane Using the Scrollbar Menu," discusses using the Split View item. See "How to Split a Pane Using the Cable Anchors" later in this chapter for information about splitting panes by direct manipulation.

When the application provides splitting functionality, you can create different views in the same pane. Splitting panes does not create separate copies of the contents; it provides a split view of the same object. Any changes made to the contents in one pane are reflected in the other splits of that pane.

The limit to the number of times you can split a pane is determined by the number of minimum scrollbars that can be displayed in the scrollbar area.

When you have split a pane, the application interactively adds the Join Views item to the items on the Scrollbar menu. See "Removing a Split Pane" later in this chapter for more information about using the Join Views item.

The following sections describe basic information about creating and removing split panes. See Chapter 16 for detailed information about creating and removing multiple split panes.

How to Split a Pane Using the Scrollbar Menu

You use the Scrollbar menu to split a pane in the following way. First, move the pointer into the scrollbar area, position it next to the place where you want to split the pane, and press MENU. The Scrollbar menu is displayed, as shown in Figure 7-7.

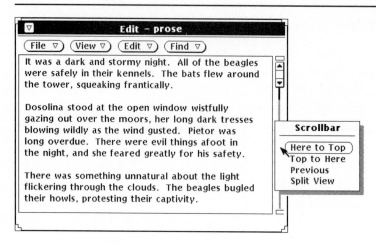

Figure 7-7   Position the pointer where you want to split the pane and press MENU.

Drag the pointer onto the Split View item on the Scrollbar menu. The item highlights, as shown in Figure 7-8.

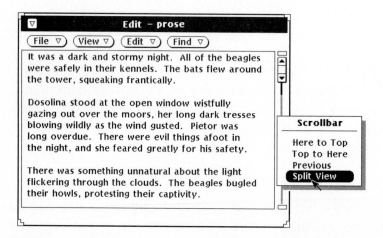

Figure 7-8   Drag the pointer onto the Split View item.

Release the MENU button. The Scrollbar menu is dismissed and the pane is split at the place the pointer occupied when you pressed MENU, as shown in Figure 7-9, *not* at the current pointer location. Each split has its own scrollbar and Scrollbar menu, and the item Join Views is added to each Scrollbar menu.

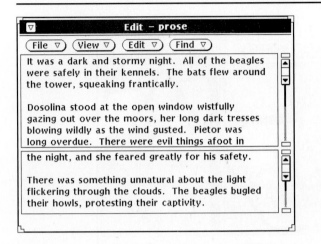

Figure 7-9 Release MENU to split the pane.

When an application normalizes scrolling, the pane split may be adjusted to the normalized unit. In this example, scrolling is normalized by the unit of a line of text. If you do not position the pointer exactly at the line break, the application may make the adjustment for you.

Panes with horizontal scrollbars can be split vertically. You split a pane that has a horizontal scrollbar in exactly the same way. Move the pointer to a place in the scrollbar area where you want to split the pane, press MENU, choose Split View from the menu, and release MENU. Figure 7-10 shows a pane with a horizontal scrollbar that has been split once. Figure 7-11 shows a pane with a vertical scrollbar that has been split twice.

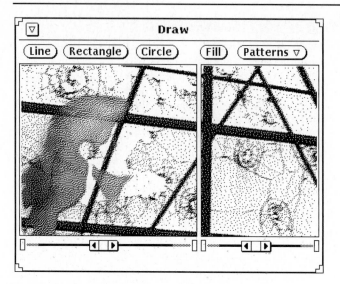

Figure 7-10   A pane with a vertical split.

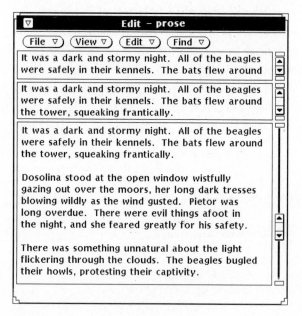

Figure 7-11   A pane that has been split twice.

Note that the smallest pane you can have is determined by the height (or width) of the minimum scrollbar. Alternatively, you can have a small pane that is the height (or width) of the scrollbar without a cable. If you try to split a pane in the region that falls between the length of the minimum scrollbar and the abbreviated scrollbar, or between the length of the abbreviated scrollbar and the scrollbar without a cable, the pane snaps to the smaller size. Figure 7-12 shows the unsplittable areas. See Chapter 16 for information about resizing panes.

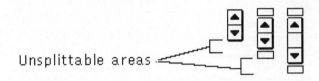

Figure 7-12   Unsplittable areas.

How to Split a Pane Using the Cable Anchors

You can use either the top or bottom cable anchor to split a pane. The cable anchors can only be dragged into the pane. The following examples show how to use the vertical scrollbar to split a text pane using the top cable anchor.

1 Move the pointer to the top cable anchor and press SELECT. The cable anchor highlights, as shown in Figure 7-13.

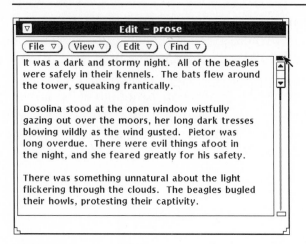

Figure 7-13   To split a pane, move the pointer to one of the cable anchors and press SELECT.

2 Drag the pointer downward. A 1-point horizontal line is displayed from the left edge of the pane to the center of the cable anchor to show where the split will occur, as shown in Figure 7-14.

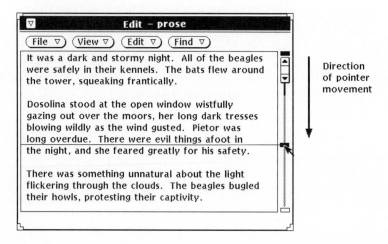

Figure 7-14   Drag the cable anchor downward.

3 Release SELECT. The pane is split, and the highlighted cable anchor that you dragged with the pointer becomes the bottom cable anchor for the pane. The highlighting is removed from the cable anchor, and each split has its own scrollbar, as shown in Figure 7-15.

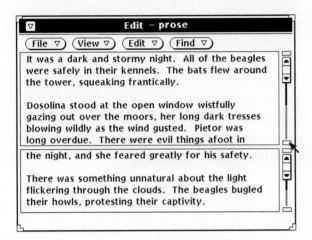

Figure 7-15   Release SELECT to split the pane.

Removing a Split Pane

When you have split a pane, the application interactively adds the Join Views item to the choices on the Scrollbar menu. The following sections describe basic information about removing split panes using the Join Views item. See Chapter 16 for detailed information about how an application determines how to redisplay multiple split panes. See "Removing a Split Pane with the Cable Anchors" later in this chapter for information about using the cable anchors to remove a split pane.

Removing a Split Pane with the Scrollbar Menu

You remove a split pane with the Scrollbar menu in much the same way that you split a pane. The steps below describe removing a split using the Scrollbar menu.

1 Move the pointer to any place in the scrollbar area next to the pane you want to remove and press MENU.

2 Drag the pointer to the Join Views item. The item highlights. The OPEN LOOK UI implementation provides visual feedback for the pane to show you that the pane will be removed when you release MENU. This visual feedback may be as simple as dimming the border of the pane or as complicated as dimming the border and the contents of the pane.

3 Release MENU.

In the example shown in Figure 7-16, both the border and the contents of the top pane are dimmed to show that it will be removed when you release MENU.

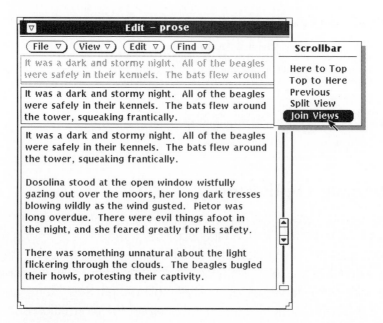

Figure 7-16 When the Join Views item is highlighted, the border and the contents of the pane are dimmed.

When you release MENU, the dimmed pane is removed, and the contents of the adjacent pane expand to fill the area previously occupied by the pane. See Chapter 16 for more information about how an application fills in split pane areas.

Removing a Split Pane with the Cable Anchors

You remove a split pane with the cable anchors in much the same way that you split a pane. You can use either cable anchor for a split pane to remove the split. The examples below show removing a split using the top cable anchor.

1 Move the pointer to the top cable anchor in the pane you want to remove and press SELECT. The cable anchor highlights, as shown in Figure 7-17.

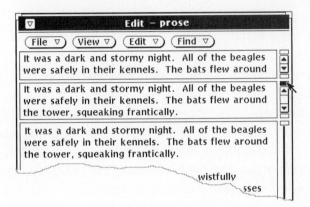

Figure 7-17   To remove a split pane, move the pointer to a cable anchor of that pane.

2 Drag the pointer downward. The cable anchor and the bounding line move with the pointer, as shown in Figure 7-18.

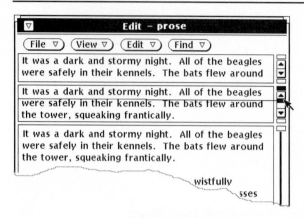

Figure 7-18 To remove a split pane, drag the pointer toward the bottom cable anchor.

3 Drag the pointer until the top and bottom cable anchor overlap. The OPEN LOOK UI implementation provides visual feedback for the pane to show you that the pane will be removed when you release MENU. This visual feedback may be as simple as dimming the border of the pane or as complicated as dimming both the border and the contents of the pane. In Figure 7-19, the border and the contents of the pane are dimmed to show that it will be removed when you release SELECT.

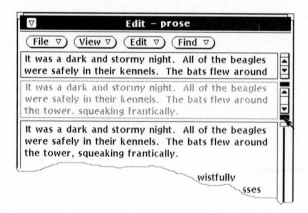

Figure 7-19 When the cable anchors overlap, both the border and the contents of the pane are dimmed.

4 Release SELECT. The dimmed pane is removed, and the contents of the adjacent pane expand to fill the area previously occupied by the pane. In the example shown in Figure 7-20, the top pane expands downward to fill the available space. See Chapter 16 for more information about how an application fills in split pane areas.

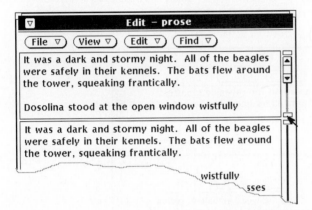

Figure 7-20 Release SELECT to remove the split view.

Page-Oriented Scrollbars

Applications with separate pages, such as document preparation systems, can use a *page-oriented scrollbar* to show this orientation. The only time a page number is displayed is when you press SELECT with the pointer over the drag area of a page-oriented scrollbar. The page number display does not prevent you from dragging the elevator.

You use the page-oriented scrollbar in the following ways:

☐ To view the page number, move the pointer to the drag area of the elevator and press SELECT. A box containing the page number is displayed to the left of the elevator.

☐ To drag the elevator, move the pointer to the drag area of the elevator and press SELECT. The page indicator is displayed and does not interfere with dragging the elevator. As you drag the pointer, the box interactively expands or contracts at the left to accommodate different numbers of digits.

The page numbers change as the text is scrolled. When you release the pointer, the view in the pane snaps to display the top of the current page. The elevator may also make a slight adjustment to reflect its position in the data accurately.

The top window in Figure 7-21 has a 1-digit page number. The bottom window has a 3-digit page number.

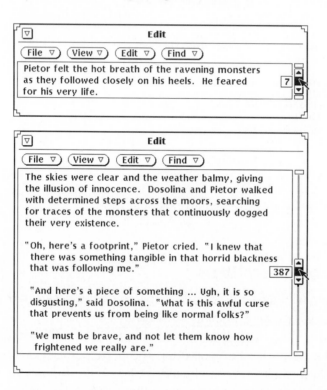

Figure 7-21   Two windows with page-oriented scrollbars.

Abbreviated and minimum scrollbars do not show page orientation, even if the application provides this scrolling feature, since they do not have a drag area.

Scrollbar Menu

The scrollbar has a pop-up menu that you access by pressing MENU in the scrolling area. See Chapter 10 for a description of scrollbar menus.

Scrolling Without Scrollbars

An OPEN LOOK UI implementation supports two additional kinds of scrolling that are not accessed from the scrollbar:

☐ Automatic scrolling
☐ Panning

Automatic Scrolling

A Level 2 implementation provides automatic scrolling. *Automatic scrolling* occurs when you select objects by pressing SELECT and dragging the pointer. When the pointer reaches the border of a pane, a scrolling list, or the beginning or end of a text field, the contents automatically scroll to display more information. A graphics application displays the next point. A text application displays the next line. A text field displays the next character. The pointer is not constrained to the boundary of the object. Automatic scrolling lets you extend selections beyond the information that is currently visible in the pane or scrolling list.

Panning

A Level 1 implementation provides a PAN modifier key—set from the Workspace Properties window—to allow you to "glue" the contents of a pane to the pointer and move them in any direction. This method of scrolling is called *panning,* because it is like moving a video camera to change the view in the lens. Applications that implement panning use the PAN modifier key to allow you to access that functionality. A Level 2 implementation provides panning functionality for panes.

When you scroll by panning, you anchor the pointer on a location that is visible in the pane. You can then move the contents to any border of the pane by dragging the pointer. The anchored contents move with the pointer. You cannot move the panning pointer outside the borders of the pane.

You initiate panning by following the steps below:

1 Move the pointer to the place where you want to start panning.

2 Press the PAN modifier key on the keyboard and then SELECT. When the pointer changes to the panning pointer, you can release the PAN modifier key.

3 Drag the pointer to a new location within the pane.

4 Release SELECT.

When the basic pointer is at the bottom of a pane, the panning pointer moves upward to keep the hot spot inside the border of the pane.

A text application can permit you to move the pointer in any direction within the pane. Alternatively, a text application can constrain panning so that the contents of the pane scroll vertically. When only vertical panning is supported, the panning pointer remains anchored at the horizontal position and can only be moved vertically within the pane.

The following examples show vertical panning in a text application. To initiate panning, first you move the pointer into the pane. In the example shown in Figure 7-22, the pointer is at the bottom of the pane to permit you to pan the contents of the pane upward.

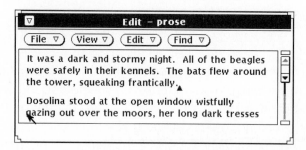

Figure 7-22   To initiate panning, move the pointer into the pane.

Then press the PAN modifier key on the keyboard and SELECT. The pointer changes to the panning pointer, as shown in Figure 7-23. When the panning pointer is displayed, you can release the PAN modifier key.

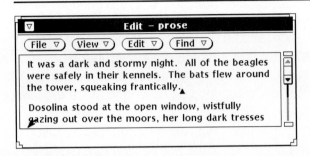

Figure 7-23   Press the PAN modifier key and SELECT.

Drag the pointer upward in the pane. The text is "attached" to the panning pointer and moves upward with it, as shown in Figure 7-24.

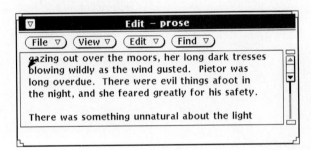

Figure 7-24   Drag the pointer to move the contents of the pane.

Release SELECT to leave the panning mode. The panning pointer changes back to the basic pointer, as shown in Figure 7-25.

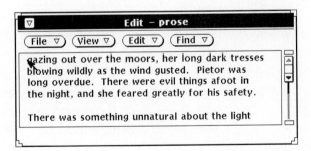

Figure 7-25   Release SELECT to leave panning mode and redisplay the basic pointer.

A text application customarily normalizes scrolling so that text is displayed line by line. The application determines whether or not scrolling is normalized.

In an application that supports unconstrained panning, you can drag the pointer in any direction and move the contents of the pane directly. The next examples illustrate how you can use panning to move the view in the pane. The left part of Figure 7-26 shows the complete image, while the right shows the portion of the image that is visible in the pane. When you initiate panning with the pointer in the middle of the image, you can move the pointer in any direction within the pane.

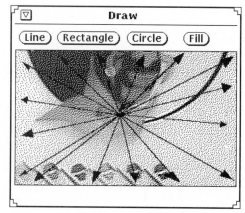

Figure 7-26 Panning is unconstrained when the image is not at the edge of the pane.

When you get to the edge of the image, the pointer stops, and you cannot move it closer to the side of the pane. For example, the pane in Figure 7-27 is at the rightmost side of the image. If you initiate panning with the pointer at the center of the pane, your movement in the right half of the pane is unconstrained. However, you cannot move the pointer into the left half of the image.

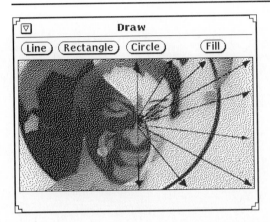

Figure 7-27   Panning is partially constrained when the edge of an image is at the side of the pane.

When the image is aligned on the right side of the pane and you initiate panning with the pointer also at the right side, you can only move the image vertically. The pointer bumps against the right side, and the panning pointer movement is restricted to directions that allow more of the image to be moved into the pane. The arrows on the right side of the pane in Figure 7-28 show the movement permitted by the panning pointer under these circumstances.

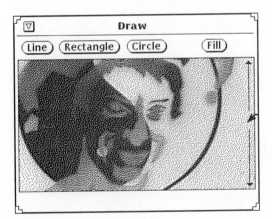

Figure 7-28   Panning is constrained when the pointer is at the edge of an image.

8

SCROLLING LISTS

A scrolling list is a list of items through which you can scroll and, in most cases, choose. Scrolling lists are most commonly displayed in a pane containing the list. They can also be displayed in property windows or control areas. A scrolling list can also stand alone in a command window.

Scrolling List Functionality

The items in scrolling lists are similar to settings: they can be exclusive or nonexclusive. A Level 1 implementation provides the following kinds of scrolling lists:

☐ A scrolling list from which you can choose one item (*exclusive scrolling list*)
☐ A scrolling list from which you can choose one or none of the items (*variation of exclusive scrolling list*)
☐ A scrolling list from which you can choose none, one, or multiple items (*nonexclusive scrolling list*)

You choose an item in an exclusive or nonexclusive list in the same way you choose exclusive or nonexclusive settings: by moving the pointer onto an item and clicking SELECT. An ADJUST click momentarily displays the question mark pointer.

Each of these kinds of scrolling lists has a required Scrolling List menu, and can be edited using items from that menu. Cut/copy/paste functionality, which uses the clipboard and the core function keys is also provided.

A Level 2 implementation provides a hierarchical scrolling list from which you can access different levels of a hierarchy, for example, a file system.

When a scrolling list is displayed in a pop-up window and the window is dismissed, the current state of the scrolling list is retained and is redisplayed when the pop-up window is invoked again. The application can clear current items from the scrolling list before redisplaying it, when appropriate.

When the scrolling list is the active input area, the OPEN LOOK UI specifies that the implementation provide minimum pattern matching functionality, as follows: You can search for items on the list by typing a letter from the keyboard. When an item on the list begins with that letter, the item is selected or made current, as specified by the application. If no item on the list matches the keyboard input, the system beeps to let you know that there is no match for that character. If you type a second character, the next item that begins with that character becomes current. Any application can implement alternative, more sophisticated, pattern matching functionality.

See the *OPEN LOOK Graphical User Interface Application Style Guidelines* for suggestions about how to implement scrolling list functionality.

Required Elements of a Level 1 Scrolling List

A Level 1 scrolling list has the following required elements:

☐ A 2-point rectangular border
☐ A scrollbar
☐ A list of text items
☐ A Scrolling List menu
☐ A one-point border around the current item or items
☐ An optional bold label followed by a colon

Figure 8-1 shows an example of a scrolling list that displays suggested alternate spellings for a spelling checker. The current item is "charade."

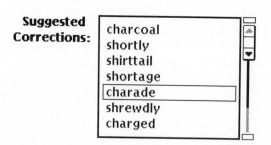

Figure 8-1 A basic scrolling list with one current item.

The Scrolling List Menu

In normal operation, when the pointer is in the scrolling list, pressing MENU displays the Scrolling List menu, as shown in Figure 8-2.

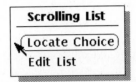

Figure 8-2   The Scrolling List menu.

When the current item has been scrolled out of view, you can quickly scroll to the current item by choosing the Locate Choice item from the Scrolling List menu. When you want to edit the list to insert, delete, or change items on the list, choose the Edit List item to put the scrolling list into edit mode. When the scrolling list is in edit mode, additional menu choices are provided that let you make changes to the items in the scrolling list. See Chapter 10 for information about the Scrolling List menu; editing scrolling lists is described later in this chapter.

Applications can add items to this Scrolling List menu.

Exclusive Scrolling Lists

An exclusive scrolling list lets you choose one item from a list of items. This is, perhaps, the most common type of scrolling list. You choose the item by moving the pointer into the rectangle of white space that contains an item on the list and clicking SELECT. The entire line for each item is active, not just the word itself. When you click SELECT, a one-point rectangle surrounds the current item. An ADJUST click momentarily displays the question mark pointer.

Figure 8-3 shows an example of a scrolling list that contains a list of available fonts. The current item in this example is "Courier."

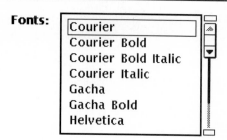

Figure 8-3   You can choose one current item from an exclusive scrolling list.

When the window containing a scrolling list with a current item is dismissed, the current item is remembered and is redisplayed the next time you open the window.

If you delete the current item while editing an exclusive scrolling list, the OPEN LOOK UI implementation specifies the first item in the list as the current item.

Variation of Exclusive Scrolling Lists

Just as a Level 1 implementation provides a variation of exclusive settings that lets you choose none of the settings, a variation of an exclusive scrolling list lets you choose none or one of the items on the list. You choose none of the items by moving the pointer to the current item and clicking SELECT to remove the current item border. An ADJUST click momentarily displays the question mark pointer.

You might see this kind of scrolling list in an application that provides a list of suggested alternate spellings when no appropriate alternate is provided on the list. Figure 8-4 shows an exclusive scrolling list with no current items. The suggested corrections are for the word "shargola."

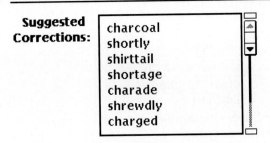

Figure 8-4   A variation of an exclusive scrolling list with no current item.

Nonexclusive Scrolling Lists

A nonexclusive scrolling list lets you choose none, one or multiple items from a list. You choose an item by moving the pointer to each item in turn and clicking SELECT. An ADJUST click momentarily displays the question mark pointer.

Figure 8-5 shows an example of a scrolling list that contains a list of possible recipients for an electronic mail message. The current items on the list indicate those people to whom you want to send the message.

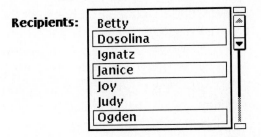

Figure 8-5   A nonexclusive scrolling list permits multiple current items.

Nonexclusive scrolling lists have three items on the Scrolling List menu, as shown in Figure 8-6:

☐ Locate Next Choice
☐ Clear All Choices
☐ Edit List

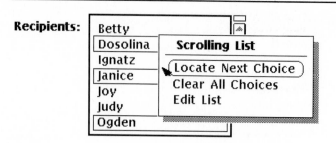

Figure 8-6 The nonexclusive Scrolling List menu.

You use the Locate Next Choice item to scroll the next choice on the list that is not visible into the scrolling list pane. You use the Clear All Choices item to quickly clear all of the current choices, leaving no current items.

Selecting Items for Editing in a Scrolling List

All scrolling lists can be edited. However, applications may restrict access to editing functionality to a limited group of users who have the appropriate permissions to make changes to a scrolling list. When you do not have permission to edit a list, the application determines whether the Edit List item on the Scrolling List menu is dimmed or not displayed.

To put a scrolling list into edit mode, choose Edit List from the Scrolling List pop-up menu. Current items are displayed with a dimmed border.

When the scrolling list is in edit mode, you select items in the same way that you select other graphic objects: to select one item, move the pointer onto the item and click SELECT. An ADJUST click toggles the state of the item.

When you select a current item, the normal selection highlighting is displayed, and the dimmed border is included in the highlighting.

Figure 8-7 shows a scrolling list in edit mode with one item selected.

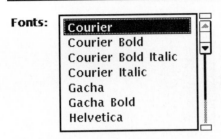

Figure 8-7 A scrolling list with one item selected.

When an application permits multiple selection, you can select multiple items by making a wipe-through selection: move the pointer onto an item and press SELECT. Drag the pointer to highlight items, and release SELECT to complete the selection. Figure 8-8 shows a scrolling list with multiple adjacent items selected.

Figure 8-8 A scrolling list with adjacent items selected.

It is useful to be able to select nonadjacent items, and you select them in the same way that you select other graphic objects: move the pointer to an item and click SELECT to select the item and clear all other selections. Move the pointer to another item and click ADJUST to add it to the selection. Clicking ADJUST on a selected item deselects it without clearing other selected items. Figure 8-9 shows a scrolling list with nonadjacent items selected.

Fonts: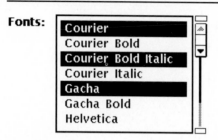

Figure 8-9   A scrolling list with nonadjacent items selected.

Using Items on the Scrolling List Menu

Once you have selected items for editing, press MENU to display the Scrolling List menu. Applications can add items to this menu to provide sort, filtering, or item numbering capabilities. Figure 8-10 shows the minimum editing Scrolling List menu.

Figure 8-10   The minimum Scrolling List menu for edit mode.

The following sections describe how to use each of these items.

Change

The Change item lets you edit the contents of one selected item at a time. When multiple items are selected, the Change item is inactive. When an item is selected and you choose Change from the Scrolling List menu, the highlighting is replaced by a fixed length text entry line with an active caret. The header of the window containing the scrolling list is highlighted, since the scrolling list is the input area.

Figure 8-11 shows a scrolling list with a text entry field.

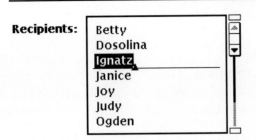

Figure 8-11   A scrolling list with a text entry field.

You can type a new entry, automatically replacing the highlighted text. Alternatively, you can move the pointer anywhere in the item and click SELECT to reposition the caret and insert or delete characters in the same way that you edit in a text field.

Pressing RETURN validates the entry, removes the text entry line, and redisplays the highlighting for the selected item, as shown in Figure 8-12.

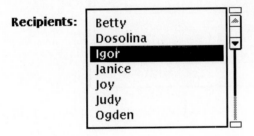

Figure 8-12   Pressing RETURN validates the entry, removes the text entry line, and redisplays the highlighting.

To change another item, move the pointer and click SELECT to highlight the item. Then press MENU to display the Scrolling List menu and choose Change again.

Properties

Some applications may provide additional information that is not displayed as part of the scrolling list. When this occurs, the application replaces the Change item on the Scrolling List menu with a window item labeled Properties. Selecting an item from the scrolling list and then choosing the Properties item displays a property window containing text fields. You edit the information in the property window and click on the Apply button to enter that information into the scrolling list. When multiple items are selected, the Properties item on the Scrolling Menu is inactive.

Figure 8-13 shows an example of a property window for a scrolling list that contains fonts. The path name showing the location of the font is an integral part of the information in the scrolling list, although that information is not displayed.

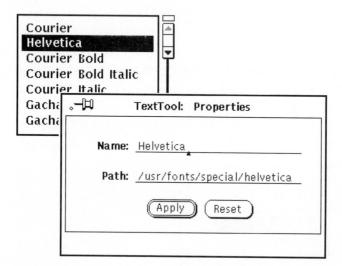

Figure 8-13   Choosing Properties from the Scrolling List menu displays a property window.

Insert

The Insert menu item lets you make multiple line entries in a scrolling list. The Insert submenu has two items that you use to position the text entry line:

□ Before
□ After

Choosing Before opens a text entry line before the first selected item in the scrolling list. When there is no selected item, the text entry line is opened before the first item in the scrolling list. When you have completed an entry, pressing the Return key validates the entry, enters the new item into the list, and moves the text entry field down one line. You can add as many items to the list as you want by typing an entry and pressing the Return key. Each time you press the Return key, the entry for that line is validated and a new text entry line is displayed. When you have entered as many items as you want, press the Return key when the active caret is at the beginning of the line to remove the text entry line.

Choosing After opens a text entry line after the last selected item in the scrolling list. When there is no selected item, a text entry line is opened after the last item in the scrolling list.

Delete

When you choose Delete from the Scrolling List menu, the highlighted items are removed from the scrolling list. The application determines whether a Notice is displayed to confirm the deletion or when there is additional information, such as a path name for font location, that is attached to an item.

End Editing

When you choose End Editing from the Scrolling List menu, any opened text entry lines are validated and closed, and the scrolling list is no longer in edit mode. The next time you press MENU, the default Scrolling List menu is displayed. You can return to edit mode at any time by choosing Edit List from the menu.

Multi-Level Scrolling Lists

In a Level 2 implementation, when a scrollable list can access multiple levels in a hierarchy, such as a file system, it has the following additional elements:

☐ Title area
☐ Scrolling buttons
☐ Levels menu
☐ Glyphs and/or text items in the scrolling list to show levels in the hierarchy

A multi-level scrolling list has one current item per level.

The elements of a multi-level scrolling list are described in general terms in the following sections. The section "Using Multi-Level Scrolling Lists" gives a more detailed example.

Title Area and Scrolling Buttons

A title area with a 1-point line beneath it contains a title in bold type, aligned left, that describes the level of the hierarchy. Scrolling buttons for moving up and down in the hierarchy are displayed to the right of the title area. The scrolling buttons are used to trace a previous path through the hierarchy, and have a Levels menu attached to them. When you have not gone to another level in the scrolling list, the default path is the first item at each level of the scrolling list that has a hierarchy. The title area and scrolling buttons are shown in Figure 8-14.

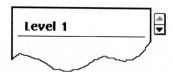

Figure 8-14   Title area of a multi-level scrolling list.

When you are at any level below the first level in the hierarchy, one dot for each level above the current level is displayed, left-justified, above the title. In the example in Figure 8-15, you are at level 2 in a hierarchy. There is one level above, represented by the dot.

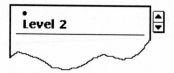

Figure 8-15   A level 2 header of a multi-level scrolling list has one dot.

One dot is added to the right of the first dot for each additional level of the hierarchy into which you descend. In the example in Figure 8-16, you are at level 3 in a hierarchy.

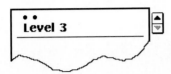

Figure 8-16   A level 3 header of a multi-level scrolling list has two dots.

Levels Menu

The scrolling buttons have a Levels menu that shows you the path you have traversed through the hierarchy. The top level is always the first item on the menu. The item for the current level is always inactive. When you have not changed levels, the only item on the menu is the top level, as shown in Figure 8-17.

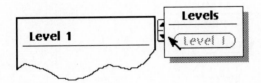

Figure 8-17   An example of a Levels menu with no history.

When you move down through levels in the hierarchy, the Levels menu expands and contracts both horizontally and vertically to accommodate the number of items and the varying lengths of the item names. The menu always displays the current path you are on in the hierarchy. For example, when you have moved down one branch to the bottom of the hierarchy and then go to the top level and move down a different branch, the information from the first branch is not maintained.

The item labels on the Levels menu use the names of the levels that are represented by the dots above the title. In the following examples, the level of the hierarchy is shown as the item label. Figure 8-18 shows examples of the Levels menu for levels 2 and 3.

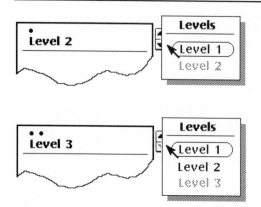

Figure 8-18   Examples of a Levels menu with a history.

When you move from level 3 back to level 2, the level 3 item is still present and active on the Levels menu, as shown in Figure 8-19.

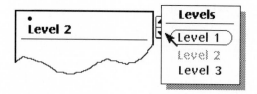

Figure 8-19   The Levels history is displayed when moved in the hierarchy.

Glyphs and/or Text Items

Multi-level scrolling lists always have a glyph that shows you whether or not there are additional levels in the hierarchy. The hierarchical glyph is displayed at the left of the item. Additional glyphs can also be used in a multi-level scrolling list and, when present, are displayed to the right of the hierarchical glyph. For example, in a file system hierarchy, glyphs representing folders and documents could be used. A folder has levels beneath it (the documents contained in the folder), but a document is at the lowest level of the hierarchy.

The default hierarchical glyph is a dot that is the same size as the dots that are displayed in the title area. This glyph is present only when there are additional levels available for the item on the list. In Figure 8-20, the glyphs displayed next to the Programs and Utilities items indicate that these items have additional levels.

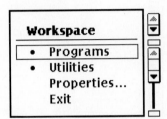

Figure 8-20   The default hierarchical glyph.

An application can replace the default glyph with another glyph and can specify a unique glyph that represents an item that does not have additional levels.

Using Multi-Level Scrolling Lists

The examples in this section describe how you use a multi-level scrolling list to access different levels when you are creating a menu.

Double-Clicking to Move Down Levels

The following examples show how to use a scrolling list to edit the Workspace menu.

Double-clicking SELECT on an item that is not at the bottom of the hierarchy makes it current, and moves you down one level in the hierarchy. In Figure 8-21, the current item, Programs, becomes the title of the next level of the scrolling list. You can make selections on nested levels of the hierarchy, but they do not become current.

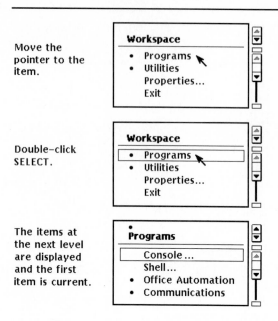

Figure 8-21   Double-clicking to move down a level in a multi-level scrolling list.

Note that the top scrolling arrow is not dimmed once you move down a level. You can click SELECT on the top arrow to move up in the hierarchy.

Suppose that you double-click on the Office Automation item to display that list. Office Automation becomes the title of the scrolling list, and another dot is added to the title area to show that you are two levels below the top, as shown in Figure 8-22.

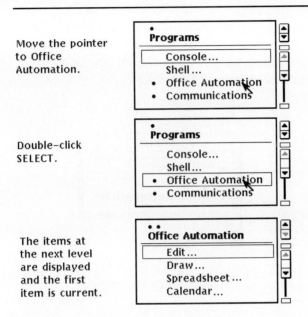

Move the pointer
to Office
Automation.

Double-click
SELECT.

The items at
the next level
are displayed
and the first
item is current.

Figure 8-22   Double-clicking to move down another level in a multi-level scrolling list.

Using the Levels Menu

When you have moved down the hierarchy in a multi-level scrolling list, you can use the items on the Levels menu to move anyplace on the hierarchical path. You display the Levels menu by moving the pointer onto the scrolling buttons at the right of the title area and pressing MENU. Figure 8-23 shows the Levels menu after you have moved down to the Office Automation level.

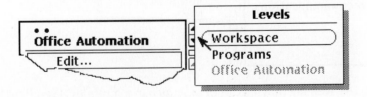

Figure 8-23   The Levels menu.

You can choose Workspace from the Levels menu to return to the top level of the hierarchy. Alternatively, you can move upward through the hierarchy without displaying the Levels menu by clicking SELECT on the top arrow.

Figure 8-24 shows the scrolling list and its Levels menu after you have clicked once on the top scrolling arrow. You are back at the Programs level of the hierarchy. The menu continues to show the Programs item, and both scrolling arrows are dark to show that you can move up or down in the hierarchy when you click SELECT.

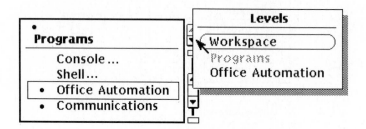

Figure 8-24   Using the Levels menu to move back up a level in a multi-level scrolling list.

Note that as you move back up through the hierarchy, the item that is current is the last choice you made to descend the hierarchy.

Suppose that you double-click SELECT on the Communications item to descend to another branch in the hierarchy. The scrolling list now contains the items Network and Telecommunications, as shown in Figure 8-25, and the Levels menu shows the Workspace, Programs, and Communications levels.

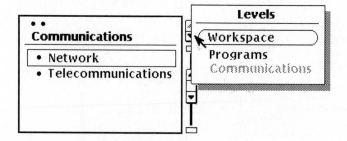

Figure 8-25   Moving down a different branch in a multi-level scrolling list replaces the item on the Levels menu.

If you double-click SELECT on Network, it is added to the Levels menu, as shown in Figure 8-26.

198

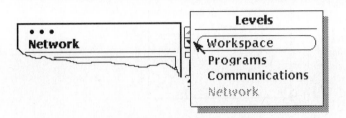

Figure 8-26   Moving down another level in a multi-level scrolling list adds another item to the Levels menu.

If you choose Programs from the menu to move up two levels, the Communications item is selected, since that is the most recent choice made at the Programs level.

Using the Scrolling Buttons to Change Levels

You can move quickly between levels that you have traversed by clicking SELECT on the up and down scrolling buttons. The path you traverse corresponds to the levels on the Levels menu. When you are at the top level and the Levels menu has no history entries, clicking SELECT on the down arrow button moves you to the first multi-level choice on the list. Figure 8-27 shows how you use the scrolling arrows to return to the Programs level with the Office Automation item selected.

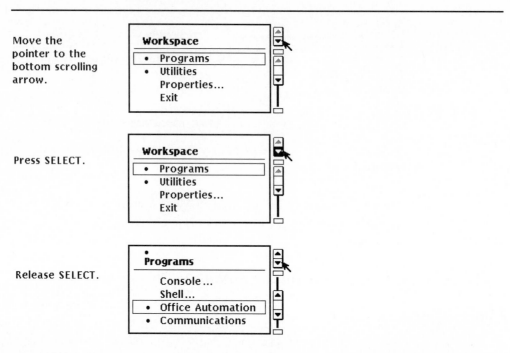

Figure 8-27 Using the scrolling arrows to move down a level in a multi-level scrolling list.

9

COLOR AND THREE-DIMENSIONAL DESIGN

This chapter describes how color is used in specific areas of the interface and provides the general guidelines on the use of color that were followed in the design of the interface. It also provides a detailed description of the three-dimensional design.

Color Philosophy

The design philosophy of the OPEN LOOK User Interface is to use color sparingly, consistently, and purposefully. Restraint is the key.

Application and Interface Regions

To understand the approach taken to color in the OPEN LOOK UI, you must know the distinction between regions that belong to the application and regions that are considered a part of the user interface.

The application usually creates one or more panes that it controls completely. The OPEN LOOK UI does not restrict the use of color within those panes. *The OPEN LOOK Graphical User Interface Application Style Guidelines* provides guidelines for the use of color in an application.

The OPEN LOOK UI restricts the use of color in the standard interface regions—the workspace, window background, scrollbars, Notices, and the panes in all pop-up windows. These regions form the part of the background against which the application-specific information is displayed. Controlling the use of color in these regions ensures that the colors used in the interface regions do not overwhelm or compete with the application, which is the primary focus of attention.

You can set the color of the following elements in the interface region from the Workspace Properties window:

☐ The workspace
☐ The background for the icon and windows of an application
☐ The selection
☐ The active caret and header highlighting that show the input area
☐ Individual controls

Palettes

To ensure that the colors in the interface work well together, the OPEN LOOK UI uses the concept of a *palette.* A palette is a set of colors that harmonize well.

Each palette is divided into three subpalettes, one for each of the following visual elements:

☐ Workspace background
☐ Window background
☐ Selection/input area

The workspace and window background palettes are neutral, lightly saturated colors. The selection/input area palette consists of bright, highly saturated colors that stand out against the neutral background colors.

You specify a system-wide palette from the Workspace Properties window. From within that palette, you choose specific colors for the workspace background, the selection, the caret, and the default window background.

You can override the default background color for any application by setting a new color from the property window of that application. All the windows for the application use this color. This provides an easy way for you to associate a base window with its pop-up windows. The icon for the application also uses this color.

In most color implementations, the borders of the window are not part of the window background. However, systems that have a limited number of highly saturated colors can display the borders of the window using the window background palette choices. In this case the window background is considered to be the window borders. The OPEN LOOK UI implementation uses aesthetic considerations to determine whether the borders or the window background display the color.

See Chapter 3 for an illustration of required window properties. See Chapter 11 for illustrations of system-wide color properties.

To offer flexibility, applications can be written that permit you to edit existing palettes and create new ones.

Use of Color for a Three-Dimensional Effect

Color in controls calls for the following elements:

☐ Text in black
☐ Outline of controls in white
☐ Window background color
☐ Highlighting color
☐ Button shadow color

Depending on the quality and resolution of a given color implementation, these elements can be applied at three different levels.

The complete use of color requires all five elements, where the highlighting color is a little darker than the background color, and the shadow color is darker than the highlighting color.

Implementations that support the use of four colors for these elements substitute black for the shadow color.

Implementations that support the use of three colors use the black-and-white design for controls, and specify a light color for the background.

The specifications described in this chapter are illustrated with black-and-white reproductions of color plates.

The outlines of buttons, menu buttons, and the scrollbar elevator create a three-dimensional effect. The top and left borders are accented with a light background color, while the bottom and right corners are accented with a dark background color.

When you press SELECT on a button or a menu item, the light and dark accents are reversed, and the button area is darkened, which gives the illusion that the button is actually pushed into the surface. This effect is equivalent to the dark-light reversal referred to in this specification as highlighting.

Individual Color for Controls

The OPEN LOOK UI allows the application (but not the user) to specify the color of individual controls such as buttons and sliders. It is recommended that this capability be used sparingly and purposefully.

Icons

When icons are shown on monochrome displays, they are always enclosed in a border. The border is needed because the black text of the label on the icon would not be clearly visible against the 50 percent gray workspace background.

On a color display, the border is not needed, since the background color can be lightly saturated and yet provide enough contrast to make the label on the icon clearly visible. In color implementations, you can choose whether or not to display borders for icons from the Workspace Properties window.

Color Guidelines

The following guidelines are included as background to help you understand the motivation behind the OPEN LOOK UI color design. These guidelines apply equally well to the design of applications.

The design must work first in black and white. Although the use of color is becoming more prevalent, a large number of the displays that an OPEN LOOK UI implementation will run on are, and will continue to be, monochrome. The basic design cannot rely on color. Each of the elements must look good on a monochrome display. When color is added, this look should be enhanced.

Use monochromatic, neutral tones for the background. The workspace is the background against which the windows are displayed. Within the windows, all the unbordered space is the background against which the various elements (such as the window menu button, pushpin, buttons, scrollbars, and application panes) are displayed. Both the workspace and the window backgrounds should use muted and lightly saturated colors.

Use color to add information to the interface. Color can be used as a code for items such as the current selection, error information, and active areas. Color codes are most effective when they meet the following criteria:

☐ They are easily identifiable
☐ They are used consistently (for example, the selection is yellow wherever it is displayed).
☐ They reflect commonly held color associations, such as red for error or critical conditions.
☐ They are restrained. Research has demonstrated that the more color codes used, the longer it takes the user to distinguish each one.

Use bright colors sparingly. Color is fun. The appropriate place to use bright or intense color is where information transfer is at a minimum. Providing a brightly colored display at power-up or log-on can create a strong first impression without getting in the way of the interface.

Allow users to set their own colors. Color preferences vary from individual to individual. Users will want to change the colors, no matter how nice the default palette is. There are many valid reasons for allowing users to set colors for the interface: personal preference, the need for variety, and individual deficiencies in color perception.

Consider color blindness when choosing colors. The most common color deficiencies are in distinguishing between red and green (8 percent of men, .4 percent of women) and blue and yellow. Designing the interface in black and white, and then adding color, ensures that color-blind individuals can use the system.

Vary brightness to show depth. Brightness can be varied as a sort of "dimmer switch" to convey dimension.

Consider the size of the object or area when choosing colors. Since large areas of saturated color tend to leave after-images and cause fatigue, never use highly saturated colors for large areas such as the background of a window. However, for small areas such as borders or small glyphs that depend on color recognition, highly saturated colors are valuable.

Consider the proximity of areas of color to avoid blending. Do not put small areas of color that need to be distinguished or identified next to or near other colors that they blend with. For example, a 1-point yellow line next to a 1-point blue line will be perceived as a 2-point green line.

Do not use spectral extremes together. Don't use red text on blue and green backgrounds. Colors at considerably different wavelengths appear to vibrate when placed together.

Use high contrast between text and background. Maximum contrast, such as white characters on a black background, or vice versa, provides the easiest character recognition.

Consider light on dark versus dark on light when choosing a typeface. The effect of screen elements "glowing" and giving off ambient light is called *halation*. Halation causes white characters on a black background to appear bolder and brighter than dark characters on a white background. It may be advisable to use a bold typeface, particularly in smaller sizes, when placing white or light characters on a dark background.

Color Plates

Figure 9-1 (see color insert) shows a three-dimensional design using the kinds of colors recommended for the OPEN LOOK UI, as follows:

☐ Workspace: Darker muted colors imply that the background is farther away. This creates a sense of depth for the icons and windows displayed on the workspace.
☐ Windows: Very light, unsaturated colors identify windows and allow you to distinguish among application windows.
☐ Selection: Saturated colors for selection allow the selection to stand out.

Figure 9-2 (see color insert) shows an example of a grayscale three-dimensional implementation.

Figure 9-3 (see color insert) shows the Summer palette. Figure 9-4 (see color insert) shows the Winter palette.

Three-Dimensional Design

The OPEN LOOK UI three-dimensional design can be implemented on grayscale and color systems that can represent images with more colors than just black and white. The following sections describe the visual elements of the three-dimensional design.

Required Color Groups

Figure 9-5 provides information about the color group required to represent the three-dimensional look. Black and white are always provided as part of the color palette. BG1 is a color that you can select from the group of valid window background colors. To produce a realistic three-dimensional effect, the BG2 and BG3 colors must be derivatives of the window background color, BG1. These color groups are used to describe the three-dimensional design.

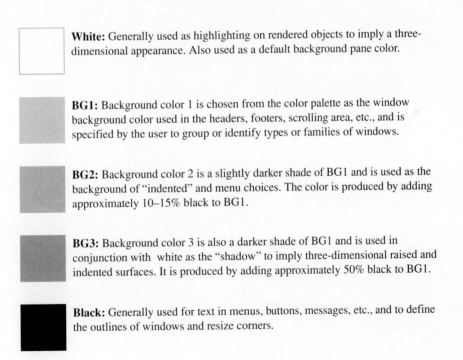

White: Generally used as highlighting on rendered objects to imply a three-dimensional appearance. Also used as a default background pane color.

BG1: Background color 1 is chosen from the color palette as the window background color used in the headers, footers, scrolling area, etc., and is specified by the user to group or identify types or families of windows.

BG2: Background color 2 is a slightly darker shade of BG1 and is used as the background of "indented" and menu choices. The color is produced by adding approximately 10–15% black to BG1.

BG3: Background color 3 is also a darker shade of BG1 and is used in conjunction with white as the "shadow" to imply three-dimensional raised and indented surfaces. It is produced by adding approximately 50% black to BG1.

Black: Generally used for text in menus, buttons, messages, etc., and to define the outlines of windows and resize corners.

Figure 9-5   Color group descriptions for three-dimensional design.

Raised and Recessed Objects

The three-dimensional look of graphic objects in the OPEN LOOK UI is achieved by using consistent highlighting and shadowing. An imaginary light source at a 45 degree angle above and to the left of the object is assumed. When the object is raised from the surface, the top and left sides of the object are white and the lower and right sides are in shadow (BG3). When the object is recessed into the surface, the light and shadow are reversed. To accentuate this recessed look, a slightly darker shade of the surface color (BG2) is applied to the recessed surface to make it appear slightly in shadow. Figure 9-6 shows examples of raised and recessed items.

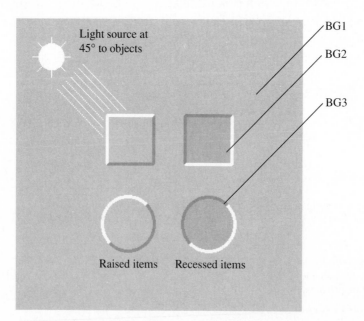

Figure 9-6   Raised and recessed objects for a three-dimensional design.

Three-Dimensional Button Design

The three-dimensional design of normal and highlighted buttons differs from that of monochrome buttons in the way depth is shown. On a monochrome system, depth is shown by using a double-thickness stroke on the lower and right sides of the button. In a three-dimensional implementation, depth is shown by a single stroke-width light and dark line, as shown in Figure 9-7. When a button is highlighted, it appears to recede into the screen. This appearance is achieved by reversing the white and BG3 colors used in the outline of the button. In addition, a slightly darker background is used in the button border to simulate a recessed and shadowed surface.

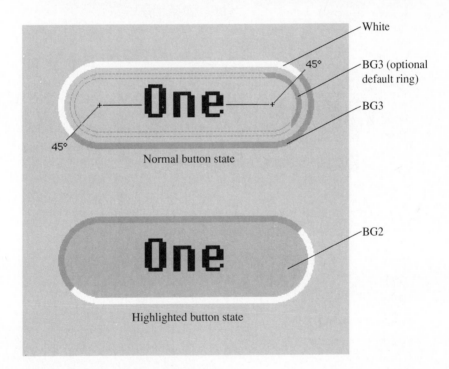

Figure 9-7   Three-dimensional buttons.

Menu buttons and abbreviated menu buttons use the same visual conventions. The menu mark is also rendered in a three-dimensional fashion. However, its shape and highlighting do not change. The filled portion of the menu symbol is BG2, as shown in Figure 9-8.

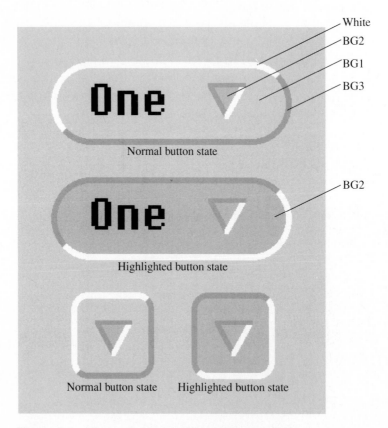

Figure 9-8   Three-dimensional menu buttons.

Menu Items

Items on menus are black text or glyphs on a field of BG1. When the pointer moves over each item, a recessed button shape is displayed as shown in Figure 9-9, with highlighting and shading exactly as for a highlighted button. Menu marks are highlighted and shaded as shown, and do not alter their appearance when an item is highlighted. The default menu item is shown with a ring of BG3.

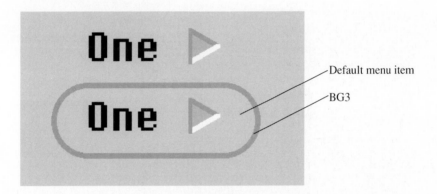

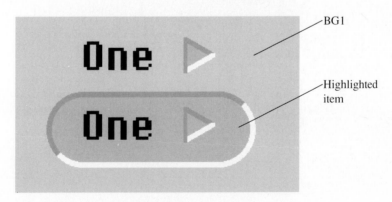

Figure 9-9   Three-dimensional menu items.

Exclusive and Nonexclusive Settings

Exclusive and nonexclusive settings are displayed on a field of BG1. The appearance and feedback are similar to those of buttons. Normal settings are raised, invoked settings are recessed. Exclusive settings are grouped together edge to edge as shown in Figure 9-10, and recess individually when set. Nonexclusive settings are separated by space. The default setting is shown with an inner rectangle of BG3.

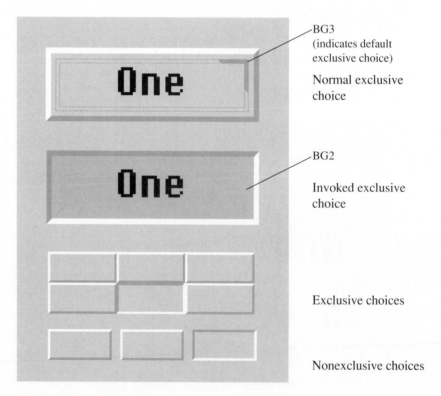

BG3
(indicates default exclusive choice)

Normal exclusive choice

BG2

Invoked exclusive choice

Exclusive choices

Nonexclusive choices

Figure 9-10   Three-dimensional exclusive and nonexclusive settings.

Check Boxes

Check boxes are displayed on a background color of BG1. An unchecked box is displayed as a raised button. When you press SELECT on a check box, the box is recessed into the surface. When you release the mouse button, the box is displayed as a raised box with a black check mark superimposed on the surface, as shown in Figure 9-11.

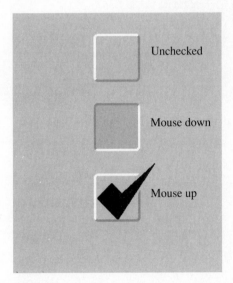

Unchecked

Mouse down

Mouse up

Figure 9-11   Three-dimensional check boxes.

Sliders

Sliders are displayed on a background color of BG1 and have a recessed "channel" and raised slider and drag box in black with a BG3 highlight. When tick marks are used, they are also raised as shown in Figure 9-12.

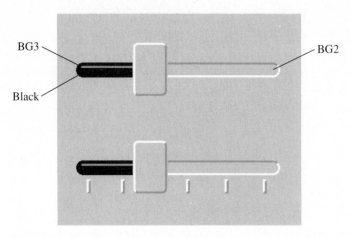

Figure 9-12   Three-dimensional sliders.

Gauges

Gauges are displayed on a background color of BG1. The gauge is a recessed surface (BG2) with a black indicator. When tick marks are used, they are also raised as shown in Figure 9-13.

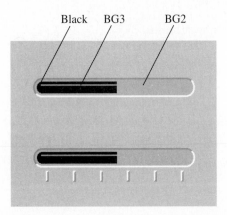

Figure 9-13   Three-dimensional gauges.

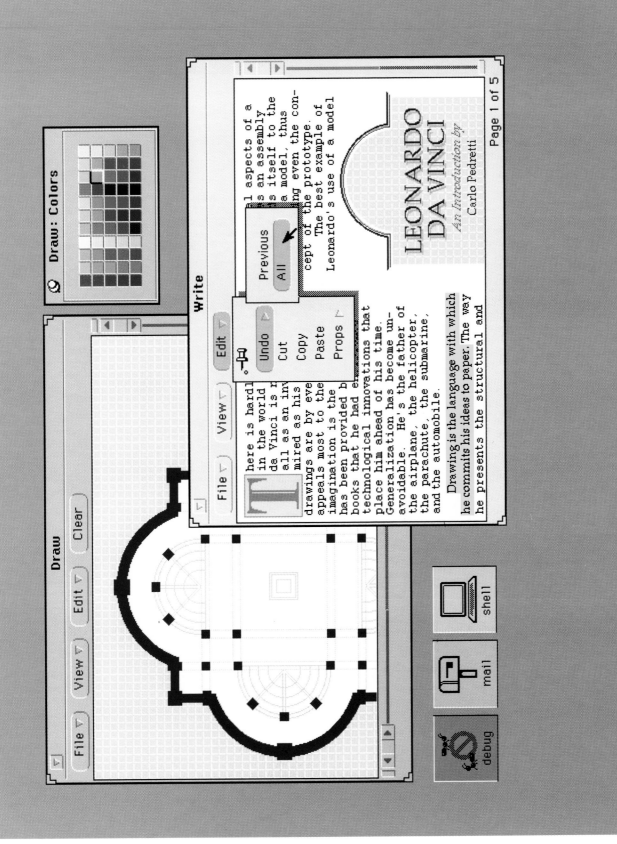

Figure 9-1 Color three-dimensional implementation—workspace, base windows, command window, menu, and icons.

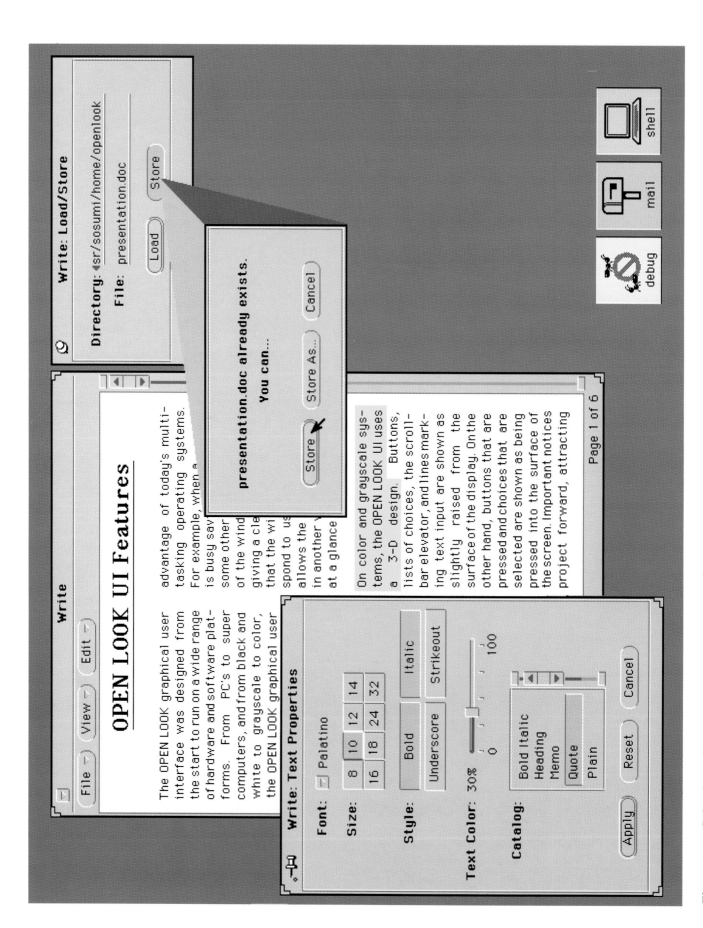

Figure 9-2 Color three-dimensional implementation—base window, property window, command window, and Notice.

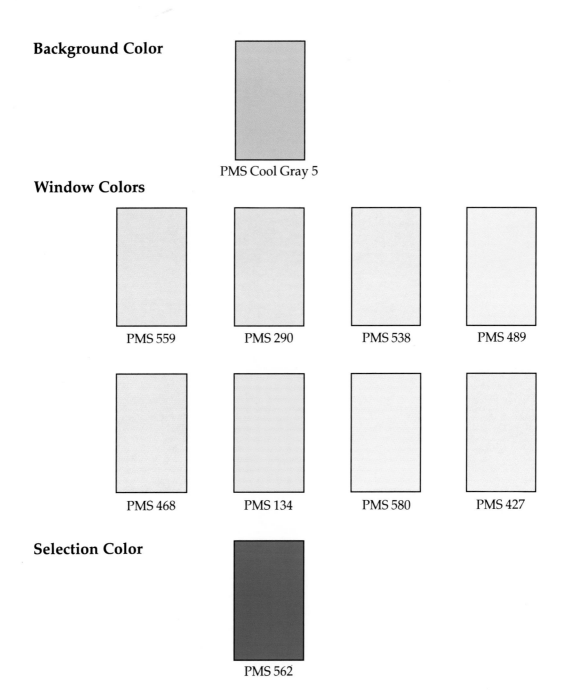

Background Color

PMS Cool Gray 5

Window Colors

PMS 559   PMS 290   PMS 538   PMS 489

PMS 468   PMS 134   PMS 580   PMS 427

Selection Color

PMS 562

Figure 9-3   Summer Palette

Background Color

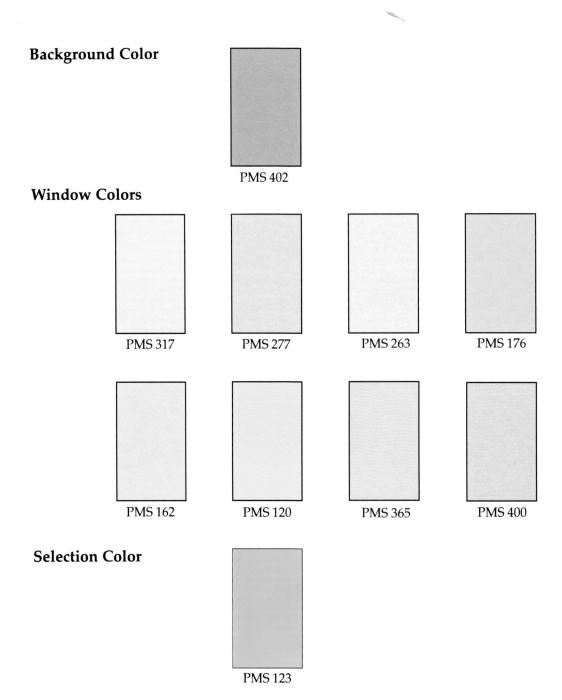

PMS 402

Window Colors

PMS 317   PMS 277   PMS 263   PMS 176

PMS 162   PMS 120   PMS 365   PMS 400

Selection Color

PMS 123

Figure 9-4   Winter Palette

Text Fields

Text fields are displayed on a background color of BG1 as a raised line made up of a white stroke above a BG3 stroke, as shown in Figure 9-14. The left end of the line is white and the right end is BG3.

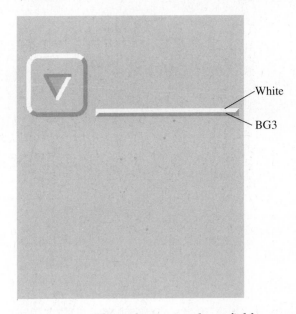

White

BG3

Figure 9-14   Three-dimensional text fields.

Scrollbars

Scrollbars, like other control elements, are displayed on a background color of BG1. User-selectable areas (the elevator and the top and bottom cable anchors) are three-dimensional, as shown in Figure 9-15. The three areas in the scrolling elevator raise and recess in the same way as buttons and settings.

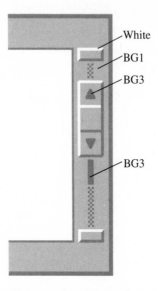

Figure 9-15   Three-dimensional scrollbars.

Window Elements

Windows have black borders, resize corners, and text elements that reside on a background color of BG2. The line below the header is a chiseled line in BG3 with a white line below it. Pane borders are BG3, as shown in Figure 9-16.

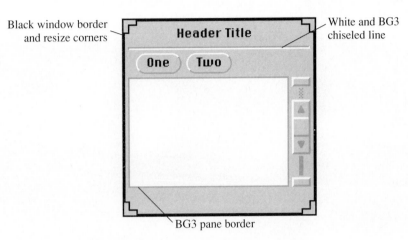

Figure 9-16 Three-dimensional window elements.

Scrolling Lists

Scrolling lists are displayed in control areas and command and property windows on a background color of BG1. The edges of the list are defined by a "chiseled" line made up of a white stroke and a BG3 stroke. Current items in the list are shown by recessed surfaces with a BG2 background color, as shown on Item 2 in Figure 9-17.

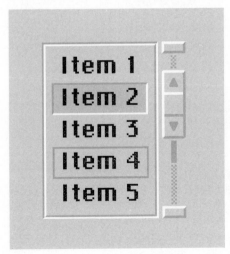

Figure 9-17 Three-dimensional scrolling lists.

PART III

REQUIRED OPEN LOOK UI FUNCTIONALITY

10

REQUIRED OPEN LOOK UI MENUS

This chapter describes the menus that are required for an OPEN LOOK UI implementation.

To promote consistency across applications and toolkits, the OPEN LOOK UI specifies and defines the following menus that are used to control workspace and window elements:

☐ Workspace menu (Level 1)
☐ Window menu (Level 1)
☐ Pop-up Window menu (Level 1)
☐ Settings menu for property window panes (Level 1)
☐ Scrollbar menu (Level 1)
☐ Scrolling List menu (Level 1)
☐ Edit menu for text and numeric fields (Level 2)

Any other menus used in an OPEN LOOK UI implementation are defined by the application. See Chapter 6 for a description of standard menu elements, and Chapter 15 for information about menu functionality.

Workspace Menu

In addition to the standard menu elements, the Workspace menu, shown in Figure 10-1, has the following elements:

☐ Title: Workspace
☐ Pushpin
☐ Items
   ▫ Programs (with a menu mark)
   ▫ Utilities (with a menu mark)
   ▫ Properties (with a window mark)
   ▫ Exit

Figure 10-1 The Workspace menu.

Programs

Programs displays a submenu with a list of application programs that you can run from the workspace. You add and delete applications from this submenu using the Workspace Properties window.

Utilities

Utilities displays a submenu with a list of utilities that you can run from the workspace. Figure 10-2 shows a Utilities submenu with the following items:

☐ Refresh (optional)
☐ Window Controls (Level 2)
☐ Clipboard (Level 2)
☐ Print Screen (optional)

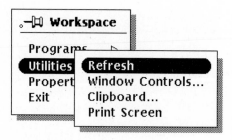

Figure 10-2 A Utilities submenu.

The OPEN LOOK UI implementation and application developers can add utilities to this menu.

In a Level 2 implementation, you can edit the Utilities submenu using the Workspace Properties window.

Refresh

Refresh redisplays all windows on the workspace.

Window Controls

A Level 2 implementation provides a Window Controls item that displays a pop-up window from which you can perform operations on multiple windows and icons that are selected on the workspace. See Chapter 16 for information about selecting multiple windows and icons. When an OPEN LOOK UI implementation supports virtual edges for the workspace, the Window Controls pop-up window can be moved onto the reserved area of the workspace. See Chapters 3 and 11 for more information about defining reserved areas of the workspace.

The Window Controls pop-up has the following elements:

☐ Pinned pushpin
☐ Buttons
  ▫ Open/Close
  ▫ Full/Restore Size
  ▫ Back
  ▫ Quit
☐ Optional resize corners

Figure 10-3 shows the default Window Controls pop-up window. The controls in this window operate on selected objects as appropriate.

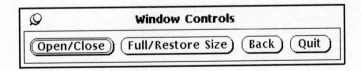

Figure 10-3   The default Window Controls pop-up window.

Open/Close. The Open/Close button (the default) opens selected icons, closes selected windows, and dismisses or cancels selected pop-up windows in the same operation.

Full/Restore Size. The Full/Restore Size button applies to all selected windows and icons, as appropriate. When Full Size is applied to a selected icon, the icon is opened, the window is displayed in the application-specified expanded size, and the window is brought to the front of the screen along with its associated pop-up windows. Any selected pop-up windows that do not recognize the Full/Restore Size command do not change size. Closing a window to an icon does not alter the Full/Restore Size setting for that window.

Back. The Back button moves selected windows or icons to the back of the screen. When the window property for Group Windows is set, unselected pop-up windows that are owned by a selected base window are also moved to the back of the screen.

Quit. The Quit button quits the selected windows or icons.

It is recommended that the Window Controls pop-up window have resize corners and that the controls redisplay to conform to the shape of the window. This allows you to configure the window in a way that is convenient for your workspace layout. Figure 10-4 shows three suggested configurations for the Window Controls pop-up with resize corners.

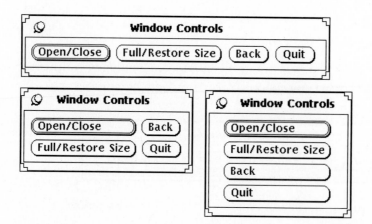

Figure 10-4   Three configurations of Window Controls when the window has resize corners.

An OPEN LOOK UI implementation can add other controls to this window that are appropriate for use with multiple selected objects. Additional controls could provide operations such as tiling selected windows and icons, or linking unrelated windows.

Clipboard

A Level 2 implementation provides a clipboard item that displays the current contents of the clipboard used by cut/copy/paste operations in a base window. As you use the clipboard, the contents of the Clipboard window are automatically updated.

The Clipboard window has the following elements, as shown in Figure 10-5:

☐ Resize corners
☐ A single scrollable pane. Allowing the pane to be split is optional.
☐ A footer

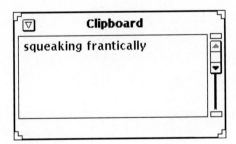

Figure 10-5   The Clipboard window.

Each OPEN LOOK UI implementation can have its own clipboard. See Chapter 17 for a description of cut, copy, and paste operations.

Print Screen

Print Screen prints an image of the objects that are currently displayed on the workspace. An OPEN LOOK UI implementation can expand the basic Print Screen capability by adding a window mark to the Print Screen item and designing a pop-up window with the following kinds of options: print the entire screen, print a region of the screen defined by a bounding box, or print a specific window on the workspace. This pop-up window could also contain options for defining a destination printer and for printing the screen to a file.

Properties

Properties displays the property window for all the properties you can set for the workspace. Chapter 11 contains a complete specification for the default contents of the Workspace Properties window.

Exit

Exit quits all elements of the workspace. Any applications running are also quit.

Customizing the Workspace Menu

In a Level 1 implementation the only part of the Workspace menu that you can customize is the Programs submenu. All other items must be provided as specified.

A Level 2 implementation allows you to customize the Workspace menu and its submenus. You edit the Workspace menu and its submenus from the Workspace Properties window. See Chapter 11 for information about workspace properties.

Base Window Menu

In addition to standard menu elements, the Window menu, shown in Figure 10-6, has the following elements:

- Title: Window
- Items
  - Open or Close
  - Full Size or Restore Size
  - Properties (with a window mark)
  - Back
  - Refresh
  - Quit

Figure 10-6   The Window menu.

Pressing MENU on an icon or on the background of a base window displays the Window menu. Window menu choices apply to the window or icon at the pointer location.

If an item name has two choices the names toggle to reflect the current state of the object at the pointer location.

Applications cannot change any of these items, nor can they add items to the Window menu. Each of the Window menu items is described below.

Open or Close

The Open label is shown when the pointer is on an icon and you press MENU. The Close label is shown when the pointer is on a base window and you press MENU. When you choose Close, the base window and its associated pop-up windows are closed to an icon. No other commands are executed.

Full Size or Restore Size

Full Size changes the size of a window to an application-defined maximum and brings it to the front of the screen. When a base window is brought to the front of the screen, its associated pop-up windows are also brought to the front, and are layered on top of the base window. When a window is not full size, the item label is Full Size. The application specifies the default window size and state of this item.

When a window size has been expanded, the item label is Restore Size. Restore Size returns an expanded window to its originally specified size. Closing a window to an icon does not alter the Full Size/Restore Size setting for that window.

When Full Size or Restore Size is selected from an icon Window menu, the icon is opened, and the window is displayed in the appropriate size and brought to the front of the screen.

Properties

Properties displays a property window that you use to set window properties. Window properties are specified in Chapter 3. The application cannot add other properties to this window.

Back

The Back option moves the window or icon to the back of the screen. When the window property for Group Windows is set, pop-up windows that are owned by a base window are also moved to the back of the screen.

Refresh

Refresh redraws the window or icon.

Quit

The Quit option quits the window or icon.

Pop-up Window Menu

In addition to standard menu elements, the pop-up Window menu, shown in Figure 10-7, has the following elements:

☐ Title: Window
☐ Items
  ▫ Dismiss or Cancel
  ▫ Back
  ▫ Refresh
  ▫ Owner?

Figure 10-7   The pop-up Window menu.

Applications cannot change any of these items, nor can they add items to the pop-up Window menu. Each of the pop-up Window menu items is described below.

Dismiss (or Cancel)

The Dismiss (or Cancel) item on the pop-up Window menu has some subtle distinctions.

Command Windows

When you dismiss a command window, it is removed from the screen. Usually the information displayed in that window is saved, whether or not a command has been executed. The next time the pop-up window is invoked, it appears as it did when it was dismissed. In this case, Dismiss is displayed as the item label.

Property Windows

When you have made no changes to a property window, or when the property window is pinned and you have applied the changes, Dismiss is displayed as the label.

When you have made changes to a property window that have not been applied, and you display the window menu, Cancel is displayed. Cancel is used to show you that the changes have not been applied and that when the property window is dismissed, the changes will be discarded. The next time you display the property window, it will show the current settings.

The Dismiss button menu has the following items, as shown in Figure 10-8:

☐ This Window
☐ All Pop-ups

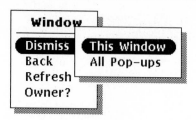

Figure 10-8   The Dismiss submenu.

You can dismiss the current pop-up window by choosing This Window. When you choose All Pop-ups, all the pop-up windows opened from a base window are dismissed together.

Back

The Back option moves the pop-up window to the back of the screen. You always move pop-up windows to the back of the screen individually from the pop-up Window menu. The window property for Group Windows only affects grouping from the base Window menu.

Refresh

Refresh redraws the pop-up window.

Owner?

The Owner? option flashes the title bar of the base window that owns the pop-up window, and brings that base window to the front of the screen.

Settings Menu

The pane of a property window has a pop-up menu with the following elements, as shown in Figure 10-9:

☐ Title: Settings
☐ Items:
   ▫ Apply
   ▫ Reset
   ▫ Apply to New Selection
   ▫ Set Default

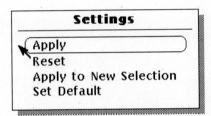

Figure 10-9   The Settings property window pop-up menu.

Applications must be sure that the items on the Settings menu always match the buttons at the bottom of the property window. If the property window has Apply and Reset buttons only, the Settings menu has Apply and Reset items. Applications cannot add items to the Settings menu. Each of the Settings menu items is described below.

Apply

The Apply item applies changes made in the property window to the selection and dismisses the property window if it is not pinned.

Reset

The Reset item returns the settings to the current values for the selection.

Apply to New Selection

When a property window has a second selection of the same kind in the same window, use the Apply to New Selection item to apply properties to the new selection. When there is only one selection, the Apply to New Selection item is not displayed. See Chapters 3 and 18 for more information.

Set Default

You can change the default settings for a property window to the settings that are displayed in the property window using the Set Default item. When this option is not available, the Set Default item is not displayed.

Scrollbar Menu

When a pane has a vertical scrollbar, the scrollbar area has a Scrollbar menu with the following required elements, as shown in Figure 10-10.

☐ Title: Scrollbar
☐ Items:
  ▫ Here to Top
  ▫ Top to Here
  ▫ Previous

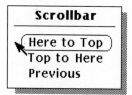

Figure 10-10   The minimum vertical Scrollbar menu.

When a pane has a horizontal scrollbar, the scrollbar area has a Scrollbar menu with the following elements, as shown in Figure 10-11:

☐ Title: Scrollbar
☐ Items:
  ▫ Here to Left

□ Left to Here
□ Previous

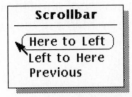

Figure 10-11   The minimum horizontal Scrollbar menu.

In a Level 2 implementation, applications that allow you to split a pane add an item labeled Split View to the Scrollbar menu. When a pane has been split, the application interactively adds an item labeled Join Views to the Scrollbar menu. Figure 10-12 shows an example of a vertical Scrollbar menu that has these two items. See Chapter 7 for a description of how to split and join panes using the Scrollbar menu. Applications can add items to the minimum Scrollbar menus.

Figure 10-12   The vertical Scrollbar menu for a pane that has been split.

Here to Top/Here to Left

This item moves the object (as defined by the application) that is next to the pointer location to the top (or left, for a horizontal scrollbar) of the pane. Suppose you want to move a line of text that is displayed in the middle of a pane to the top of the pane. You can do so with the following steps:

1 Move the pointer so that it is in the scrollbar area next to the line of text.

2 Press MENU to display the Scrollbar menu at the pointer location.

3 Choose the Here to Top item.

4 Release MENU. The Scrollbar menu is dismissed, and the view in the pane is repositioned so that the line next to the pointer is at the top of the pane. The position of the pointer does not change.

Top to Here/Left to Here

This item moves the first object at the top (or left) of the pane to the pointer location. Suppose you want to move a line of text that is displayed at the top of the pane down, so that you can see the text immediately above it. You can do so with the following steps:

1 Move the pointer so that it is in the scrollbar area next to the place where you want the top line to move.

2 Press MENU to display the Scrollbar menu at the pointer location.

3 Choose the Top to Here item.

4 Release MENU. The Scrollbar menu is dismissed, and the view in the pane is repositioned so that the line of text that was at the top of the pane is now positioned next to the pointer. The position of the pointer does not change.

Previous

This choice returns the contents of the pane to the previous scrolling position.

Scrolling List Menu

The pane of each scrolling list has a pop-up Scrolling List menu with a minimum set of required items, as shown in Figure 10-13:

☐ Title: Scrolling List
☐ Items:
  ◌ Locate Choice
  ◌ Edit List

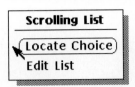

Figure 10-13   The minimum Scrolling List menu.

When the current item is not visible in the scrolling list, use the Locate Choice item to quickly scroll to it.

A nonexclusive scrolling list changes the Locate Choice item to Locate Next Choice, and also has a Clear All Choices item to allow you to clear the current items quickly.

When a scrolling list can be edited, the Scrolling List menu has an Edit List item. Choosing the Edit List item from the Scrolling List menu puts the scrolling list in edit mode and provides the following minimum set of required items, as shown in Figure 10-14.

☐ Change or Properties
☐ Insert
  ▫ Before
  ▫ After
☐ Delete
☐ End Editing

Figure 10-14   The minimum Scrolling List edit menu.

Applications can add items to either of these Scrolling List menus. See Chapter 8 for information about using scrolling lists.

Locate Choice

This choice is the default item. Choosing it scrolls the current item so that it is visible.

Edit List

Choosing it puts the scrolling list into edit mode to allow you to insert, delete, or change items in the list.

Change

This choice is displayed on the menu when all information about an item is visible in the scrolling list. Choosing it adds a text line and an active caret to the selected item in the list to allow you to edit the information. This item is the default. When there is no selection or when there are multiple selections in the scrolling list, this item is inactive.

Properties

This choice is displayed instead of the Change item on the Scrolling List menu when a scrolling list has additional editable information that is attached to the items. Choosing it displays a property window that allows you to change the properties of selected items in the scrolling list and edit additional information that is not visible in the scrolling list itself. When there is no selection in the scrolling list or when there are multiple selections, this item is inactive.

Insert

This menu item displays a submenu that contains the items Before and After.

Before

This choice inserts a text field with an active caret before the first selected item in the scrolling list. When there is no selected item, it inserts a text field at the start of the scrolling list. You use this text field to enter new information into the scrolling list. This item is the default. When there is no selection in the scrolling list, this item is inactive.

After

This choice inserts a text field with an active caret after the last selected item in the scrolling list. When there is no selected item, it inserts a text field at the end of the scrolling list. You use this text field to enter new information into the scrolling list. When there is no selection in the scrolling list, this item is inactive.

Delete

This choice deletes selected items from the scrolling list and does not store the text on the clipboard. When there is no selection in the scrolling list, this item is inactive.

End Editing

This choice validates and completes any editing that is in process and takes the scrolling list out of editing mode. When a scrolling list is edit only, this item is not required.

Text Field Edit Menu

In a Level 2 implementation, the text area of each text field has a pop-up Edit menu. The shaded area in Figure 10-15 shows the text area from which you can display the Edit menu for a numeric field, a type-in field, and a text pane.

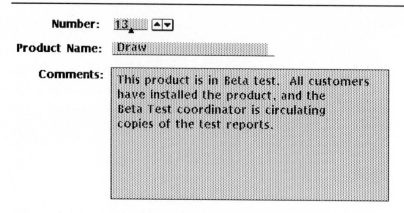

Figure 10-15   The shaded areas show the part of the text field from which you can display the Edit menu.

The Edit menu has the following minimum required elements, as shown in Figure 10-16:

☐ Title: Edit
☐ Items:
  ▫ Undo
  ▫ Cut
  ▫ Copy
  ▫ Paste
  ▫ Delete

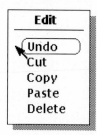

Figure 10-16   The minimum text field Edit menu.

Applications can add items to the minimum text field Edit menu.

Undo

This choice is the default item. It undoes the last action in the text field.

Cut

This choice removes selected text from the text field and stores it on the clipboard. When no text is selected, this item is inactive.

Copy

This choice puts a copy of selected text from the text field onto the clipboard. When no text is selected, this item is inactive.

Paste

This choice inserts the contents of the clipboard at the caret location in the text field. When the clipboard contains inappropriate data, the application displays a Notice. When the clipboard is empty, this item is inactive.

Delete

This choice deletes selected text from the text field, and does not store the text on the clipboard. When no text is selected, this item is inactive.

11

Workspace Properties

Introduction

Global preferences are set from the Workspace Properties window, which you access from the Workspace menu. In addition, each base window has a property window that is used for setting individual window properties.

This chapter describes the minimum requirements for a basic set of user-settable properties, specifies the required workspace properties, and shows suggested designs and layouts for these properties. An OPEN LOOK UI implementation can add other user-settable properties to this minimum set and should include options to tailor the implementation to specific hardware or software. For example, if the hardware supports adjustable volume and sound, the controls for a system "beep" could be set with a slider rather than using an option for "on" or "off." The figures in this chapter show a combination of Level 1, Level 2, recommended, and optional workspace properties.

When Workspace Properties Take Effect

Some workspace properties apply to future events and do not change the properties of windows or icons already displayed on the workspace. For example, changing the default color setting for windows never changes the background color of any windows already displayed. In an OPEN LOOK UI implementation of any level, the properties that apply to future events are set when you click SELECT on the Apply button. The next time you display a window, it uses the new settings to determine what properties to display.

Other properties, such as changing the selection color, are global and must be the same everywhere on the workspace. For example, you cannot set green for the selection color in one window and blue for the selection color in another window. For global properties that affect the entire workspace, the level of implementation determines when changes are applied.

☐ In a Level 1 implementation, you must click SELECT on the Apply button, exit the workspace, and reenter it to apply global properties such as selection color or keyboard mappings.

☐ When a Level 2 implementation can support the immediate application of global properties, clicking SELECT on the Apply button applies global properties to all objects currently displayed on the workspace. When a Level 2 implementation cannot support it, you must exit the workspace and reenter it to apply global properties.

Control Area

The Workspace Properties window has the following suggested elements:

☐ A header with the following elements
  ▫ A Pushpin
  ▫ The title "Workspace: Properties"
☐ A control area with two controls
  ▫ Category abbreviated menu button
  ▫ Factory/Custom exclusive settings
☐ A pane to contain the property settings
☐ Apply and Reset buttons centered at the bottom of the pane

The layout and design of the control area are determined by the OPEN LOOK UI implementation. Figure 11-1 shows the suggested elements with Category and Settings on the same line.

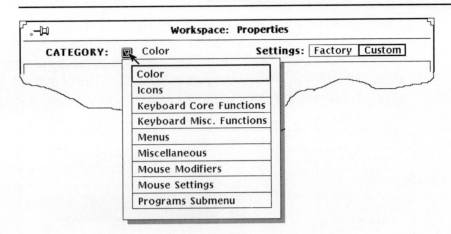

Figure 11-1 Workspace Properties window control area.

The Category abbreviated menu button on the left side of the control area shows the category for the pane that is displayed in the property window. The menu shows all the Workspace Properties window categories:

☐ Color (Level 2)
☐ Icons (Level 1)
☐ Keyboard Core Functions (Level 1)
☐ Keyboard Miscellaneous Functions (Level 1)
☐ Menus (Level 2)
☐ Miscellaneous (Level 1)
☐ Mouse Modifiers (Level 1)
☐ Mouse Settings (Level 1)
☐ Programs Submenu (Level 1 only)
☐ Workspace Menu (Level 2 only)

Each of these categories is described in detail later in this chapter. When you choose a category from the menu, the name to the right of the menu button changes to reflect the new category, and the property window displays a pane with the category settings.

The Workspace Properties window always has a Settings category that offers two choices:

☐ Factory
☐ Custom

The Factory setting is the same for all levels of implementation and is used to display the default settings for the OPEN LOOK UI implementation as read-only information. No controls are displayed in the pane. Since you cannot change any of the settings, the Apply and Reset buttons are inactive. Figure 11-2 shows the Color category with the Factory setting chosen.

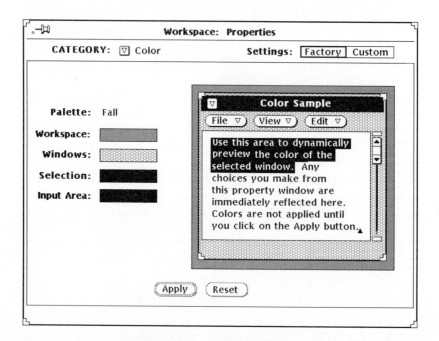

Figure 11-2   The Color category with factory settings.

In a Level 1 implementation, clicking SELECT on the Custom setting redisplays the contents with the appropriate controls, using the default settings. When the controls are displayed, you can make changes to the settings for that category. Figure 11-3 shows the Color category with the Custom setting chosen. Changes are applied when you click SELECT on the Apply button.

Figure 11-3   The Workspace Properties control area with Level 1 custom settings.

In a Level 2 implementation, you can save a variety of custom settings, using your own naming conventions. The Settings category for a Level 2 implementation has an abbreviated button with a window mark, followed by a text field. Figure 11-4 shows an example of a color category for a Level 2 implementation. In this example, the Settings choices are displayed on a second line below the Category choices.

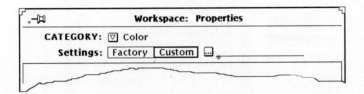

Figure 11-4   The Workspace Properties control area with Level 2 custom settings.

When you choose Custom, the default choices are displayed. To choose a different custom setting, type the name of the custom setting in the text field and press Return. To display an editable scrolling list containing the current custom settings, click SELECT on the abbreviated button at the left of the text field. A pop-up window containing a scrolling list is displayed. You can choose one of the choices in the scrolling list to enter it into the text field, or you can create a new custom setting (add it to the list).

The Color Category

On color systems, the Color category settings, shown in Figure 11-5, are used to define the color properties of the workspace. The Workspace, Windows, and Selection categories are required for a Level 2 implementation. The Input Area category is an optional setting.

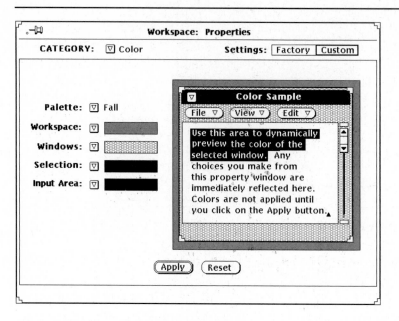

Figure 11-5   Color category.

Note: Black-and-white patterns are used as representations of different colors on the palettes.

Each color control is an abbreviated menu button. Any changes made to the color settings are immediately reflected in the Color Sample window at the right. In this way, you can preview the choices before applying them. The area around the Color Sample window shows the chosen workspace color.

The changes displayed in the Color Sample area are not applied until you click SELECT on the Apply button.

The Color Palette Menu

Figure 11-6 shows the Palette menu.

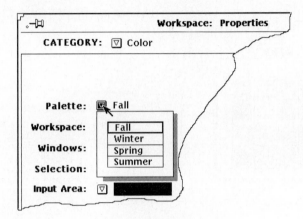

Figure 11-6 Color category, Palette menu.

The Workspace Palette Menu

Figure 11-7 shows an example of the Workspace Palette menu with 16 color choices. The number of choices on this palette is determined by the color capabilities of your OPEN LOOK UI implementation. The color of the workspace is a global property.

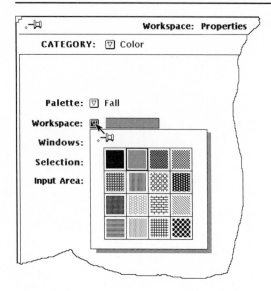

Figure 11-7   Color category, Workspace menu.

The Windows Palette Menu

The Windows palette menu is the same as the Workspace palette menu. The color that you choose from this menu sets the default background color for any new windows you open. You can choose a different background color from the property window for the application. Setting a color from the property window for the application overrides the default selection from the Workspace Properties window. The Windows color that you choose does not affect the background color of windows already displayed. It applies to any new windows you open after you click SELECT on the Apply button. Some OPEN LOOK UI implementations may require you to quit the workspace and reenter it before this property is applied.

The Selection Palette Menu

Figure 11-8 shows an example of the Selection menu. The color you choose from this menu determines the color that is used for highlighting text selections. The color you choose is displayed in the highlighted text of the Color Sample window. The Selection color is a global property.

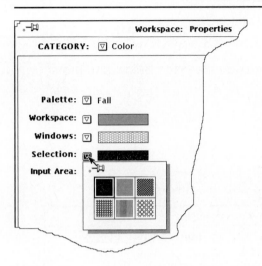

Figure 11-8   Color category, Selection menu.

The Input Area Palette Menu

The color you choose from the Input Area palette sets the color for the active caret and for the highlighting of the header that shows the active input area. Figure 11-9 shows an example of the Input Area palette menu. The Input Area color is a global property.

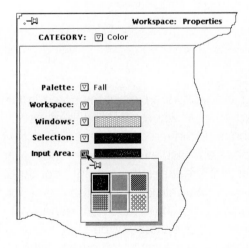

Figure 11-9   Color category, Input Area menu.

The Icons Category

The Icons category settings are listed below and are shown in Figure 11-10.

☐ Location (Level 1)
☐ Border (Level 2)
☐ Align to Grid (Level 2)
☐ Grid Origin (Level 2)
☐ Grid Spacing (Level 2)

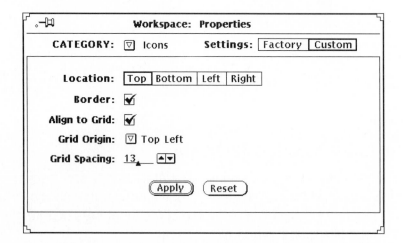

Figure 11-10   Icons category settings.

The Location Setting

Use the Location setting to specify the side of the screen that icons move to when an application is started up or when a window is closed. When you use the Top setting, the first icon is displayed at the upper left corner of the workspace. Subsequent icons are displayed one icon width to the right of the previous icon. When the last icon reaches the top right corner of the screen, the next icon is moved one icon height down from the top of the screen, and a second row is formed following the same placement pattern. This same pattern is used for each of the other settings. When you use the Bottom setting, the first icon is displayed in the lower left corner. When you use the Left setting, the first icon is displayed in the upper left corner. When you use the Right setting, the first icon is displayed in the upper right corner. The Location setting applies to future placement of icons and does not affect the location of any icons already displayed on the workspace.

The Border Setting

Use the Border setting check box to choose whether or not to display the icon borders for unselected icons in a color implementation. The Border setting is a global property.

The Align to Grid Setting

Use the Align to Grid check box to choose whether or not you want the icons to snap to the invisible grid intersections on the workspace. The Align to Grid setting is a global property.

The Grid Origin Setting

Use the Grid Origin setting to determine whether you want the grid to originate at the top left, the top right, the bottom left, or the bottom right corner of the screen. Grid origin always refers to the physical screen, and does not change if you define virtual edges for the workspace. The Grid Origin setting is a global property.

The Grid Spacing Setting

Use the Grid Spacing numeric field to determine the number of points between the horizontal and vertical lines for the workspace grid. The Grid Spacing setting is a global property.

See Chapter 3 for more information about icon placement and the workspace grid.

The Keyboard Core Functions Category

The Keyboard Core Functions category is shown in Figure 11-11 with the following functions:

☐ Copy (Level 1)
☐ Cut (Level 1)
☐ Help (Level 1)
☐ Paste (Level 1)
☐ Properties (Level 1)
☐ Undo (Level 1)
☐ Stop (Level 2)

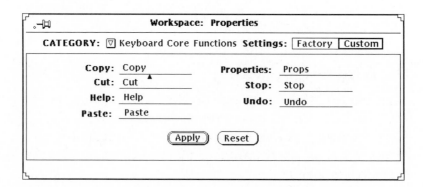

Figure 11-11   Keyboard Core Functions category.

To define a keyboard equivalent for these core functions, move the caret to the field to be defined, and press the equivalent key sequence. When you press a key, the key name is displayed in the field as it is labeled on the keycap. For example, pressing Ctrl types Ctrl in the text field, pressing Shift types Shift, pressing Alt types Alt, pressing A types A, and so on. Keyboard settings are global properties.

The Keyboard Miscellaneous Functions Category

The Keyboard Miscellaneous Functions category, shown in Figure 11-12, includes the following functions:

☐ Cancel (Level 1)
☐ Default Action (Level 1)
☐ Next Field (Level 1)
☐ Previous Field (Level 1)
☐ Character Back (Level 2)
☐ Character Forward (Level 2)
☐ Delete Character Back (Level 2)
☐ Delete Character Forward (Level 2)

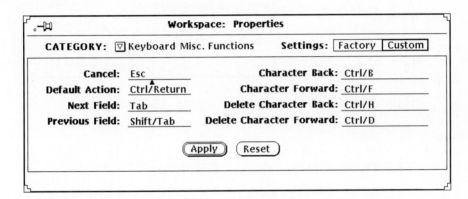

Figure 11-12   Keyboard Miscellaneous Functions category.

To define a keyboard equivalent for these miscellaneous functions, move the caret to the field to be defined, and press the equivalent key sequence. When you press a key, the key name is displayed in the field as it is labeled on the keycap. For example, pressing Ctrl types Ctrl in the text field, pressing Shift types Shift, pressing Alt types Alt, pressing A types A, and so on. A slash (/) is printed to show modification. Keyboard settings are global properties.

The Menus Category

The Menus category, shown in Figure 11-13, contains the following settings:

☐ Drag-Right Distance (Level 1)
☐ SELECT mouse press (optional)
☐ MENU mouse click (Level 2)

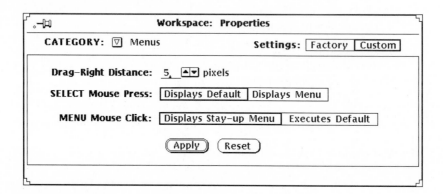

Figure 11-13   Menus category.

The Drag-Right Distance Setting

The Drag-Right Distance setting allows you to specify how far you must drag the pointer to the right to display a submenu. The default distance is 5 pixels. The Drag-Right Distance is a global property.

The SELECT Mouse Press Setting

The optional SELECT Mouse Press setting allows you to specify the way button menus are displayed when you press SELECT. The SELECT Mouse Press is a global property.

☐ When you choose the Displays Default setting, pressing SELECT when the pointer is on a menu button in a control area displays the default setting within the button border as specified in Chapter 5 for Level 1 implementations.

☐ When you choose the Displays Menu setting, pressing SELECT when the pointer is on a menu button in a control area displays the button menu. This option lets you make selections and choose from menus using only one mouse button. Choosing from a menu with SELECT works in the same way as using MENU, as described in Chapter 15.

The MENU Mouse Click Setting

The Level 2 MENU Mouse Click setting allows you to choose how menus are displayed when you click MENU. The MENU Mouse Click is a global property.

☐ When you choose Displays Stay-up Menu, menus operate as specified for Level 1 implementations, allowing both press-drag-release and click-move-click operations, as described in Chapter 15.

☐ When you choose Executes Default, clicking MENU for a pop-up menu immediately executes the default choice from the menu. See Chapter 15 for more information about using this option. When you choose this option, the click-move-click method is disabled. Instead, clicking MENU on a menu button in the control area briefly displays the menu.

The Miscellaneous Category

The Miscellaneous category, shown in Figure 11-14, is used to define the following settings:

☐ System beeping (Level 1)
☐ Scale at Startup (Level 2)
☐ Set Input Area (Level 2)
☐ Scrollbar Placement (optional)
☐ Set Virtual Edges (optional)
☐ SELECT Always Brings Window Forward (Level 2)

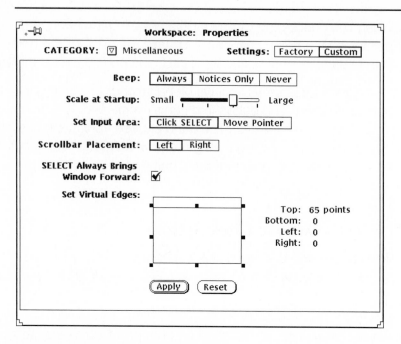

Figure 11-14 Miscellaneous category.

The Beep Setting

Use the Beep setting to specify when you want the system to beep: Always, for Notices Only, or Never. The Always setting does not set a continuous beep. It permits you to hear all beeps that are generated by both the OPEN LOOK UI implementation and the applications displayed on the workspace. The OPEN LOOK UI implementation specifies that the system beeps for important messages, when clicking SELECT on a menu button cannot execute the default because the default is inactive and when you set the workspace as the input area. Applications are not restricted to beeping for these purposes, and can implement beeping to notify you of other application-specific functions. The Beep setting is a global property.

The Scale at Startup Slider

Use the Scale at Startup slider to specify the initial scaling size for applications when they are first started. You can use the property window that you access from the application's Window menu to specify scale at startup the next time you start up the application. The Scale at Startup setting applies to future invocations of application windows and does not affect any applications already displayed on the workspace.

Some OPEN LOOK UI implementations may display exclusive settings for Scale at Startup instead of using a slider.

The Set Input Area Setting

Use the Set Input Area setting to specify whether you must click SELECT to type or simply move the pointer into the window to set the input area. Set Input Area is a global property.

When the Move Pointer option is set, the highlighting of the window header with the input area is changed to two-point lines at the top and bottom of the window header as specified in Chapter 3.

The Scrollbar Placement Setting

Use the Scrollbar Placement setting to specify whether vertical scrollbars are positioned at the right or left side of the pane. Horizontal scrollbars are always positioned below the pane. The Scrollbar Placement setting is a global property.

The SELECT Always Brings Window Forward Setting

Use the SELECT Always Brings Window Forward check box when you want the window brought to the front of the screen any time you click SELECT anywhere in the window. If you do not choose this option, clicking SELECT in a pane to set the insert point does not automatically bring the window to the front of the screen if it is partially obscured. This setting is a global property.

The Virtual Edges Setting

Use the Virtual Edges setting to define an artificial edge to the screen. Windows treat the virtual edge of the screen as the actual edge of the screen. The OPEN LOOK UI implementation must provide a way for a specific class of applications to display in the area between the virtual edge and the physical edge of the screen. Icons can be moved directly beyond the virtual edge of the screen.

Press SELECT on one of the grab handles and drag the bounding box to define a virtual edge. Virtual edges are not mutually exclusive—they can be set on one, two, three, or four sides of the screen. As you drag the grab handle, the number of points between the physical edge of the screen and the virtual edge of the screen is displayed in the readonly field to the right.

When you apply properties to set virtual edges, a 1-point line is displayed on the workspace to show the dividing line between the workspace area and the virtual edge or edges. Set Virtual Edges is a global property.

See Chapter 3 for more information about the virtual edge setting.

The Mouse Modifiers Category

The Mouse Modifiers category, shown in Figure 11-15, is used to change the default mouse modifier keys.

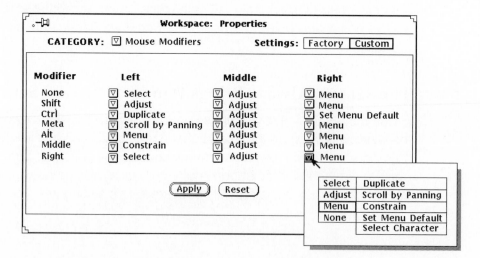

Figure 11-15   Mouse Modifiers category.

Each abbreviated menu button has the same menu, shown in Figure 11-15, which contains all the possible functions. The controls form a table that you read by finding the column representing the mouse button and the row representing a specific modifier.

For example, LEFT modified by None means SELECT. LEFT modified by Ctrl means DUPLICATE. LEFT modified by Alt means MENU.

Mouse Modifiers are a global property.

The Mouse Settings Category

The Mouse Settings category, shown in Figure 11-16, is used to set the following mouse characteristics:

☐ Enable/disable scrollbar pointer jumping (Level 1)
☐ Enable/disable pop-up pointer jumping (Level 1)
☐ Set mouse acceleration (optional)
☐ Set the multi-click timeout factor (optional)

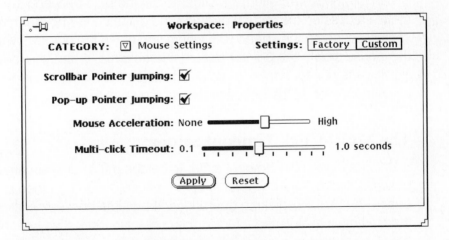

Figure 11-16   Mouse Settings category.

The Scrollbar Pointer Jumping Setting

When the Scrollbar Pointer Jumping check box is checked, the pointer tracks the movement of the scrolling buttons and jumps ahead of the scrollbar elevator. When the check box is not checked, scrollbar pointer jumping is disabled. See Chapter 7 for more information about scrollbar pointer jumping. Scrollbar pointer jumping is a global property.

The Pop-up Pointer Jumping Setting

When the Pop-up Pointer Jumping check box is checked, the pointer jumps to a pop-up window when it is displayed and, when appropriate, the input area is set to that pop-up window. When the check box is not checked, the pointer never jumps to pop-up windows. See Chapter 3 for more information about pointer jumping. Pop-up pointer jumping is a global property.

The Mouse Acceleration Slider

Use the Mouse Acceleration slider to set the ratio between the distance the mouse moves on the mouse pad and the distance the pointer moves on the screen based on the speed with which you move the pointer. When you move the mouse slowly, the pointer does not accelerate. When you move the mouse quickly, the pointer moves a greater distance the higher the mouse acceleration slider is set. Mouse Acceleration is a global property.

The Multi-Click Timeout Slider

Use the Multi-Click Timeout slider to set the maximum permitted time between clicks—when you release the mouse button and then press it again—for multiple clicking operations. If the time between clicks is longer than the multi-click timeout factor, the clicks are treated as separate events, not as a single command. Multi-click timeout is a global property.

The Programs Submenu Category

The Programs Submenu category settings are used to define the applications that are displayed on the Workspace menu. Figure 11-17 shows the Programs Submenu category settings. Note that the scrolling list shows sample applications that are not a required part of an OPEN LOOK UI implementation.

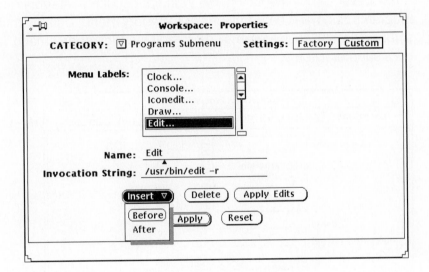

Figure 11-17   Programs Submenu category.

The property window contains an editable scrolling list that you use to define the name and the file system location of the applications that are accessed from the Programs item of the Workspace menu. The information you type in the Name field becomes the label on the Programs submenu for that application.

Add a new item to the menu by typing the item name and invocation string in the text field and clicking SELECT on the Insert button.

Edit an existing item name, or change the invocation string, by clicking SELECT on an item in the scrolling list. The item name is displayed in both the Name field and the invocation string in the Invocation String field. Revise or edit the existing information, and click SELECT on the Apply Edits button.

Delete an item from the scrolling list by clicking SELECT on the item and then clicking SELECT on the Delete button.

As with all property windows, properties are not applied until you click SELECT on the Apply button. Since the items on the scrolling list may change, a change bar is displayed next to the entire scrolling list if you make any changes to the existing menu.

The Workspace Menu Category

In a Level 2 implementation, the Workspace Menu category replaces the Programs Submenu category on the Category menu. Use the multi-level scrolling list shown in Figure 11-18 to edit the Workspace menu items and any of its submenu items.

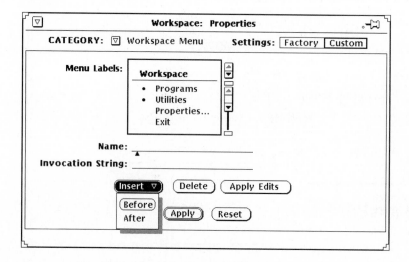

Figure 11-18 Workspace Menu category.

12

FILE MANAGER

An OPEN LOOK File Manager provides such basic functions as browsing, copying and deleting files, and initiating programs. This chapter describes the elements and functionality for a basic File Manager implementation. Any File Manager implementation can provide additional functionality to augment the basic functionality specified in this chapter. Implementations of the File Manager that run in a network environment should provide a method with which you can access other parts of the network as part of the File Manager functionality.

Introduction

The File Manager displays glyphs to represent directories, data files, and applications in the file system. These glyphs can be selected and operated on directly or indirectly within the File Manager base window. You operate on glyphs directly by selecting, dragging, and releasing them over folders and panes within the File Manager. You operate on glyphs indirectly by selecting and cutting or copying them to the clipboard, and then pasting them elsewhere in the file structure within the File Manager window. The File Manager thus provides both a direct and intuitive way for you to manage your files and maintains consistency with the familiar cut/copy/paste clipboard paradigm.

When the File Manager glyphs are moved out of the File Manager and onto the workspace, they become independent icons, providing you with a way to start applications without using the Workspace menu. When supported by an application, you can drag appropriate glyphs from the File Manager directly onto an application pane to load the file into the application.

From within an application that provides a Browse button—following the recommendations in the *OPEN LOOK Graphical User Interface Application Style Guidelines*—you can access the File Manager and browse through the file structure that is displayed in the File Manager window. Suppose that you want to load a document into a word processing application. When you use the Browse button, the File Manager window automatically opens, comes to the front of the screen, and displays the files in the appropriate folder. You then use a control in the File Manager to load the file. The File Manager is dismissed and returns to its previous location and state.

File Manager Functionality

This section outlines the basic functionality the File Manager must provide. The functionality is explained later in this chapter.

A File Manager implementation has the following visual elements:

☐ A required base window configuration (described in detail in the following section)
☐ File Manager glyphs that represent data files, applications (executable files), and folders (directories)

A File Manager implementation requires the following functionality:

☐ A way to associate each data file with its appropriate application so that the application automatically starts when you select and open a data file
☐ A way to support interactions between the File Manager and other applications
☐ Two ways to manipulate File Manager glyphs:
  ▫ Direct manipulation—by dragging and dropping selected glyphs onto a folder, the File Manager pane, a separate application pane, an independent icon, or the workspace
  ▫ Using the clipboard for cut/copy/paste operations
☐ The following file management operations:
  ▫ Create folder
  ▫ Create file
  ▫ Display folder contents
  ▫ Change folders
  ▫ Rename files and folders
  ▫ Delete files and folders
  ▫ Change file properties
  ▫ Sort (by name, size, and date)

The following sections describe the elements of the File Manager and its functionality.

The File Manager Base Window

The File Manager base window has the following required elements:

☐ A control area
☐ A scrollable *path pane,* which is used to show the operating system hierarchy or ancestor chain
☐ A scrollable *folder pane,* which is used to display the contents of the folder at the end of the path pane
☐ A footer for error and informational messages

These elements are shown in Figure 12-1.

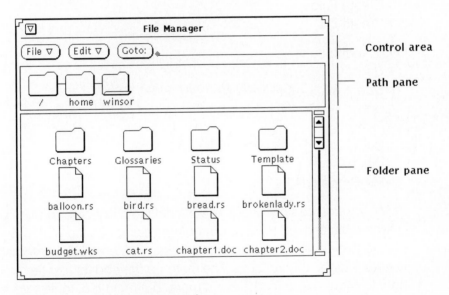

Figure 12-1   The File Manager base window.

The basic kinds of File Manager glyphs are:

☐ Folders
☐ Data files
☐ Applications

The glyphs for folders and data files are shown in Figure 12-1. Folders can be closed or opened. The last folder in the path pane of the base window is always open, indicating that the contents of that folder are displayed as glyphs in the scrollable pane below.

The following sections describe the elements of the control area, the path pane, and the folder pane. Later sections in this chapter contain information about how to use the File Manager and describe additional types of glyphs.

Elements of the Control Area

The control area has the following required controls:

□ File menu button
  ▫ Open
  ▫ Print
  ▫ Create Folder
  ▫ Create File

□ Edit menu button
  ▫ Undo
  ▫ Select All
  ▫ Copy
  ▫ Paste
  ▫ Cut
  ▫ Delete
  ▫ File Properties

The control area can have an optional Goto button and text field.

When you use the Browse button from an application to open the File Manager, a Load menu button (with Load File and Cancel items on the menu) is added to the control area. The Goto button and its text field move to the right to allow space for the Load menu button in the control area, as shown in Figure 12-2.

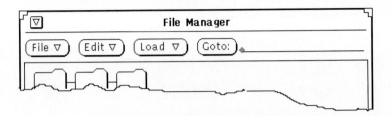

Figure 12-2 A Load menu button is displayed in the control area when you open the File Manager from an application.

The File Menu

The items on the File menu are described briefly in this section.

Open opens any selected glyph in the path or folder pane and automatically starts the application bound to that glyph.

Print prints selected data files. If the glyph is not a data file and, therefore, cannot be printed, an error message is displayed in the footer of the File Manager base window.

Create Folder creates a new folder.

Create File opens an editor window.

The Edit Menu

The items on the Edit menu are described briefly in this section.

Undo undoes the last operation.

Select All selects all the files in the folder pane.

Copy puts a copy of selected file names from the folder pane on the clipboard.

Paste copies or moves files by inserting selected file names that are stored on the clipboard into the folder pane.

Cut puts a copy of selected file names from the folder pane on the clipboard and removes the file glyph from the File Manager.

Delete deletes selected files from the folder pane.

File Properties displays a property window showing system information about the selected object or objects such as the file name, size, date, and type.

Figure 12-3 shows an example of how the contents of the File Properties window might look when one data file object is selected. The contents of the File Properties in this example shows typical UNIX® operating system file information.

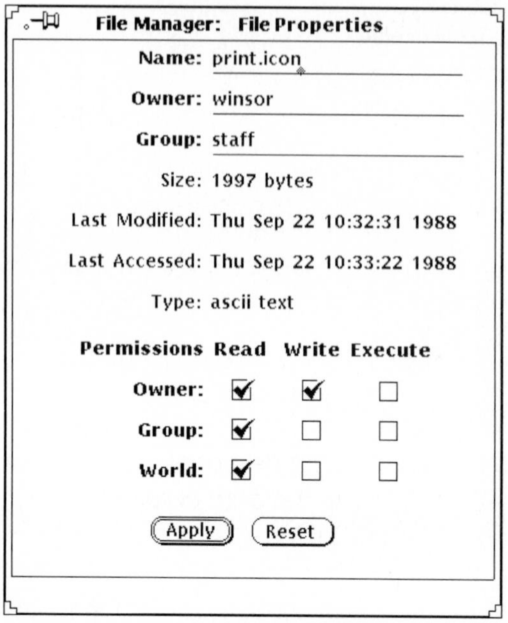

```
┌─────────────────────────────────────────────┐
│ ₀─▯▯   File Manager:  File Properties          │
│              Name: print.icon_____  │
│             Owner: winsor_____   │
│             Group: staff_____   │
│              Size: 1997 bytes                  │
│     Last Modified: Thu Sep 22 10:32:31 1988    │
│     Last Accessed: Thu Sep 22 10:33:22 1988    │
│              Type: ascii text                  │
│                                                │
│   Permissions Read  Write Execute              │
│       Owner:   ☑     ☑      ☐                  │
│       Group:   ☑     ☐      ☐                  │
│       World:   ☑     ☐      ☐                  │
│                                                │
│          ( Apply )   ( Reset )                 │
└─────────────────────────────────────────────┘
```

Figure 12-3   An example of the File Properties window.

The information shown in this File Properties window is an example that is specific to the UNIX operating system. Implementations of the File Manager for different operating systems show statistics appropriate to that operating system.

You use the File Properties window shown in this example to change the Name, Owner, Group, and Permissions of the selected object. Additional read-only information is displayed about the selected object. When you change properties and click SELECT on the Apply button, the new properties are applied to the selected object.

When multiple glyphs are selected, all choices are indeterminate. See Chapter 3 for information about indeterminate properties and Chapter 4 for information about indeterminate settings.

The Goto Button and Text Field

You can type a path into the Goto text field and click SELECT on the Goto button to open that folder. Alternatively, you can type a file name and click SELECT on the Goto button to select a data file or application.

Elements of the Path Pane

The path pane shows the path of the folder for the information that is displayed in the folder pane. The required elements of the path pane follow:

☐ A pane large enough to accommodate the folder and the text labels
☐ A scrollbar that is displayed only when the window is too small to contain the complete path
☐ A selectable folder. The minimum contents of the pane is a folder that shows the bottom of the file structure.
☐ A selectable closed folder with the name for each folder in the hierarchy
☐ A pop-up Path Commands menu with the following items:
  ▫ Open
  ▫ File Properties

In Figure 12-4, which shows these elements of the path pane, the home folder is selected, and the Path Commands pop-up menu is displayed.

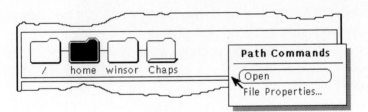

Figure 12-4   The elements of the path pane.

When you resize the base window so that not all the folders fit in the pane, a horizontal scrollbar is displayed for the path pane, as shown in Figure 12-5.

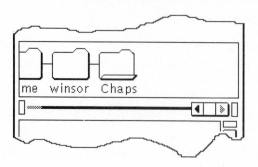

Figure 12-5   The path pane is scrollable when it is too small to display the entire path.

Elements of the Folder Pane

The folder pane displays the contents of the open folder in the path pane. The folder pane has the following elements:

□ A pane, with a scrollbar when the contents cannot be completely displayed, that contains selectable named glyphs
□ A pop-up Folder Commands menu with the following required items:
  ▫ Open
  ▫ Delete
  ▫ File Properties
□ Named glyphs representing the contents of the folder

The Folder Commands Pop-up Menu

The pop-up menu is shown in Figure 12-6.

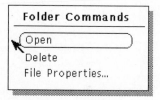

Figure 12-6   The pop-up Folder Commands menu.

The Folder Pane Glyphs

The folder pane displays the contents of the folder in the path pane with one named glyph for each file. Each glyph in the folder pane represents one of three types of files:

☐ Folder: directory
☐ Data file: a text, graphics, or other data file
☐ Application: an executable program

These glyphs are typically two-thirds the size of the default icon size. The unselected and selected File Manager default glyphs for each of these file types are shown in Figure 12-7.

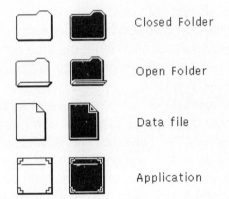

Closed Folder

Open Folder

Data file

Application

Figure 12-7   The default File Manager glyphs, unselected and selected.

The folder is always displayed and can be represented as either open or closed, as shown in Figure 12-7. Some File Manager implementations may display folders only in the closed state. Data file and application glyphs can be displayed in different ways, as explained in the paragraphs that follow.

Folder Files. Folder files are always displayed as an open or closed folder and have either a selected or unselected state. Figure 12-8 shows examples of closed folders with the folder name centered beneath the glyph.

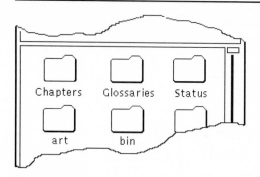

Figure 12-8   Examples of folders in a folder pane.

Data Files. The File Manager default is to bind each data file glyph to the default text editor. Any data file can be bound to a specific application. When data files are bound to a specific application other than the default text editor, the image area for the application's icon design can be displayed within the border of the standard data file glyph.

In the examples shown in Figure 12-9, the data files with a .rs suffix are bound to a graphics editor and display an image of the Draw application glyph within the border of the data file. Data files with a .wks suffix are bound to a spreadsheet and display an image of a grid representing a spreadsheet application within the border of the data file. Other files that are not bound to a specific application are, by default, bound to the default text editor. The data files with the suffix .doc in Figure 12-9 are bound to the default text editor and, therefore, show no glyph within the border of the data file.

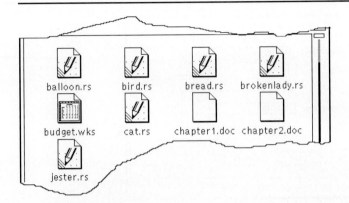

Figure 12-9   Examples of data files with application images.

Applications. An application can use either the standard File Manager application glyph or the icon image specific to the application. For example, an application named "Snapshot" that is used to capture screen images could be displayed in either of the ways shown in Figure 12-10.

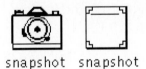

Figure 12-10   An application can use either its own icon image or the File Manager application glyph.

The File Manager Properties Window

The File Manager Properties window is displayed when you choose Properties from the control area.

The settings in the File Manager Properties window are specific to the operating system. The example shown in Figure 12-11 shows a suggested File Manager Properties category that is specific to the UNIX operating system.

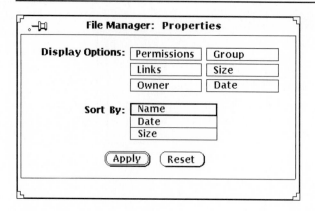

Figure 12-11 A suggested UNIX operating system File Manager Properties category.

A File Manager implementation can add other properties to this window, such as a way for you to specify your default printer.

Each setting in this example is described in the following paragraphs.

Display Options

Any display options that you choose are displayed in the folder pane, followed by the file name.

Sort By

You can choose the order in which the contents of the folder pane are displayed. Sort the contents alphabetically by name; in reverse chronological order by date, with the most recent files first; or by size with the largest files first.

Binding

This section describes *binding*—logically connecting data files, glyphs, and applications to File Manager functionality. The following kinds of binding are required elements of a File Manager implementation:

☐ Binding a specific glyph to a data file or application so that the glyph image is displayed in the folder pane instead of the default File Manager glyph

☐ Binding a specific application to a data file so that the application is automatically invoked when you open the data file

These methods of binding can be used separately or together. For example, you can bind an application to a data file without displaying a special glyph in the border. A glyph image can be bound to a data file without binding the application. A printer command can be specified for a data file.

Default Bindings

When no default bindings are provided, the File Manager default is to bind all data files to the text editor.

It is recommended that a File Manager implementation provide a standard set of default bindings in a dedicated file that is read by the File Manager during initialization. This file should include standard system bindings for applications (such as the console window and shell windows, and mail, calendar, and clock applications) and data files (including standard editing tools such as edit and draw applications). When appropriate, bindings for a spreadsheet and data base application may also be provided. Each application should specify a bind entry as part of the installation script.

Some operating systems have built-in file typing. When available, use file typing to identify data files for binding. When file typing is not available, use name patterns and/or magic numbers.

Using the File Manager

You can perform many operations in the File Manager either by using the clipboard to cut, copy, and paste File Manager glyphs, or by directly manipulating glyphs by selecting them, and then dragging and dropping the glyphs onto the destination.

This section describes how to use the File Manager to perform the following functions:

☐ Change folders
☐ Copy, move, and rename files
☐ Use the glyphs in the folder pane

Changing Folders

This section describes how to change folders in the file structure. You can change folders in the following ways:

☐ Type the name of a folder in the path in the Goto text field and click SELECT on the Goto button.
☐ Move to a higher level in the file system using folders in the path pane.
☐ Move to a lower level in the file system using folders in the folder pane.

Each of these methods is explained in the paragraphs that follow.

Using the Goto Text Field

To open any folder in the file system hierarchy, type a path name for a folder in the Goto text field and click SELECT on the Goto button.

Using Folders in the Path Pane

You can display the contents of a folder higher up in the chain that is displayed in the path pane by following these steps:

1 Move the pointer to the folder and click SELECT.
2 Press MENU to display the Path Commands pop-up menu.
3 Move the pointer onto the Open item and release MENU. The folder is opened, and any folders to the right of the open folder are closed and removed from the display in the pane.

To accelerate these steps, you can move the pointer to a folder and double-click SELECT to open the folder without displaying the menu. While the folder is being opened, the busy pointer is displayed, as shown in Figure 12-12.

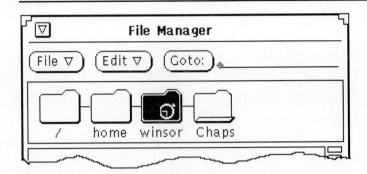

Figure 12-12   Double-click SELECT on a folder to open it.

The Chaps folder is closed and removed from the path pane, and the winsor folder is selected and opened, as shown in Figure 12-13. The contents of the folder are displayed in the scrollable folder pane.

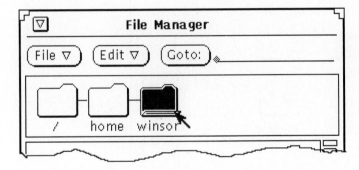

Figure 12-13   The new folder is opened.

You do not need to move up in the chain folder by folder. You can move the pointer to any folder in the chain and double-click SELECT to display the contents of any folder in the path pane.

Using Folders in the Folder Pane

You use the folders displayed in the folder pane to move farther down in the path. You change the display in the folder pane using one of two methods:

☐ Move the pointer to a folder in the folder pane and click SELECT. Press MENU to display the pop-up menu for the folder pane, drag the pointer onto the Open item, and release MENU.
☐ Move the pointer to a folder in the folder pane and double-click SELECT.

Using either method, the folder highlights in the same way. While the files are opening, the pointer changes to the standard busy pointer. In the example shown in Figure 12-14, the contents of the Chapters folder are being opened and the busy pointer is displayed.

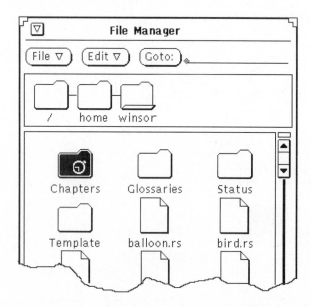

Figure 12-14 While the folder is being opened, the busy pointer is displayed.

When you open the new folder, the older folder, winsor in this example, is closed. The new folder, Chapters, is opened at the end of the chain in the path pane. The contents of the folder pane change to reflect the contents of the Chapters folder, as shown in Figure 12-15.

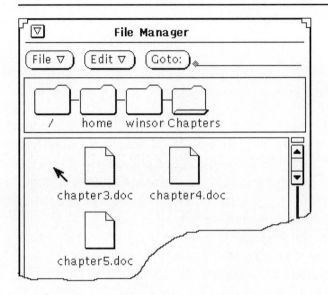

Figure 12-15   The folder pane displays the contents of the new folder.

The Chapters folder in this example contains only data files. You cannot move any farther down the path in this folder. To view the contents of other folders, double-click SELECT on a folder in the path pane, and then choose another folder from the folder pane.

Opening Files

This section tells you how to use data file and application glyphs in the folder pane. Following the OPEN LOOK UI selection paradigm, you can select and operate on multiple objects within the File Manager folder pane. The specific File Manager implementation determines how the Open item is displayed when multiple objects are selected. When the implementation supports opening multiple objects, the Open item is active. When the implementation does not, the Open item is inactive.

You can open selected data files and applications from the folder pane in two ways:

☐ Move the pointer to a data file or an application in the folder pane and click SELECT. You can click ADJUST on additional data file or application glyphs to select them. Press MENU to display the pop-up menu for the folder pane, drag the pointer onto the Open item, and release MENU. All selected data file or application glyphs are opened.

☐ Move the pointer to a data file or application in the folder pane and double-click SELECT.

Once a glyph has been opened, it becomes an independent base window with all the properties and functionality of any other base window on the workspace. Closing the window displays the icon for the application on the workspace. Applications determine the way windows opened from the File Manager are displayed as icons on the workspace. See Chapter 3 for more information about icon specifications.

For data files, an application window—determined by binding—is opened and the data file is displayed in that application window. The File Manager automatically opens the default editor application if no other application is specified.

For applications, the application is opened. A new file is not automatically loaded.

Copying and Moving Files

You can copy or move files within the file structure in either of two ways:

☐ Direct manipulation
☐ Using the clipboard

Direct Manipulation

Press the DUPLICATE Modifier key and SELECT to copy a glyph, or press SELECT to drag a glyph. Drag a glyph onto a folder. Folders are the only objects that accept move operations for all glyphs. When you move any glyph onto a folder, you get visual feedback indicating whether or not you can add the glyph to the folder. Release SELECT to copy or move the glyph.

When copying or moving glyphs, the File Manager implementation determines what visual feedback is displayed. For example, when a folder under a glyph accepts input, the folder highlights and may open to show that the move or copy can be performed, as shown in Figure 12-16.

Figure 12-16   A folder that accepts input opens and highlights.

Folders that are write-protected (do not accept input) either display a glyph showing that the folder is locked within the border of the folder, or display a lock in the border of the folder when you drag the glyph over the folder, as shown in Figure 12-17.

Figure 12-17   A folder that does not accept input displays a lock.

If an error occurs during the move/copy operation, the system beeps and the appropriate error message is displayed in the footer of the File Manager base window.

An optional method for showing write-protected folders is for the File Manager implementation to display a write-protected glyph consistently in the border of folders that do not accept input.

Using the Clipboard

Click SELECT and use Cut or Copy to put the file name on the clipboard, and then use Paste to insert the file name at the appropriate place in the file structure.

This section provides examples of using direct manipulation to copy and move files. See Chapter 17 for information about how to use the clipboard for copy and move operations. Figure 12-18 shows the folder pane that is used for the direct-manipulation copy and move examples.

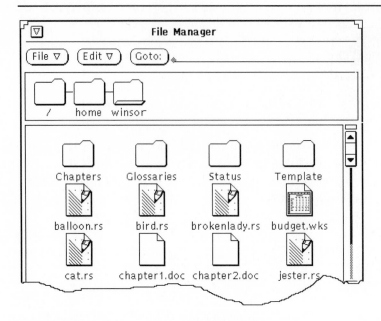

Figure 12-18   An example of a folder pane.

Copying a File by Direct Manipulation

Suppose that you want to put a copy of the chapter1.doc data file in the folder named Chapters. To do this by direct manipulation, use these steps:

1 Move the pointer to the chapter1.doc glyph and press the DUPLICATE modifier key and SELECT. The glyph highlights to show that it is selected.

2 Then move the pointer. The pointer changes to the duplicate pointer, and you drag an outline of the glyph as you move the pointer.

3 To copy the file in the same folder, drag the glyph outline anywhere in the folder pane where the hot spot of the pointer is not over a folder, as shown in Figure 12-19.

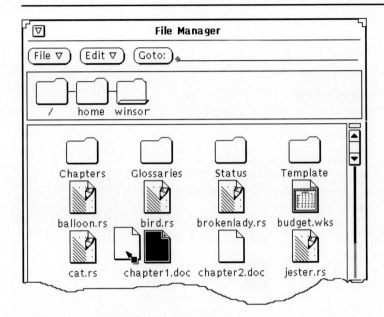

Figure 12-19   To copy a glyph, press DUPLICATE and SELECT and drag the glyph to a blank area of the folder pane.

4 Release SELECT.

A File Manager implementation assigns a new file name in one of two ways:

☐ The suffix .copy is appended to the name of the data file.
☐ A pop-up window is displayed with a text field in which you type the new file name.

In this example, files are arranged alphabetically. The file is inserted immediately after the original document, as shown in Figure 12-20.

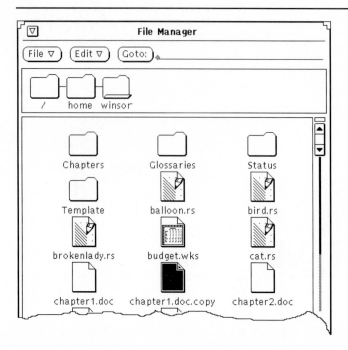

Figure 12-20   The copy of the data file is inserted in proper sort order.

You can rename the file by displaying the File Properties command window, typing a new name in the Name field, and clicking SELECT on the Apply button.

You can copy or move a number of files at the same time by selecting several files (click SELECT on the first file and then click ADJUST to select additional files) and dragging them. Outlines of the selected files drag as a group. The position of the hot spot of the pointer determines the target destination for the copies of the files. If the hot spot of the pointer is over a folder that accepts input, the files are copied into that folder. If the hot spot is anywhere else in the folder pane, the copies are put in the current folder.

Moving a File by Direct Manipulation

Now you want to move chapter1.doc.copy into the Chapters folder by direct manipulation. The operation is exactly the same as copying except that you do not need to press a modifier key with SELECT to initiate the move.

1 This time, press SELECT and drag the glyph border for the chapter1.doc.copy data file so that the hot spot of the pointer is on the Chapters folder. The folder is highlighted and may be open to show you that the data file will be put inside the folder, as shown in Figure 12-21. When the folder does not have write permission, it does not open, and a lock is displayed in the border of the folder to show you that you cannot move a file into that folder.

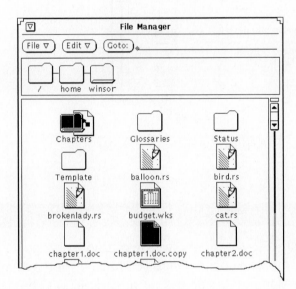

Figure 12-21 When an icon is moved over a folder with proper permissions, the folder opens and highlights.

2 Release SELECT to put the data file into the folder. The data file is removed from the folder pane, and the folders redisplay, since the longest file name in the folder has been moved to another folder. Figure 12-22 shows the folder pane after the data file has been moved.

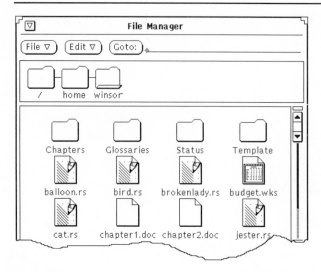

Figure 12-22   The data file is moved to the new folder.

File Manager Icons on the Workspace

You can select any File Manager glyph and drag it off the File Manager base window onto the workspace. Once you have moved a glyph outside the borders of the File Manager base window, an operating system link is created to the application. From the user's perspective, the glyph becomes an independent application icon with all the properties and functionality of any icon on the workspace. The application specifies the appearance of the data file icon when it is displayed on the workspace. It is recommended that the name of the glyph be displayed inside the border of the icon when it is on the workspace. You cannot drag any icon that is displayed on the workspace back into the File Manager pane.

When these icons are displayed on the workspace, you open them in the same way as you open any other icon on the workspace—by choosing Open from the Window menu or by double-clicking SELECT on the icon.

When a data file is opened, a base window for the application that is bound to that data file is displayed, and the data file is loaded into the application window.

When an application is opened, the base window for that application is opened. No file is loaded.

The following list suggests some common ways to use this functionality:

□ Invoke an application by dragging it from the File Manager window onto the workspace. This is an alternative way to access an application without using the Workspace menu. The application starts when you release SELECT.
□ Drag a frequently accessed data file onto the workspace.

Figure 12-23 shows an example of the workspace with File Manager glyphs displayed as icons on it.

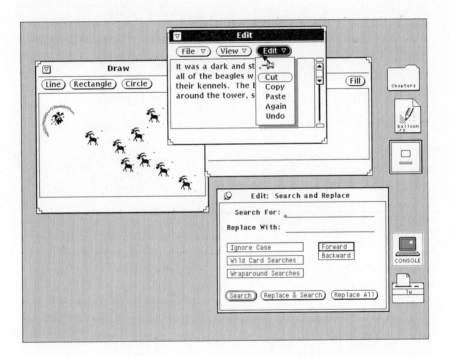

Figure 12-23   File Manager glyphs displayed as icons on the workspace.

Interactions Between the File Manager and Applications

The File Manager interacts directly with applications in two ways:

☐ You can drag a data file from the File Manager and drop it onto an application pane to load the file into the application.
☐ From within an application, you can open the File Manager window, browse, load a selected file into the application, and close the File Manager window.

The OPEN LOOK UI implementation must provide a protocol that supports interactions between applications developed with that implementation and the File Manager.

Loading a File by Direct Manipulation

The following example shows how to load a file into an application pane by direct manipulation. In Figure 12-24, you have pressed SELECT and dragged the glyph for the file romance.doc from the File Manager onto the pane of the Edit application.

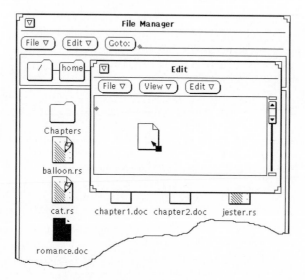

Figure 12-24   Dragging a data file onto the pane of an application.

When you release SELECT, the file is loaded into the application, as shown in Figure 12-25. The beginning of the file is displayed in the pane, and the active caret is positioned at the beginning of the file.

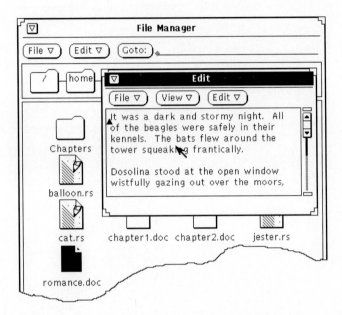

Figure 12-25   The file is loaded into the application.

13

PROCESS MANAGER

Introduction

A Level 3 implementation may provide a Process Manager application, which allows you to view running processes and choose whether or not to display messages from processes that communicate with the Process Manager. The Process Manager provides a central place for you to look for system messages, especially for processes or programs such as printer daemons, which do not have a window in which to display status messages.

The Process Manager requires a standardized message protocol, which is not specified in this book, so that applications may communicate with the Process Manager. Any Process Manager implementation can provide additional functionality to augment the basic functionality specified in this chapter.

Process Manager Functionality

No specific visual design is required. The following functionality must be provided:

☐ A way to display a selected and a comprehensive list of processes that you are running, including an identification number and a process name
☐ A way to choose whether or not to display system messages for one or more processes
☐ A way to clearly identify messages with their originating processes
☐ A way for the Process Manager to send messages to itself
☐ A way to store and/or print a log of messages from each process
☐ A way to select and terminate one or more processes for which you have permission

14

KEYBOARD AND MOUSE SPECIFICATIONS

This chapter describes keyboard and mouse device independence, Level 1 and Level 2 keyboard and mouse functions, customization of the keyboard through a single user interface, keyboard mappings, and mouse specifications.

Device Independence

An OPEN LOOK UI implementation is designed to work with three mouse button functions: SELECT, ADJUST, and MENU. These mouse button functions are accessible from a one-, two- or three-button mouse as well as directly from the keyboard.

An OPEN LOOK UI implementation allows flexible mapping of functions to mouse buttons and keyboard keys.

The default assignments for a three-button mouse are as follows:

☐ LEFT = SELECT
☐ MIDDLE = ADJUST
☐ RIGHT = MENU

You use modifier keys with a mouse button to access the three functions on systems with a one- or two-button mouse. You can change the mouse button and default modifier key assignments from the Workspace Properties window.

Although the OPEN LOOK UI does not require a particular physical keyboard, it does require a minimum set of keyboard functions. These keyboard functions are defined in terms of functionality, not in terms of a specific key on the keyboard.

For example, the key that you use to dismiss a pop-up window without issuing a command is the CANCEL key. The default mapping for CANCEL is the Esc key, but you can assign CANCEL to a different function or modifier key.

In a Level 1 implementation, you define the mappings for keyboard functions from the Workspace Properties window.

In a Level 2 implementation, a more sophisticated mechanism called the virtual keyboard is provided. See "Virtual Keyboards" later in this chapter for more information about the virtual keyboard.

The minimum acceptable keyboard for an OPEN LOOK UI has *up-down encoded* function and modifier keys—it can discriminate between pressing a function or modifier key down and releasing it—and has the following keys:

□ Shift
□ Control (or equivalent modifier key)

When you use the Caps key, it changes the keyboard to Caps mode for the whole workspace.

Accelerators provide a quick way to access functions from the keyboard without using the mouse. Accelerator functions are mapped either to function keys or to modified keys such as Ctrl/K so that you do not need to type more than two keystrokes to access a function.

See "Keyboard Mapping" later in this chapter for more information.

Level 1 Keyboard Functions

A Level 1 implementation provides a basic required set of functions for the keyboard and the mouse. The functions that are required for a Level 1 implementation are:

□ Mouse button functions (SELECT, ADJUST, and MENU)
□ Mouse modifiers
□ Core functions
□ Pop-up window accelerators
□ Text field navigation functions

You can reassign the default setting for all required keyboard and mouse functions in a Level 1 implementation from the Workspace Properties window. See "Keyboard Mapping" later in this chapter for information about default settings.

Mouse Modifiers

You can access additional functionality by pressing a modifier key in conjunction with one of the mouse button functions. The number of modifier keys available for these functions depends on your hardware configuration. You may be able to assign only a subset of these modifiers if your keyboard does not have enough available modifier keys. You change the default for the mouse modifiers using the Mouse Settings category on the Workspace Properties window.

Table 14-1 shows the mouse modifier functions required for a Level 1 implementation.

Table 14-1   Mouse modifier functions required for a Level 1 implementation.

DUPLICATE	Copy the selected object by dragging.
PAN	Scroll by panning.
CONSTRAIN	Constrain the direction of a dragging operation to only the x or y coordinate, depending on the direction in which you move the pointer to initiate dragging. You can release and then press the CONSTRAIN modifier during a single drag to allow you to change the direction of the constraint dynamically.
SETMENUDEFAULT	Set the current item in the menu as the menu default.

Core Functions

A Level 1 implementation requires a set of *core functions* that are mapped to the keyboard. You change the default for the core functions using the Keyboard Core Functions category on the Workspace Properties window.

Table 14-2 shows the core functions required for a Level 1 implementation.

Table 14-2   Core functions required for a Level 1 implementation.

CUT	Put a copy of the selected object onto a clipboard and then delete the object from the workspace. This key can also be used as a mouse modifier for Quick Move operations. See Chapter 17 for more information about quick operations.
COPY	Make a copy of the selected object and put it onto a clipboard.
PASTE	Insert a copy of the data on a clipboard at the insert point. This key can also be used as a mouse modifier for Quick Duplicate operations.
UNDO	Undoes the last operation. If the last operation is an undo, restores the last operation. Applications may implement multiple levels of undo functionality.
HELP	Display a Help window for the object under the pointer.
PROPERTIES	Display a property window for the selected object.

Pop-up Window Accelerators

A Level 1 implementation requires two *pop-up window accelerators* that are mapped to the keyboard, as described in Table 14-3. These accelerators can be used in all pop-up windows: command windows, property windows, Help windows, and Notices.

You change the default for the pop-up window accelerators using the Keyboard Settings category on the Workspace Properties window.

Table 14-3   Pop-up window accelerators required for a Level 1 implementation.

DEFAULTACTION	Execute the default button command and dismiss the pop-up window.
CANCEL	Dismiss the pop-up window without choosing an action.

Text Field Navigation

A Level 1 implementation requires two *text field navigation* keys that are mapped to the keyboard, as described in Table 14-4. You change the default for the text field navigation keys using the Keyboard Miscellaneous Functions category on the Workspace Properties window.

Table 14-4   Text field navigation functions required for a Level 1 implementation.

NEXTFIELD	Move the caret to the next input area in the pane and select the contents of the field. When the caret is in the last input area, move the caret to the first input area.
PREVFIELD	Move the caret to the previous input area in the pane and select the contents of the field. When the caret is at the first input area, move the caret to the last input area.

Level 2 Functions

A Level 2 implementation provides an expanded set of functions for the keyboard and the mouse that includes all Level 1 functionality. This expanded set defines a minimum list of keyboard functions. Any OPEN LOOK UI implementation or application can define and use additional functions. When additional functions are defined, a mechanism is provided to permit you to modify the keyboard mapping.

Applications are encouraged to use the specified virtual function names rather than hard-wired keyboard mappings as part of their application design so that you can change these mappings from the Workspace Properties window.

Keyboard equivalents provide a way to access all required functionality from the keyboard, allowing mouseless operation. You can also assign these mouse button functions to specific keys on the keyboard. If you assign mouse button functions to keys on the keyboard, the functionality is available both from the mouse buttons and from the keyboard keys. Using these mouse button equivalents provides all the functionality available from the mouse buttons. Selection and visual feedback are identical for both mouse and mouseless operations.

Mouseless Operations

A Level 2 implementation allows you to move the pointer using the arrow keys on the keyboard, and to access mouse button functions from function keys assigned to the SELECT, ADJUST, and MENU mouse button functions. Table 14-5 shows the pointer movement and mouse function keys required for a Level 2 implementation.

Table 14-5   Pointer movement and mouse functions required for a Level 2 implementation.

POINTERUP	Move the pointer up 1 pixel (repeats and accelerates).
POINTERDOWN	Move the pointer down 1 pixel (repeats and accelerates).
POINTERRIGHT	Move the pointer right 1 pixel (repeats and accelerates).
POINTERLEFT	Move the pointer left 1 pixel (repeats and accelerates).
SELECT	Equivalent to SELECT on the mouse.
ADJUST	Equivalent to ADJUST on the mouse.
MENU	Equivalent to MENU on the mouse.

Core Functions

A Level 2 implementation requires an additional core function key that is mapped to the keyboard. You change the default for the core functions using the Keyboard Core Functions category on the Workspace Properties window. The additional core function required for a Level 2 implementation is shown in Table 14-6.

Table 14-6   Core function required for a Level 2 implementation.

STOP	Cancel pending operations in the window under the pointer. Cancel modal operations in process.

Text Caret Movement

A Level 2 implementation requires the following set of *text caret movement functions* that are mapped to the keyboard. You change the default for the text caret movement functions using the Keyboard Settings category on the Workspace Properties window. Text motions cause the text view to scroll in all text areas if necessary to keep the insert point visible. Table 14-7 shows the text caret motion functions required for a Level 2 implementation.

Table 14-7   Text caret movement functions required for a Level 2 implementation.

CHARFWD	Move the insert point forward one character. Beep when insert point is at the last printable character of the file.
CHARBAK	Move the insert point backward one character. Beep at the start of a file.
ROWDOWN	Move the insert point down one row in the current column (or to the end of the next row if column is past the end of the next row).
ROWUP	Move the insert point up one row in the current column (or to the end of the previous row if column is past the end of the previous row).
WORDFWD	Move the insert point after the last printable character of the next word, not including any end-of-line character when the word is at the end of a line (or the current word if the insert point is within a word).
WORDBAK	Move the insert point before the first character of the previous word (or the current word if the insert point is within a word).
LINESTART	Move the insert point before the first character of the current line. When the insert point is already there, no action.
LINEEND	Move the insert point after the last printable character of the current line, not including the end-of-line character. When the insert point is already there, no action.

Table 14-7 (continued)

DOCSTART	Move the insert point before the first character of the document. When the insert point is already there, no action.
DOCEND	Move the insert point after the last printable character of the document. When the insert point is already there, no action.
PANESTART	Move the insert point to the first row and column of the viewing area. When the insert point is already there, no action.
PANEEND	Move the insert to the last row and column of the viewing area. When the insert point is already there, no action.

Text Editing Functions

A Level 2 implementation requires the following set of text editing functions that are mapped to the keyboard. You change the default for the text editing functions using the Keyboard Settings category on the Workspace Properties window. Table 14-8 shows the text editing functions required for a Level 2 implementation.

Table 14-8   Text editing functions required for a Level 2 implementation.

DELCHARFWD	Delete the character to the right of the insert point.
DELCHARBAK	Delete the character to the left of the insert point.
DELWORDFWD	Delete the word to the right of the insert point.
DELWORDBAK	Delete the word to the left of the insert point.
DELLINEFWD	Delete from the insert point to the end of the line.
DELLINEBAK	Delete from the insert point to the beginning of the line.
DELLINE	Delete the entire current line.

Text Selection Functions

A Level 2 implementation requires the following set of text selection functions that are mapped to the keyboard. You change the default for the text selection functions using the Keyboard Settings category on the Workspace Properties window. Table 14-9 shows the text selection functions required for a Level 2 implementation.

Table 14-9   Text selection functions required for a Level 2 implementation.

SELCHARFWD	Adjust the selection one character forward.
SELWORDFWD	Adjust the selection to the end of the current word, then words forward.
SELLINEFWD	Adjust the selection to the end of current line, then lines forward.
UNSELCHARBAK	Deselect one character backward..
UNSELLINEBAK	Deselect one line backward.

Scrolling Accelerators

A Level 2 implementation requires the following set of scrolling accelerators. You can use these accelerators to scroll the contents of a pane with the input area without moving the pointer to the scrollbar. These accelerators are equivalent to clicking SELECT on various parts of vertical and horizontal scrollbars. See Chapter 7 for more information about scrolling. Table 14-10 shows the scrolling accelerators required for a Level 2 implementation.

Table 14-10   Scrolling accelerators required for a Level 2 implementation.

SCROLLUP	Scroll the view up one screen (same as moving the pointer to the cable above the elevator of a vertical scrollbar and clicking SELECT).
SCROLLDOWN	Scroll the view down one screen (same as moving the pointer to the cable below the elevator of a vertical scrollbar and clicking SELECT).
SCROLLLEFT	Scroll the view left one screen (same as moving the pointer to the cable left of the elevator of a horizontal scrollbar and clicking SELECT).
SCROLLRIGHT	Scroll the view right one screen (same as moving the pointer to the cable right of the elevator of a horizontal scrollbar and clicking SELECT).
SCROLLTOP	Scroll the view to the top of the data (same as clicking SELECT on the top cable anchor).
SCROLLBOTTOM	Scroll the view to the bottom of the data (same as clicking SELECT on the bottom cable anchor).
SCROLLRIGHTEDGE	Scroll the view to the right edge of the data (same as clicking SELECT on the right cable anchor).
SCROLLLEFTEDGE	Scroll the view to the left edge of the data (same as clicking SELECT on the left cable anchor).
PAGEUP, PAGEDOWN	Page scrolling operations are defined by application-specific accelerators. These accelerators are usually mapped to Page Up, Page Down, Home, and End on a keyboard.

Input Area Navigation

A Level 2 implementation requires the following input area navigation keys that are mapped to the keyboard, as described in Table 14-11. You change the default for the input area navigation keys using the Keyboard Settings category on the Workspace Properties window.

Table 14-11   Input area navigation accelerators required for a Level 2 implementation

NEXTWINDOW	Cycle the active input area to the next window (least recently used).
PREVWINDOW	Cycle the active input area to the previous (most recently used) window. When repeated, continue down the stack to the next most recently used window.
TOGGLEINPUT	Toggle the input area between the two most recently used windows.

Soft Function Keys

Applications are encouraged to use the function keys to provide functionality specific to the individual application. A Level 2 implementation provides a Function Keys item on the Workspace Utilities submenu that you can use to display and use the function keys that are specified by individual applications.

The Function Keys window is a pop-up window. It always shows information that is specific to the keyboard you are using, and displays the keys as close to actual size as possible. For example, when your system has a keyboard with 15 function keys, the window shows 15 function keys. If your keyboard has ten function keys, the window shows ten function keys, and so on. Figure 14-1 shows an example of the Function Keys pop-up window with ten function keys and their numeric labels.

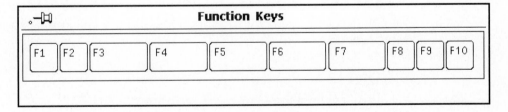

Figure 14-1   The Function Keys pop-up window.

The Function Keys window is displayed centered at the bottom of the screen. When you change the input area to a window that uses the function keys, the Function Keys window is automatically updated to reflect the new set of functions. If you change the input area to a window that does not use the function keys, the Function Keys window is updated to clear the labels.

In addition to displaying the functions assigned for each application, you can use the virtual keys in the Function Keys window to activate the functions on the key labels. You do this by moving the pointer to any one of the keys and clicking SELECT. When you press SELECT, the key highlights in the same way a button in the control area highlights. When you release SELECT, the key is activated, invoking the function on the key label.

Figure 14-2 shows an example of keys that a text formatting application might assign to a ten-function keyboard.

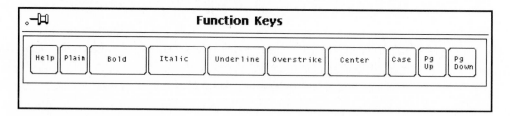

Figure 14-2   An example of a Function Keys window for a text formatting application.

When the application has more functions than the number of function keys, the Function Keys facility assigns the function "More" to one of the function keys. Clicking SELECT on the More key cycles through the complete list of functions on the remaining function keys.

Figure 14-3 shows an example of the Function Keys window for a text formatting application with 15 functions and the last key assigned to the More function.

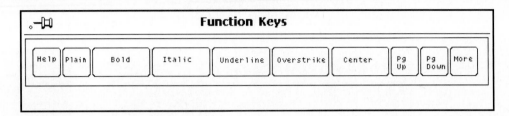

Figure 14-3   An example of a Function Keys Window for a text formatting application with a More key.

Clicking SELECT on the More key changes the functions displayed in the Function Keys window, as shown in Figure 14-4. Clicking SELECT again on the More function key redisplays the first set of functions.

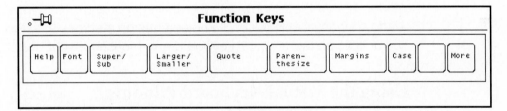

Figure 14-4   Clicking SELECT on the More key displays additional functions for the text formatting application.

Virtual Keyboards

A Level 2 implementation provides a way to examine and map the functions on the keyboard. Use the Virtual Keyboard item on the Workspace Utilities submenu to display a window that contains an image of function keys, mouse buttons, or the full keyboard, depending on what you specify. You can use this *virtual keyboard* to change the mapping of the keys by direct manipulation. The virtual keyboard is also used to specify international character sets and binding of accelerators. The Virtual Keyboard window is shown in Figure 14-5.

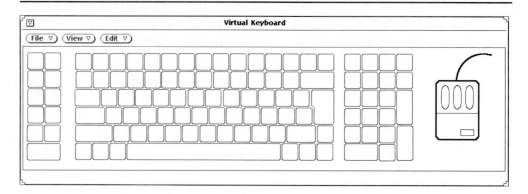

Figure 14-5   The Virtual Keyboard window.

The key names that would be displayed on the keys of the Virtual Keyboard window are for the window with the active input area. The Virtual Keyboard window for any OPEN LOOK UI implementation matches exactly the configuration of keys on the physical keyboard and mouse for your system.

Using the Virtual Keyboard Window

You can use the Virtual Keyboard window to customize the mapping of OPEN LOOK UI function keys, accelerators, core operations, and mouse functionality. You do this by editing the contents of each key individually from a property window or by manipulating existing key names by selecting them and dragging them to a new location. You can save customized mappings in files that can be stored and reloaded on your own system or another system to provide portability for your customized mappings.

You can display all or part of the keyboard, as you choose, by selecting items from the View button menu in the control area.

The function keys interactively display the functions that are appropriate for the active input area. For example, if you are using a graphics application that has specific functions bound to the function keys at the top of the keyboard, displaying the Virtual Keyboard window shows you how the function keys are mapped.

One use for the Virtual Keyboard window is to customize your mouse and keyboard for right- or left-handed use.

Multiple Language Support

When an implementation provides support for multiple languages, the OPEN LOOK UI implementation provides a LANGUAGE function key. When you press and hold the LANGUAGE key, a Character Sets pop-up window is displayed showing keys that correspond to the top row of function keys. Labels on those function keys correspond to different language capabilities. In the example shown in Figure 14-6, the keys are labeled Help, ASCII, Office, Math, Logic, Greek, ISO, Show, Set, and More, and correspond to F1 through F10 on the physical keyboard.

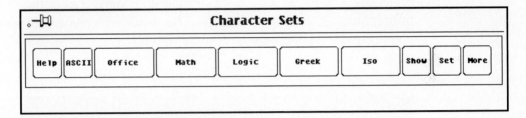

Figure 14-6   The Character Sets window.

The keys Show, Set, and More are always displayed. The remaining keys display the available keyboard maps by name.

Pressing the More key changes the names of the keycaps in the window to cycle through all available keymaps. Pressing Show opens the Virtual Keyboard window displaying the entire keyboard with the corresponding keymaps. You can type directly on the physical keyboard to access those symbols, or click SELECT on the image on the screen to type a character.

While you hold down the Language key, the chosen language is bound to the keyboard. In this way, you can easily access a few characters or symbols from another language or alternate character set interactively, and then return to typing on your usual alphanumeric configuration. For example, to type a few Greek characters in English text, hold down the Language key, press the Greek key, and then type some characters. When you release the Language key, the Character Sets window is dismissed and the primary character set is restored to English.

Typing Set sets the keymap that is highlighted to be the primary character set. When you release the Language key, the Character Set window is dismissed.

For example, to change the keyboard character set from English to Greek, hold down the Language key, press the Greek key, and then press the Set key. When you release the Language key, the Character Sets window is dismissed and the primary character set is Greek. Any alphabetic key you press on the keyboard types the corresponding Greek character at the active text insert point.

If you do not press the Set key, the primary character set is restored when the Language key is released.

If you do not know which keys correspond to the characters for the language you have selected, hold down the Language key and press the Show key. The Virtual Keyboard window is displayed or updated with the appropriate labels on the keycaps. This window remains on the screen when you release the Language key, and it can be closed to an icon or dismissed separately.

Keyboard Mapping

This specification describes the mapping of keyboard functions in terms of a "reference" keyboard layout. The OPEN LOOK UI specifies a number of functions that are bound to specific keys on any individual keyboard. The reference keyboard, shown in Figure 14-7, is not intended to suggest that this is an ideal keyboard design. It simply contains enough modifier and function keys to assign each required Level 1 and Level 2 function to an individual key.

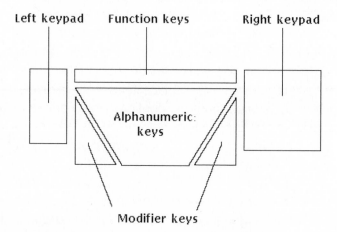

Figure 14-7   The reference keyboard layout.

Any keyboard meeting the minimum requirements can use combinations of keys to provide the functionality, as described briefly in the paragraphs that follow.

When your keyboard has up-down encoded alphanumeric keys, you can access additional modifiers by pressing Control with an alphanumeric character. For example, if your keyboard lacks a "Meta" key, you can assign an alphanumeric key to that function—the "M" key would provide a good mnemonic. When you press this assigned key with Control (Ctrl/M) it works as if you had pressed Meta. Ctrl/M, Ctrl/X would then generate a Meta/X command. You can release the M key, and as long as Control is pressed, it acts as the Meta modifier.

When your keyboard does not have a left keypad, you can assign the functions to single modified alphanumeric keys such as Ctrl/X or Ctrl/S. It is suggested that, for ease of use, you keep these functions on the opposite side of the keyboard from the mouse.

Although any keyboard has a limited number of function keys, you can "create" additional function keys in a Level 2 implementation by using the soft function key facility and assigning one of the existing function keys to More. When you press a designated modifier for FKEYS (for example, Ctrl/F), a window is displayed that shows the currently assigned functions for the function keys. Pressing More cycles through a set of assigned functions. When the names of the keys change on the screen, the function listed on the display can be accessed by pressing the corresponding key on the keyboard. Refer back to "Soft Function Keys" in earlier this chapter for more information.

If your keyboard does not have any function keys, pressing this FKEY modifier can change the top row of numeric keys to correspond to the display shown on the screen. For example, after you press Ctrl/F and while you hold down Ctrl, 1 corresponds to F1, 8 corresponds to F8, and = corresponds to F12. Additional functions may be also be assigned to modified alphanumeric keys.

For any given keyboard, a combination of these methods provides the functionality specified for the OPEN LOOK UI. See "Level 1 Keyboard Functions," "Level 2 Functions," and "Sample Keyboard Maps" earlier in this chapter for more information.

Sample Keyboard Maps

This section provides sample mouse and keyboard function default mapping assignments. Not all of the modified mouse functions need to be mapped initially. In fact, when hardware limitations exist, it may not be possible to assign all of the modifiers simultaneously. Table 14-12 shows suggested default mappings for mouse functions.

Table 14-12   Suggested default mappings for Level 1 mouse functions.

Mouse buttons	Three	Two	One
SELECT	Left	Left	Left
ADJUST	Middle	Shift/Left	Shift/Left
MENU	Right	Right	Ctrl/Left
DUPLICATE	Ctrl/Left	Ctrl/Left	Alt/Left
CONSTRAIN			
SETMENUDEFAULT	Ctrl/Right	Ctrl/Right	Shift/Ctrl/Left

Table 14-13 shows suggested default mappings for the optimum condition in which the keyboard contains labeled keys for all required functions. Suggested mappings for the Sun4 and PC-style keyboards are also included in this table.

Some keyboards have both an Enter and a Return key. The OPEN LOOK UI implementation determines whether the keyboard hardware makes a distinction between these two keys. When the Enter and Return keys use different scan codes, the implementation can choose whether to make a functional distinction between these keys or to define them as equivalent.

Table 14-13 Suggested default mappings for Level 1 keyboard functions.

Keyboard Functions	Reference	Sun Type-4	PC Style
CUT	Cut	L10 (Cut)	Ctrl/X
COPY	Copy	L6 (Copy)	Ctrl/C
PASTE	Paste	L8 (Paste)	Ctrl/V
UNDO	Undo	L4 (Undo)	Ctrl/U
HELP	Help	"L11" (Help)	F1
PROPERTIES	Props	L3 (Props)	Ctrl/P
DEFAULTACTION	Enter*	Enter	Shift/Return
CANCEL	Esc	Esc	Esc
NEXTFIELD	Next	Tab	Tab
PREVFIELD	Prev	Shift/Tab	Shift/Tab

* When the keyboard for your implementation makes a distinction between Enter and Return keys.

Mouse Specifications

This section describes the specifications for the mouse buttons in an OPEN LOOK UI implementation and includes specifications for using mouse buttons.

Damping Factor

A single click is defined when the mouse button is released within a specified number of pixels of the down stroke. The pixel movement limit is called the *damping factor*. The damping factor allows you to inadvertently move the mouse a few pixels without initiating a drag. The OPEN LOOK UI implementation specifies a damping factor for mouse clicks. The damping factor may be different for different implementations.

Multi-Click Selecting

You can use multiple clicking on mouse buttons or their equivalents as a quick way (an accelerator) to perform some specific functions. For example, double-clicking SELECT on an icon is an accelerator for Open. Double-clicking SELECT on a window header is an accelerator for Full Size. See Chapter 17 for information about multi-click selecting.

You can set the maximum length of time permitted for multi-click operations (the multi-click timeout factor) from the Workspace Properties window. The multi-click timeout measures the amount of time that elapses between the release and press of the mouse button.

Mouse Button Actions

Selecting objects in an OPEN LOOK UI implementation occurs on the down stroke of a mouse button or its equivalent, and other selections are cleared.

When the pointer is moved beyond the damping factor, the current selection is maintained. When the pointer is not moved beyond the damping factor, other selections are cleared when you release SELECT.

Initiation of an action (such as invoking a menu, setting the insert point, and executing a command on a button or menu item) occurs on the up stroke of a mouse button or its equivalent.

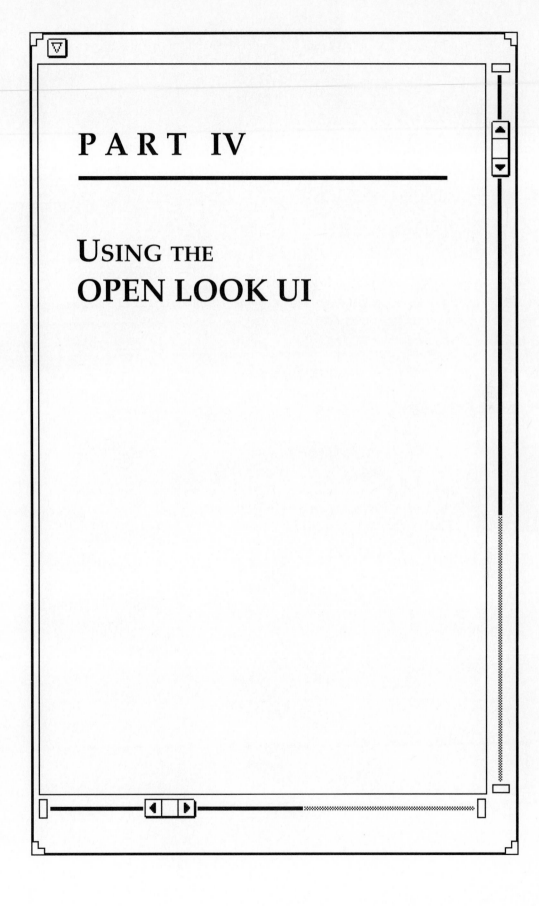

PART IV

USING THE
OPEN LOOK UI

15

USING MENUS

This chapter tells you how to view and choose from menus and how to change the default settings on a menu. It also gives the specifications for menu placement.

Choosing from Menus

There are two ways you can view and choose from any menu:

□ Press-drag-release
□ Click-move-click

Press-Drag-Release

Press-drag-release works as follows:

1 Press MENU. The menu appropriate for the pointer location is displayed.

2 While holding down the MENU mouse button, drag the pointer from control to control on the menu. When the pointer is on a control, the visual feedback appropriate for that control (described in Chapter 4 and in Chapter 6) is displayed. Items highlight and a setting shows a bold border. When the pointer is off the control, it returns to its normal condition.

3 When the pointer is on the control you want, release MENU. The action is initiated, and the menu group is dismissed.

Moving the pointer off the menu and releasing MENU dismisses the menu without making a choice.

A Level 2 implementation has an option that you can set to activate the default setting of pop-up menus without moving the pointer. This option is explained in detail under "Using Pop-up Menus" later in this chapter. When this option is set, click-move-click functionality for menus is not available.

Click-Move-Click

Click-move-click displays a menu so that it stays on the screen. You do not need to keep pressing the MENU button. You can click MENU on a menu button to display a button menu. When you click on a control to activate it, the action is performed and the menu group is dismissed. Click MENU off a control to display a pop-up menu. Click-moveclick works as follows:

1 Click MENU. The menu appropriate for the pointer location is displayed on the screen and stays up.

2 Move the pointer to the control you want to choose. The controls on the stay-up menu work the same as controls in a control area. There is no visual feedback as you move the pointer across the controls, unless you press the mouse button.

3 When the pointer is on the control you want, click SELECT or MENU to choose it. When you click on the control, the visual feedback appropriate for that control is displayed: Items highlight, and settings show a 2-point border. Clicking SELECT or MENU on a menu item displays the submenu. The originating menu item displays the standard busy pattern, and does not accept further input.

When you click SELECT or MENU anywhere off the active area of the menu controls, the menu group is dismissed from the screen.

These selection mechanisms are described more completely later in this chapter.

Using Menu Buttons

This section describes how you use menu buttons from a control area to display button menus using the press-drag-release and the click-move-click method.

Viewing Button Menus With Press-Drag-Release

When menu buttons are displayed in a control area, you view the contents of a button menu by pressing MENU. The button highlights, and the menu is displayed. The default control has a 1-point default ring around it. The pointer never jumps onto the menu. Drag the pointer onto the menu, moving the pointer from control to control, as explained in Chapter 5. When a control is highlighted or the pointer is on the pushpin, the default ring is not displayed.

When a menu has a pushpin, dragging the pointer onto the pushpin pops it into the hole. Moving the pointer off the pushpin pops it out of the hole.

When a menu has exclusive settings, the default setting displays the default when the pointer is not in the menu. When the pointer is on the menu, the current setting is displayed, and no default is shown.

When a menu has nonexclusive settings, the nonexclusive settings accurately reflect the state of the object. If a setting is "on" for the selection, the setting has a bold border. If the setting is "off" for the selection, the setting has a one-point border. The setting that is under the pointer is the only one that toggles to show a change of state.

Drag the pointer onto a control in the menu and release MENU to make a choice. When the pointer moves onto the menu, the originating menu button in the control area is highlighted. Drag the pointer off the menu and release the MENU button when no selection is desired.

When a menu has items, each menu item—an item that is followed by a menu mark—has a submenu attached to it and has an active region that always displays a submenu whether or not you drag the pointer to the right. The submenu region is shown in Figure 15-1.

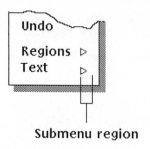

Figure 15-1   Submenu region for a menu item.

To highlight items in a menu without displaying a submenu, drag the pointer vertically from item to item anywhere to the left of the submenu region. You can drag the pointer through the menu to a specific item without submenus flashing on the screen. Figure 15-2 shows the direction in which you move the pointer to highlight menu items without displaying submenus.

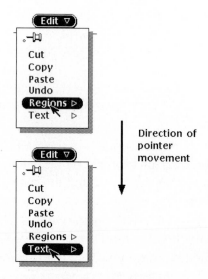

Figure 15-2   Drag the pointer vertically from item to item to highlight a menu item without displaying the submenu.

When the pointer is on a menu item, you display the submenu by dragging the pointer to the right so that it moves beyond the drag-right distance you set from the Workspace Properties window. The pointer does not jump, but remains on the highlighted item. The submenu is positioned relative to the

318

pointer location. The default item is aligned with the originating item and is automatically highlighted. The left side of the highlighting is positioned under the pointer. The originating item remains highlighted. See "Menu Placement" at the end of this chapter for specifications on submenu placement.

Figure 15-3 shows a submenu in which the items are glyphs that are larger than the originating menu item. When this occurs, the larger item is centered relative to the originating item.

Figure 15-3   To display a submenu, drag the pointer to the right in a menu item.

You can drag the pointer within the submenu to highlight a different item, drag the pointer off the submenu to the top, bottom, or right to redisplay the default ring for the menu group, or drag the pointer off the submenu to the left to dismiss the submenu and keep the originating menu displayed. Once the pointer moves beyond the left side of the submenu, the submenu is dismissed, regardless of where the pointer is positioned horizontally on the screen.

When a control on a submenu is highlighted, release MENU to activate the control and dismiss the menu group. Drag the pointer off the menu and release MENU to dismiss the menu group without activating a control. Release MENU when the pointer is on a menu item to activate the default control from the submenu and dismiss the menu group.

To display another submenu at the same level, drag the pointer to the left to dismiss the submenu, and then drag down to the next menu item and to the right to display another submenu. Figure 15-4 shows how you can move the pointer to dismiss one submenu and display another.

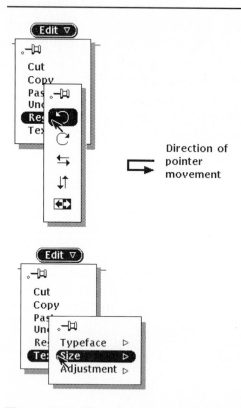

Figure 15-4   Drag the pointer to the left to dismiss a submenu, and then down and to the right to display a different submenu.

Viewing Button Menus with Click-Move-Click

When you click MENU on a menu button, the button menu is displayed and remains on the screen until the next mouse click. The menu button displays the standard busy pattern while the button menu is displayed. Clicking SELECT or MENU on a control activates the control and dismisses the menu group.

When the control is a menu item, clicking MENU anywhere on the item displays the submenu in stay-up mode. The originating item displays the standard busy pattern and accepts no further input. Clicking SELECT anywhere on the item executes the default from the submenu without displaying it and dismisses the menu group.

Clicking SELECT or MENU anywhere off the stay-up menu controls dismisses the menu group from the screen and does nothing else.

You can combine click-move-click and press-drag-release operations. When a menu is displayed in stay-up mode, you can press MENU, drag the pointer to a menu item, and drag the drag-right distance to display the submenu. You can also click MENU on a menu item to display the submenu for that item in stay-up mode. When you press MENU, the item is highlighted, as shown in Figure 15-5.

Figure 15-5   Press MENU on a menu item to highlight it.

When you release MENU, the submenu is displayed in stay-up mode. The submenu is positioned to the right of the item, and the originating item displays the standard busy pattern, as shown in Figure 15-6.

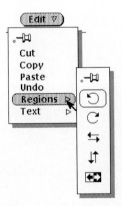

Figure 15-6   Release MENU to display a stay-up submenu from a menu in stay-up mode.

The submenu is displayed with the default control aligned with the originating menu item and the left side of the menu aligned one point to the right of the default ring. You can move the pointer anywhere on the workspace, and the menu group remains displayed on the screen. All menu controls except the busy controls are active, not just the controls on the submenu. If you decide you want to choose a control from the menu rather than the submenu, simply move the pointer to a control and click SELECT or MENU. The control is activated and the menu group is dismissed.

To display another submenu and dismiss the first submenu without choosing a control, move the pointer to a different menu item, as shown in Figure 15-7.

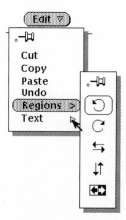

Figure 15-7   To display a different submenu, move the pointer to a different menu item.

Then click MENU. The submenu for that menu item is displayed. In the example shown in Figure 15-8, the Regions submenu is dismissed and the Text submenu is displayed.

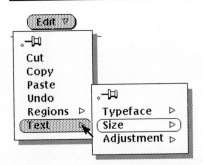

Figure 15-8   Click MENU to dismiss one submenu and display a different one.

In the preceding example, if you decide that you want to redisplay the Regions submenu when the Text submenu is displayed, move the pointer back to the Regions item and click MENU. The Text submenu is dismissed, and the Regions submenu is redisplayed.

Using Pop-up Menus

This section describes how to view and choose from pop-up menus with press-drag-release and click-move-click.

Viewing and Choosing from Pop-up Menus with Press-Drag-Release

When you press MENU to display a pop-up menu, it is displayed in the following way, as shown in Figure 15-9:

☐ The pointer does not move on the workspace.
☐ The top-level menu of the menu group is displayed with the pointer positioned a few points to the left of the default item.

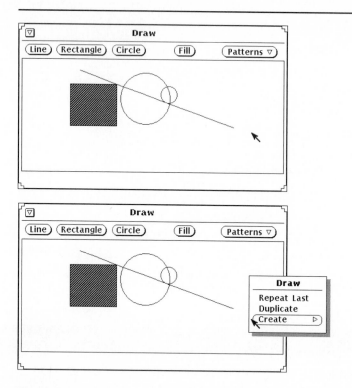

Figure 15-9   When a pop-up menu is displayed, the pointer does not move.

The pointer is positioned slightly off the default item to prevent you from inadvertently choosing an item from the pop-up menu. You must move the pointer a short distance to the right and release MENU to choose the default. In this example, moving the pointer onto the Create item by dragging the pointer to the right displays the Create submenu.

You make other choices from pop-up menus exactly the same way as you do from button menus: Move the pointer to a different control and release MENU to make a choice. Move the pointer off the menu and release MENU to dismiss the menu without making a choice.

As with button menus, moving the pointer to the right on a menu item displays the submenu, as shown in Figure 15-10. The pointer remains at the same location, and the submenu is positioned as appropriate for the pointer location.

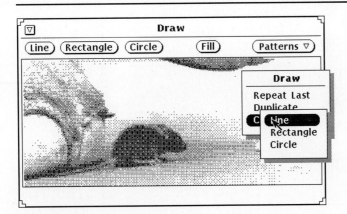

Figure 15-10   Sample pop-up menu group.

A Level 2 Option for Executing the Menu Default

A Level 2 implementation provides options to change pop-up menu default behavior. You set this option from the Workspace Properties window.

When the Executes Default option is set, the pointer is positioned a few points onto the left edge of the default control of a pop-up menu, highlighting it immediately. The Executes Default option suppresses click-move-click functionality for all menus.

Clicking MENU displays the menu, activates the default control, and dismisses the menu. Alternatively, you can press MENU to display the menu with the default control highlighted, as shown in Figure 15-11, move the pointer to a different choice, and release MENU if you do not want to use the default setting.

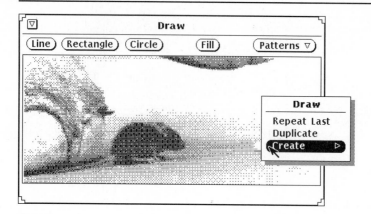

Figure 15-11   When the Executes Default option is set, the pointer is positioned on the default item.

In this example, releasing MENU while the Create menu item is highlighted executes the default item on the Create submenu and dismisses the pop-up menu.

Viewing and Choosing from Pop-up Stay-up Menus

When you click MENU on any area of the screen that is not a menu control, the appropriate pop-up menu is displayed and remains on the screen until you choose an action or dismiss the menu. As with normal pop-up menu displays, the pointer is positioned a few points to the left of the default item.

In all other respects, choosing from a pop-up menu in stay-up mode is the same as choosing from a button menu in stayup mode.

Pinning a Menu

This section describes how you pin a menu. When a menu has a pushpin, you choose it by moving the pointer to a menu button and pressing MENU, as shown in Figure 15-12.

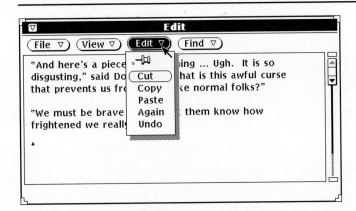

Figure 15-12   To pin a menu, first display it.

Drag the pointer to the pushpin, and pop the pin into the pinhole, as shown in Figure 15-13.

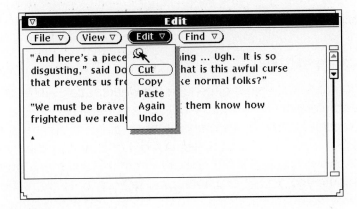

Figure 15-13   Drag the pointer to the pushpin; it pops into the hole.

Release MENU. The pinned menu becomes a pop-up window, as shown in Figure 15-14.

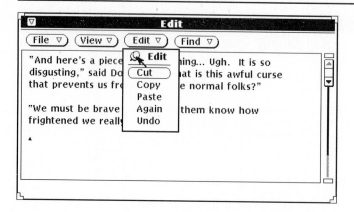

Figure 15-14   A menu that is pinned is a pop-up window.

The highlighting is removed from the originating menu button, and the menu becomes a pop-up command window with all the attributes and functionality of a command window:

☐ Title
☐ Pushpin
☐ Pop-up Window menu

If you do not want to pin the menu to the workspace, with MENU pressed, move the pointer off the pushpin and it pops out again.

When a menu is pinned, the name of the originating control becomes the title of the pop-up window that is displayed. For example, the pinned pop-up window shown in Figure 15-14 originated from the Edit menu button.

The first time you pin a menu, the upper left corner is anchored at the upper left corner of the menu it replaces. When the pinned menu is moved, it remembers its new location. If you dismiss the pinned menu and pin it again, the position of the pinned menu is determined by its location the last time it was displayed.

The size of the pinned menu may not be the same as the size of the unpinned menu, since the pop-up window must be large enough to permit the title of the control to fit completely in the header, regardless of the scale setting of the window. The guideline for menu titles is the same as for pop-up windows: When there is enough room, the title is preceded by the name of the application followed by a colon.

As a general rule, items on a pinned menu retain the same orientation as the items on the originating menu. When items are displayed vertically, there may not be room in the header to display the name of the application as well as the menu name. In such a case, the name of the application is dropped from the header, as shown in Figure 15-14.

When a menu is already pinned and you display the menu again, the pushpin is dimmed, as shown in Figure 15-15, so that you cannot pin the menu a second time. The contents of the pinned menu window are not updated to match the contents of the menu. For example, if a menu window displays an item that is not dimmed, and that item is dimmed on the transient menu, the button in the menu window need not dim.

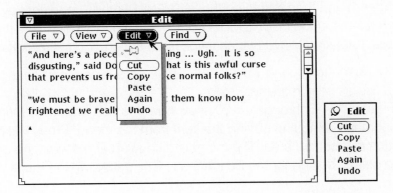

Figure 15-15 Displaying a button menu when the menu is already pinned.

Changing Menu Defaults

This section tells you how to change the default settings on menus. You can change a menu default at any time by using a SETMENUDEFAULT modifier key in conjunction with MENU. The option to specify the SETMENUDEFAULT modifier key is set from the Workspace Properties window and is described in Chapter 11.

You can press or release the SETMENUDEFAULT modifier key to display the default controls for the menu group either before or after pressing MENU to display a button menu. As you drag the pointer over the menu, the visual feedback depends on whether or not you have pressed the modifier key. If you have not pressed the modifier, the feedback is the normal feedback for the control. If you have pressed the SETMENUDEFAULT modifier, controls do not show the normal feedback. Instead, the default ring is displayed and follows the pointer as it moves from item to item within the menu. When you drag the pointer to the right on a menu item when the SETMENUDEFAULT modifier is pressed, the submenu is not displayed.

When a menu group is displayed, the pointer is not on a menu, and you press the SETMENUDEFAULT modifier, the default controls for that menu group are displayed.

When the SETMENUDEFAULT key and the MENU button are both pressed, you set the default in one of two ways:

☐ By releasing MENU (which sets the default and removes the menu from the screen) and then releasing the SETMENUDEFAULT modifier key
☐ By releasing the SETMENUDEFAULT modifier key (which sets the default) and then releasing MENU (which invokes an action or dismisses the menu)

By using the second way of setting the default, you can change the default and use an item in a single step.

Figures 15-16 through 15-20 show how you can change a menu default for a submenu without choosing the item from the menu. Press MENU on a menu button in a control area. The menu is displayed and shows the default setting. The default setting for the Edit menu is Cut, as shown in Figure 15-16.

Figure 15-16   To change a default setting on a submenu, first display the menu.

Drag the pointer to the Regions item and then right to display the submenu, as shown in Figure 15-17.

Figure 15-17   Drag the pointer to the right to display the submenu.

Suppose you now decide that you want to change the default setting to the item just below the highlighted item. Continue pressing MENU, and press the modifier key on the keyboard. The highlighting is removed from the button under the pointer location, and the default settings for the entire menu group are displayed, as shown in Figure 15-18.

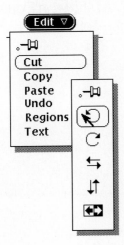

Figure 15-18   Pressing MENU and the SETMENUDEFAULT modifier key removes the highlighting from the items in the menu and displays the default rings.

Drag the pointer to the item you want for the new default in the submenu. The default ring moves with the pointer, as shown in Figure 15-19.

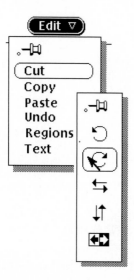

Figure 15-19   The default ring follows the movement of the pointer.

To change the modifier without choosing the button, first release MENU and then release the SETMENUDEFAULT modifier key. The default is set for the submenu, and the menu group is dismissed, as shown in Figure 15-20. As usual, the pointer remains at the position of the default button on the submenu.

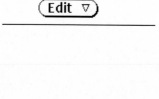

Figure 15-20   Releasing MENU and then the SETMENUDEFAULT modifier key sets the default and dismisses the menu group.

You can set the default and execute the command by changing the order in which you release the MENU button and the SETMENUDEFAULT key. The following examples show how to set the pushpin on a submenu as the default and then pin up the menu.

Since a menu item does not display the submenu while the SETMENUDEFAULT key is pressed, to change the default for a submenu, first press MENU and drag the pointer into a submenu, as shown in Figure 15-21.

Figure 15-21   To change a default setting for a submenu, press MENU and drag the pointer to the right in a menu item.

Keep pressing the MENU button and press the SETMENUDEFAULT key. As previously described, the default rings for the menu group are displayed, as shown in Figure 15-22.

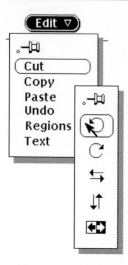

Figure 15-22   The default rings for the menu group are displayed.

Drag the pointer to the pushpin, as shown in Figure 15-23.

Figure 15-23   The default ring follows the pointer to the pushpin.

You want to set the pushpin as the default, and also pin the Regions submenu. To do this, first release the SETMENUDEFAULT key and continue to press MENU. This action sets the pushpin as the default. When you release the SETMENUDEFAULT key, the normal feedback for the control is displayed. In this example, the pushpin is pushed in and the highlighting is displayed for the Regions item, as shown in Figure 15-24.

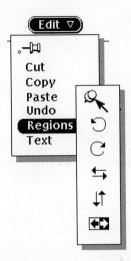

Figure 15-24 Releasing the SETMENUDEFAULT modifier with MENU pressed sets the default and pushes in the pushpin.

Next release MENU. The menu group is dismissed, and the pinned window is displayed, as shown in Figure 15-25.

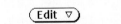

Figure 15-25 Releasing MENU sets the default, executes the command, and dismisses the menu group.

You can press MENU and the modifier key in any combination and at any time. The highlighted item under the pointer gives you visual feedback that the command will be executed when you release MENU.

You set defaults on menus with exclusive or nonexclusive settings in the same way.

Menu Placement

This section describes the specifications for the placement of submenus and pop-up menus. See Chapter 6 for a description of menu button menu placement.

Submenu Placement

When you are viewing submenus, the default item is always aligned horizontally with the originating menu item. The vertical positioning of the submenu depends on the location of the pointer when you drag the pointer past the drag-right distance.

Leftmost Submenu Placement

Once the drag-right distance is reached, the submenu is displayed, with the submenu positioned under the pointer as appropriate.

For example, if you press MENU and drag the pointer into the menu item from the left, the submenu is displayed when the pointer moves beyond the drag-right distance set in the Workspace Properties window, as shown in Figure 15-26. The default drag-right distance is 5 points. This is the leftmost position for any submenu using press-drag-release.

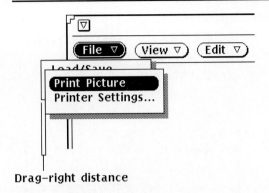

Drag-right distance

Figure 15-26   Leftmost placement for submenus.

Rightmost Submenu Placement

The horizontal positioning of the submenu at the right of menu items depends on how you drag the pointer into the submenu region. The right-most position for a submenu results when you drag the pointer into the highlighting area from the right, as shown in Figure 15-27. The left side of the menu is 5 points to the right of the left side of the menu mark.

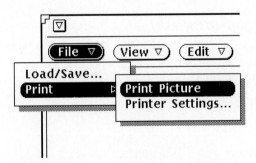

Figure 15-27   Rightmost placement of submenus.

Submenu placement at screen edges

When the pointer is so close to the right side or the bottom of the screen that there is not enough room to display the submenu in the usual way, menus and submenus are layered. The horizontal alignment is maintained, and the pointer moves horizontally to the left so that the pointer is positioned on the left side of the highlighting for submenus, and to the right of the default ring for pop-up menus. Figure 15-28 shows a pop-up menu group with the normal submenu alignment on the left, and the adjusted placement for the same menu when it is at the right side of the screen. The drop shadow never moves off the screen.

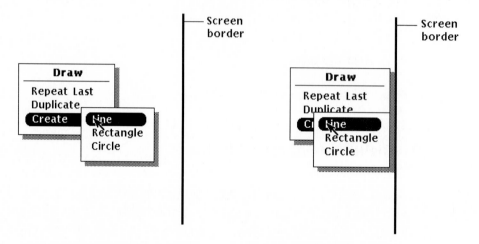

Figure 15-28   Submenu alignment on the right border of the screen.

Figure 15-29 shows a pop-up menu group with the normal menu alignment on the left, and the adjusted placement for the same menu when it is at the bottom of the screen. The pointer moves up and to the left so that it is positioned on the left side of the highlighting for the submenu and to the left of the default ring for pop-up menus.

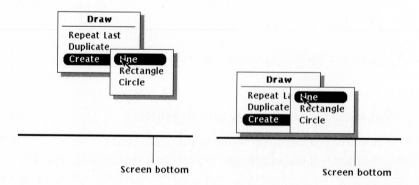

Figure 15-29   Submenu alignment at the bottom of the screen.

338

Submenu Placement for Stay-up Menus

When you use click-move-click to display menus in stay-up mode, clicking anywhere within the menu item displays the submenu. The position for stay-up menus is the same as for menus displayed to the right of a menu button in a control area: the default item aligns with the originating item, and the left side of the menu aligns with the right side of the busy feedback on the button menu, as shown in Figure 15-30.

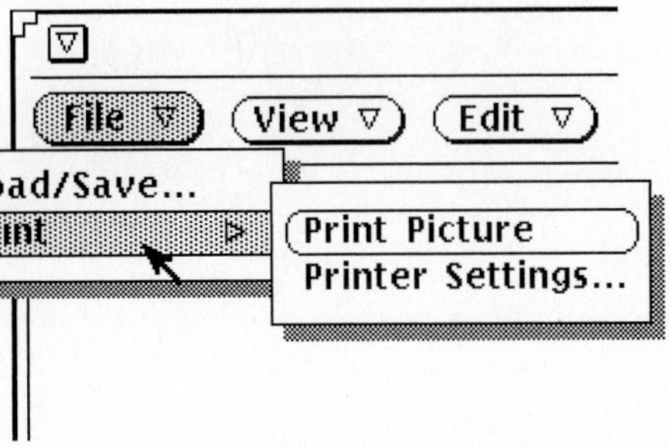

Figure 15-30 Placement for submenus in stay-up mode.

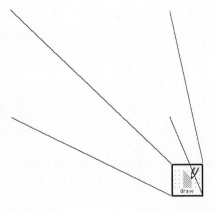

16

SELECTING AND OPERATING ON WINDOWS, ICONS, AND PANES

The select-then-operate paradigm is the foundation of the OPEN LOOK User Interface. In this paradigm, you select an object first, and then you manipulate the object directly (by dragging) or choose an operation to be performed from a menu or the keyboard. The object (or objects) for selection can be a window, an icon, a pane, or text or graphics within an application.

This chapter explains how to select and operate on windows and icons. It also tells you how to select and operate on panes and embedded objects.

Opening Icons and Closing Windows

When you open an icon, the implementation provides some visual feedback. In the example shown in Figure 16-1, thin lines momentarily radiate from each corner of the selected icon to show you where the window will be placed.

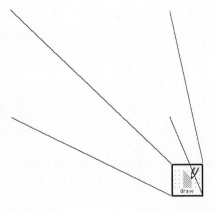

Figure 16-1   An icon with open lines.

Any time you close a window to an icon—using the Window menu button or the Window menu—the implementation provides the same sort of visual feedback as when you open an icon. In the example in Figure 16-2, thin lines radiate from the corners of the window to show the placement of the icon.

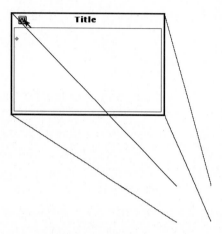

Figure 16-2   A window with close lines.

Selecting Windows and Icons

You can select single or multiple windows and icons. Table 16-1 summarizes how you use mouse buttons to select windows and icons.

Table 16-1   Selecting windows and icons.

Action	Pointer on Workspace Background	Pointer on Icon or Window Background
Click SELECT	All selections are cleared.	Object at pointer location is selected and brought to front of the screen. Any other objects are deselected.
Drag SELECT	Traces a bounding box. All objects falling entirely within box are selected.	Objects are dragged. A bounding box defining the shape of each selected object is displayed, and the group of bounding boxes move with the pointer.
Click ADJUST	No operation.	Toggles the state of the object under the pointer, selecting if not selected, deselecting if selected. Object is not brought to the front.
Drag ADJUST	Traces a bounding box. The state of all objects falling entirely within bounding box is toggled.	Toggles the state of the object under the pointer, selecting if not selected, deselecting if selected.
Click MENU	Workspace menu is displayed. Selection is not affected.	Window menu is displayed in the stay-up mode. Selection is not affected.
Press MENU	Workspace menu is displayed. Selection is not affected.	Window menu is displayed. Selection is not affected.

You can select a window or windows and manipulate them directly (for example, by pressing SELECT and dragging). In addition, you can select multiple windows and/or icons and operate on them by using controls from the Window Controls pop-up that you access from the Workspace menu. See Chapter 10 for more information about the Window Controls pop-up.

Selecting a Window

You select a window by clicking SELECT anywhere in the window background. The window is brought to the front of the screen and the border thickens, as shown in Figure 16-3.

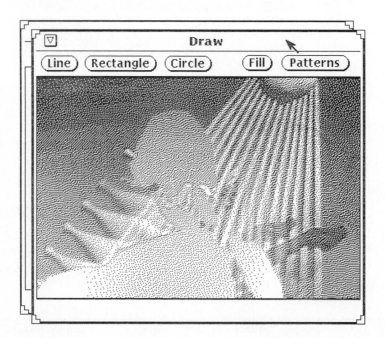

Figure 16-3 A selected window that overlaps an unselected window.

Selecting an Icon

You select an icon by moving the pointer to it and clicking SELECT. The border of the selected icon thickens, as shown in Figure 16-4. The icon on the left is selected, and the icon on the right is not selected.

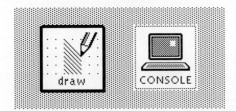

Figure 16-4   A selected and an unselected icon.

In a color implementation, when you set the borderless icon option from the Workspace Properties window, unselected icons are borderless; selected icons have a border.

Selecting Multiple Windows and Icons with ADJUST

You select several windows and icons for the same operation by clicking SELECT to select the first object, and then clicking ADJUST to extend the selection. Clicking ADJUST on a selected object toggles it to the opposite state. If a window is selected, clicking ADJUST deselects it. Windows and icons selected when you click ADJUST are not moved to the front of the screen. The following examples show the steps for selecting multiple windows and icons using SELECT and ADJUST.

1 Move the pointer to the background of a window and click SELECT. The border of the selected window thickens, as shown in Figure 16-5.

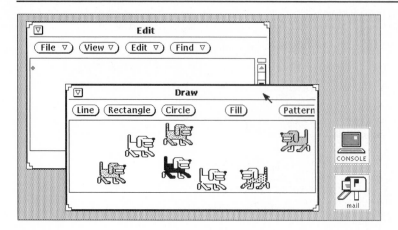

Figure 16-5 To select a window, move the pointer onto the window background and click SELECT.

2 To add another icon or window to the selected group, move the pointer onto an icon or onto the background of a window and click ADJUST. In Figure 16-6, the Mail icon is added to the selection.

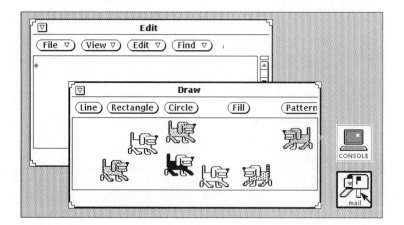

Figure 16-6 To add an icon to the selected group, move the pointer onto the icon and click ADJUST.

3 To add another window or icon to the selected group, repeat this procedure. In Figure 16-7, moving the pointer to the Edit window and clicking ADJUST adds the Edit window to the selected group.

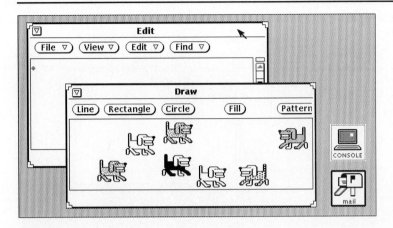

Figure 16-7   To add a window to the selected group, move the pointer onto the window background and click ADJUST.

The selected group now consists of the Draw and Edit windows and the Mail icon.

Selecting Multiple Windows with a Bounding Box

You select multiple windows and icons with a *bounding box* by pressing SELECT and dragging the pointer to define a bounding box, as shown in the following examples.

1 Move the pointer to an area outside of the group of objects to be selected.

2 Press SELECT and drag the pointer to define a bounding box that completely encloses the objects you want to select, as shown in Figure 16-8. Note that the Shell window is not completely contained within the bounding box, and therefore, will not be selected.

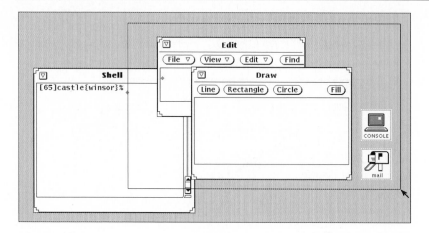

Figure 16-8   Press SELECT and drag the pointer to define a bounding box.

3 Release SELECT. The objects within the bounding box are selected. In Figure 16-9, the Edit and Draw windows and the Console and Mail icons are selected.

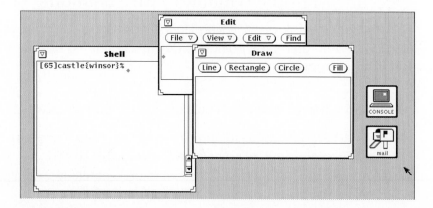

Figure 16-9   Release SELECT to select the objects within the bounding box.

Displaying the Window Controls Pop-up

When you select windows and icons, you can operate on them from the
Window Controls pop-up window that you access following these steps:

1 Move the pointer to the workspace.

2 Press MENU. The Workspace menu is displayed.

3 Drag the pointer to the right in the Utilities item. The Utilities submenu is
displayed.

4 Drag the pointer onto the Window Controls item. The item highlights.

5 Release MENU. The Window Controls pop-up is displayed, the menu group
is dismissed, and the pointer jumps to the default button, as shown in
Figure 16-10.

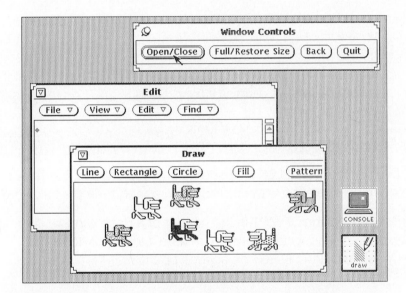

Figure 16-10   Displaying the Window Controls pop-up.

Click SELECT on the Open/Close button. The two selected windows, Draw
and Edit, are closed and remain selected. The selected Draw icon is opened
and the icons remains selected. Figure 16-11 shows the workspace after you
click SELECT on the Open/Close button.

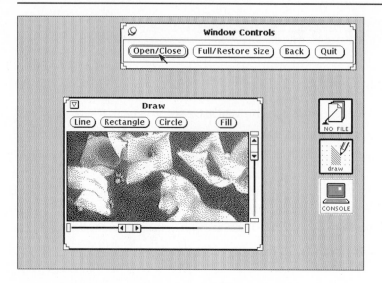

Figure 16-11   Click SELECT on a Window Controls button to operate on selected windows and icons.

You can leave the Window Controls pop-up displayed so that it is available for other operations, or dismiss it by clicking SELECT on the pushpin.

Double-Click Selecting

Double-clicking SELECT is used as an accelerator—a shortcut way to perform an operation without displaying a menu—in the following ways:

☐ Double-clicking SELECT in the header of a base window is an accelerator to expand a window to full size or restore it to its previous size.
☐ Double-clicking SELECT on an icon opens it.

Moving Windows and Icons

You can move selected windows and icons one at a time or in groups by dragging SELECT on a selected object, as shown in the following examples. The OPEN LOOK UI implementation determines whether border boxes that represent the outline of selected objects are displayed or whether the object is dragged directly.

1 Move the pointer to one of the selected windows or icons and press SELECT. Consider the position of the objects relative to the sides of the workspace, since you cannot move either windows or icons completely off the workspace.

2 Drag the pointer to move the group. In the example shown in Figure 16-12, a border box for each selected object moves with the pointer to show the location of all the moved objects.

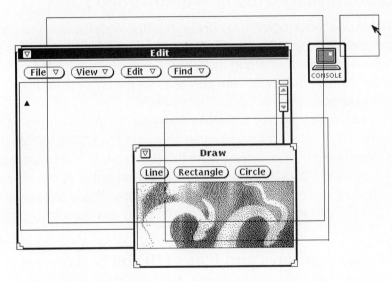

Figure 16-12   Border boxes are dragged with the pointer when you move a group of selected windows and icons.

3 When a group of objects is positioned at the new location, release SELECT. The windows and icons are moved to the new location and remain selected. You can perform another operation on the same objects, or click SELECT on the workspace to deselect them.

Ordinarily, when you make a selection of any kind on the workspace using SELECT, any other selection is cleared when you press SELECT. However, you may want to move a window without clearing the current text or graphics selection. To permit this, when you press SELECT on a window or icon, the OPEN LOOK UI implementation waits until you release SELECT to clear a selected text or graphics object. When you drag windows or icons beyond

351

the 5-pixel damping factor, the current text or graphics selection is maintained and is not cleared. When you release SELECT without moving the pointer, the window or icon at the pointer location is selected and any other selection is cleared as usual.

Moving a window with an active insert area does not change the insert point. Releasing SELECT moves the objects to the new location. The objects remain selected.

Constrained Moving of Windows and Icons

When you move objects by dragging, the movement is unconstrained—you can move the object in any direction. There are times when it is useful to move an object either along the x or the y coordinate of the screen to keep it positioned horizontally or vertically relative to some other object displayed on the workspace.

You can constrain any dragging operation by pressing the CONSTRAIN modifier key before, during, or after pressing SELECT to initiate the drag. You set the constrain modifier key from the Workspace Properties window. When you press the CONSTRAIN modifier, the movement is constrained to the direction in which you are dragging the pointer. If you release and then press the CONSTRAIN modifier during a single drag, you can change the direction.

Moving Windows and Icons Off the Screen

You can move part of a selected window or icon off the screen, but you can never move a window or icon completely off the screen. It is suggested that OPEN LOOK UI implementations bump the side of the window against the side of the screen before it can move off the screen. This makes it easy for you to position a window at the side of the screen. When you move the window past a threshold distance, say 10 pixels, the side of the window is moved off the side of the screen.

The minimum amount of a window or icon that must be displayed at the edge of the screen is a strip equal to the width of a resize corner, as shown in Figure 16-13. This strip allows you to select and manipulate the object, dragging it back onto the workspace by the visible portion. When you move part of a selected window or icon off the screen in any direction, the pointer stops when the minimum amount of the object is reached, and you cannot drag it any farther off the screen.

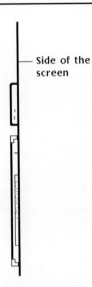

Side of the
screen

Figure 16-13 Minimum amount of windows and icons visible at the side of
the screen.

Resizing a Window

When a window has resize corners, you can shrink or expand the borders of
an individual window. The window is anchored at the corner that is diagonal to
the resize corner you use, and the viewing area expands and contracts relative
to the anchored corner. The contents of the pane are always anchored at the
upper left corner of the pane, regardless of which resize corner you use. The
area of the window is adjusted, but the contents do not change scale.

You change the size of a window using the resize corners, as follows:

1 Move the pointer to one of the resize corners of a window and press
SELECT. The resize corner highlights, as shown in Figure 16-14.

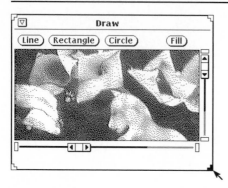

Figure 16-14   To resize a window, move the pointer to one of the resize corners and press SELECT.

2 Drag the pointer to a new location. A border box is displayed to show the dimensions of the new window. Note that the resize corner remains highlighted at the original location, as shown in Figure 16-15. It is not dragged with the pointer.

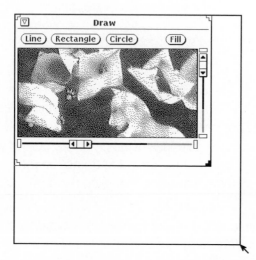

Figure 16-15   Drag the pointer to adjust the area of the window.

3 Release SELECT. The window is redisplayed in its new size, as shown in Figure 16-16. The contents of the pane are anchored at the upper left corner, regardless of which resize corner you use. Note that more of the

354

image is displayed in the larger pane, as specified by the graphics application. The title is recentered in the header, and another button in the control area is partly visible.

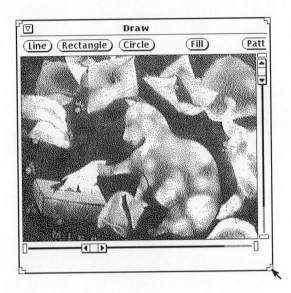

Figure 16-16 Release SELECT to complete the resizing of the window.

The following examples show you how to use the resize corners to make a text window smaller.

1 Move the pointer to one of the resize corners and press SELECT. The top right resize corner is used in the example shown in Figure 16-17.

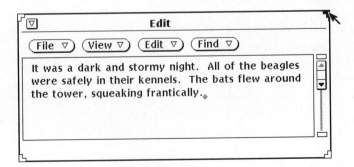

Figure 16-17 Move the pointer to a resize corner and press SELECT.

2 Drag the pointer to change the area of the window. In the example shown in Figure 16-18, you drag the pointer upward and to the left.

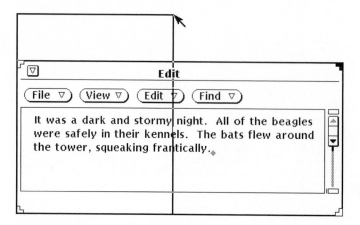

Figure 16-18   Drag the pointer to resize the window.

3 Release SELECT. The area of the window is adjusted. Note that the text in the example shown in Figure 16-19 is redisplayed to conform to the size of the new pane. This happens when it is specified by the application. The application did not specify that the buttons in the control area should be repositioned.

Figure 16-19   Release SELECT to readjust the area of the resized window.

When you resize an application with more than one pane, the application determines how to allocate the area of the panes to adjust to the resizing, keeping all panes visible when possible.

Selecting Panes

You can select a pane when the application developer has specified that an operation such as setting properties, resizing, or deleting can be performed on it. See Chapter 3 for a description of panes.

Normally, panes have a 1-point border. When you select a pane, the border thickens 1 additional point. The width of the active area at the border is determined by the OPEN LOOK UI implementation and the application. To help you position the pointer correctly, when the pointer is on the border of a selectable pane, the target pointer is displayed. When the target pointer is displayed, select the pane by clicking SELECT. The border thickens, as shown in Figure 16-20.

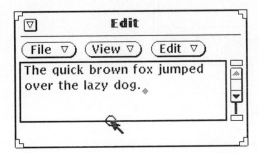

Figure 16-20   A selected pane.

You can select additional panes within the same window by clicking ADJUST on the border. You cannot select a pane in one application and then click ADJUST to select a pane in a different application window. If you click ADJUST on a pane in a different application window, the first pane is deselected, and the pane under the pointer is selected.

You can apply properties specified by the application to that pane. As an example, suppose a text editing application has a property setting for word wrapping. You select the pane, display the property window, set Word Wrap, and click SELECT on the Apply button to apply the setting to the entire document, not just the text that is visible in the pane.

Resizing Split Panes

When a window has more than one pane, or when panes have been split, the selected pane displays resize handles that you can use to adjust the total area of the pane. See Chapter 7 for information about using the cable anchors to split a pane. When you select a pane that can be resized, it displays *resize handles* on the sides of the pane that can be adjusted, as shown in Figure 16-21.

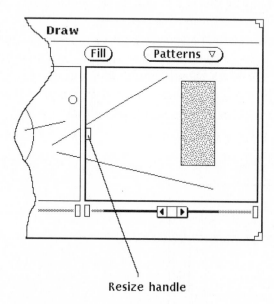

Resize handle

Figure 16-21   A selected pane with a resize handle.

Press SELECT on the resize handle, and drag it toward the center of the pane to reduce the area of the pane; drag it away from the center of the pane to increase the area of the pane. The adjacent pane automatically expands or contracts in relationship to the changes in the resized pane.

The contents of a split pane are always anchored at the upper left corner of the originating pane, and the view of the data is expanded or contracted from that anchored point. The minimum size of a split pane is the length of the minimum scrollbar, as described in Chapter 7. You cannot use the resize handle to remove a split pane. See Chapter 7 for information about how to remove a split pane.

The following steps and examples tell you how to shrink a pane with the resize handle.

1 Move the pointer to the resize handle and press SELECT. The resize handle highlights, as shown in Figure 16-22.

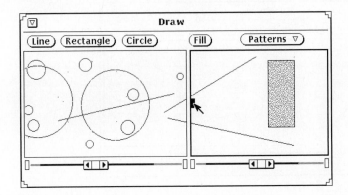

Figure 16-22   Press SELECT on a resize handle in a selected pane.

2 Drag the pointer in the direction to be resized. You can drag the pointer into the pane, or outward toward the adjacent pane. In the example shown in Figure 16-23, the pointer is dragged into the pane.

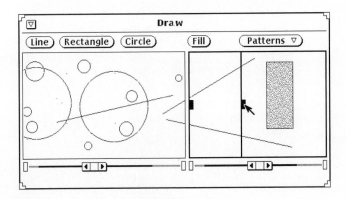

Figure 16-23   Drag the pointer to resize a pane.

3 Release SELECT to readjust the area between the two panes. The resize handle is no longer highlighted. The contents of the smaller pane are anchored in the upper left corner, and you no longer have a continuous view split into two panes, as shown in Figure 16-24.

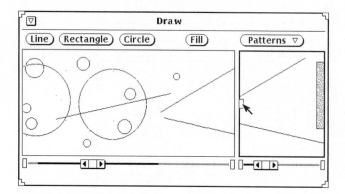

Figure 16-24   Release SELECT to readjust the area between the two panes.

When a pane can be resized in more than one direction, each side of the pane that can be resized has a resize handle. Figure 16-25 shows a pane that has been split into four. The pane in the upper right corner has been selected and displays two resize handles.

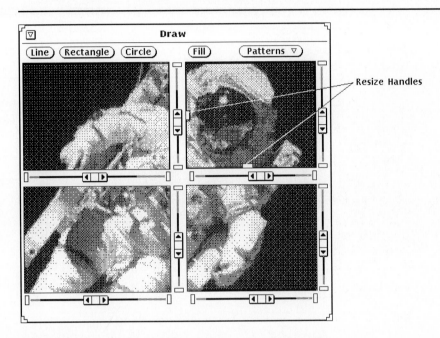

Figure 16-25   A selected pane with two resize handles.

Multiple Split Panes

Once you start creating complicated splits of the same pane, the way panes are resized or removed may depend on the specific OPEN LOOK UI implementation.

The way split panes can be resized depends on the order in which you created them. Looking at the split panes shown in Figure 16-25, you cannot determine in what order they were created. They can be created in (at least) the two ways shown in Figure 16-26.

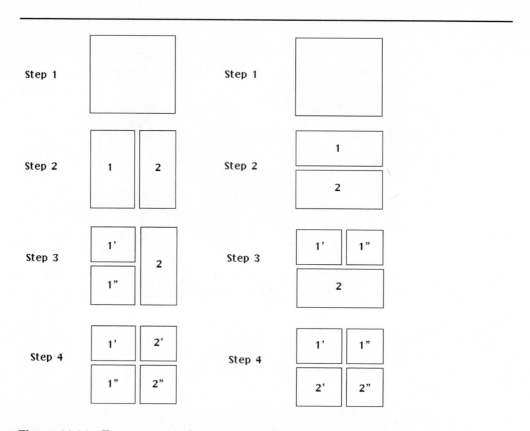

Figure 16-26 Two ways to split a pane into four.

When one pane is split into two, the two splits are related to each other and move together. You can adjust the sizes of panes 1' and 1" without changing the sizes of 2' and 2" in either configuration, as shown in Figure 16-27.

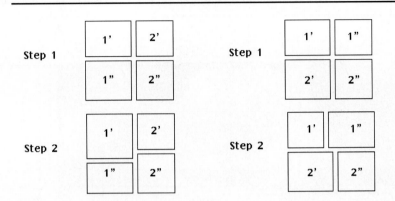

Figure 16-27 Resizing related panes.

However, if you expand or contract the 1' pane in the left example horizontally, or the 1' pane in the right example vertically, the borders of the related pane also expand or contract. The adjacent panes (2' and 2") also contract or expand, and keep the spaces between the panes the same, as shown in Figure 16-28.

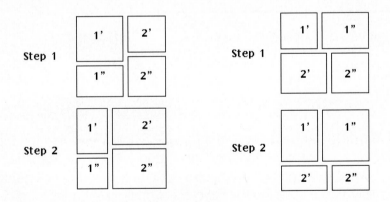

Figure 16-28 Resizing related panes.

If the top two panes are related, such as those of the spaceman shown in Figure 16-25, you can create splits, as shown in Figure 16-29. The contents of each expanded pane are anchored in the upper left corner of the pane.

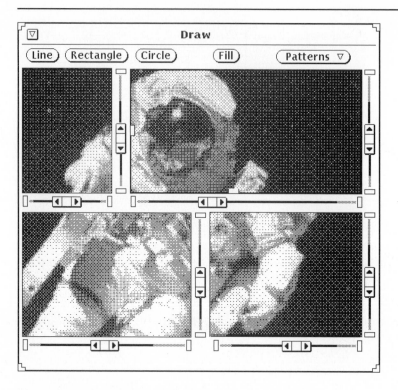

Figure 16-29   A pane with four splits.

Removing a Split Pane

You can remove a split pane using the Join Views item on the Scrollbar menu. See Chapter 7 for information about using the Scrollbar menu to remove a split pane. You can also remove a split pane by selecting it and pressing and releasing the Delete key on the keyboard, or choosing a delete function from the application menu, if one is provided.

You can remove multiple splits in the same window by selecting several panes and deleting them. You ordinarily cannot delete a primary pane from an application (however, some applications may permit you to). When selecting and deleting multiple split panes, the panes rearrange according to their relationship when they were created.

For example, if you delete the selected pane (the upper right pane in Figure 16-29), the pane at the upper left fills in that area, as shown in Figure 16-30.

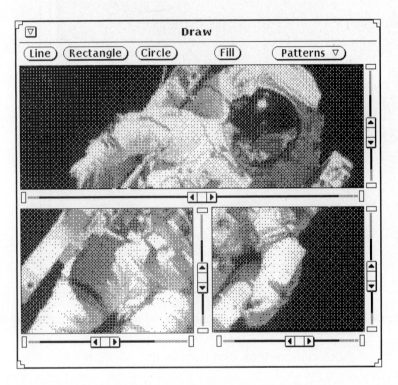

Figure 16-30   How the panes in Figure 16-29 look after one pane is deleted.

If you select the upper pane and the lower left pane in Figure 16-30, and delete them, the pane at the lower right of the window fills in the space occupied by the other two panes, as shown in Figure 16-31.

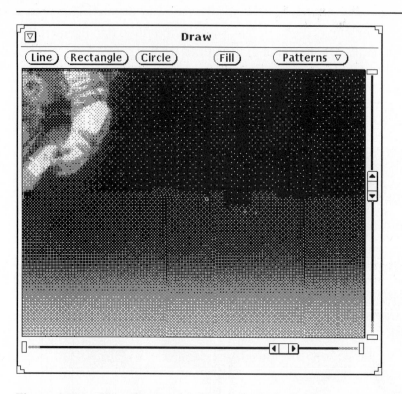

Figure 16-31 How the panes in Figure 16-30 look after two panes are deleted.

When there is more than one way for the panes to fill in the space left by a deleted split, the OPEN LOOK UI implementation specifies a rule, such as "Always fill from the left and from the top" or some other rule, that the toolkit can implement. The panes shown in Figure 16-32 are three split views of the same pane. If you select and delete the middle pane, 1 double-prime, the pane to either the right or the left could fill in the vacant space, as determined by the implementation.

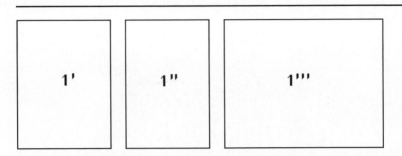

Figure 16-32 The implementation decides how to fill when the middle pane is deleted.

Selecting Embedded Objects

When the OPEN LOOK UI implementation supports *embedded objects*—for example, a publishing application with both formatted text and container objects (usually called *frames*) that themselves may contain text, graphics, or other objects—you must be able to click on the border of any container such as a pane or a frame to select it. Since the border of the container may be very small, it is recommended that the application change the pointer to the target pointer when it is on the border of a selectable object.

Recommendations for handling embedded objects are provided in the *OPEN LOOK Graphical User Interface Application Style Guidelines*.

17

SELECTING AND OPERATING ON TEXT AND GRAPHICS

Introduction

You select text and graphic objects in basically the same way that you select windows or icons—using SELECT and ADJUST.

One way to operate on text and graphics in an OPEN LOOK UI implementation is with the cut/copy/paste operations. CUT, COPY, and PASTE are core functions that are provided from the keyboard. You can change the Cut, Copy, and Paste default keys from the Workspace Properties window. An application can also provide cut/copy/paste functions from a menu.

Cut/copy/paste operations use the clipboard to keep track of selected objects. The clipboard temporarily stores text, images, and other types of objects. It does not store selected windows or icons.

You can also move and copy selected text and graphics by moving the pointer onto the selection, pressing SELECT, and dragging it with the pointer.

In a Level 2 implementation, you can view the contents of the clipboard at any time by clicking on the Clipboard item on the Workspace menu. A window showing the contents of the clipboard is displayed.

A Level 2 implementation provides a way to move text to the current insert point (Quick Move) and copy text to the current insert point (Quick Duplicate) while maintaining the current selection and the current item on the clipboard.

Table 17-1 summarizes text and graphics selection for the OPEN LOOK UI.

Table 17-1   Selecting text and graphics.

Action	TEXT		GRAPHICS	
	Off Selection	On Selection	Off Object	On Object
Click SELECT	Insert point is set at the pointer location.	When SELECT is released, insert point is set at pointer location and selection is cleared	All selections are cleared.	Object at pointer location is selected. Any other objects are deselected.
Drag SELECT	Text is highlighted as pointer is dragged (wipe-through selection).	Text move pointer is displayed. When you release SELECT, text is moved to pointer location if that location is outside the highlighted area.	Traces a bounding box. All objects falling entirely within the box are selected. The pointer must begin outside the objects to be selected.	A bounding box defining the shape of each object is displayed, and the group of bounding boxes moves with the pointer as you drag objects.
Click ADJUST	Extends the highlighting to the pointer location either extending the beginning or the end of the current.	Moves the end of the highlighting to the pointer location. Beginning of selection is preserved.	No operation.	Toggles the state of the object under the pointer, selecting if not selected or deselecting if selected.
Drag ADJUST	Adjusts an existing selection as the pointer is dragged (wipe-through). Beginning of selection is anchored at insert point.	Adjust an existing selection as pointer is dragged (wipe-through). Beginning of selection is anchored at insert point.	Traces a bounding box. All objects falling entirely within the box are toggled.	Toggles the state of the object under the pointer, selecting if not selected or deselecting if selected.

370

Selecting Text

You replace text in an OPEN LOOK UI implementation by selecting characters and then typing new text from the keyboard or pasting it in from the clipboard. The selected characters are deleted when the first character is typed.

You insert text by setting the insert point in an input area and typing text from the keyboard or pasting it in from the clipboard.

Wipe-Through Text Selection

The following steps and examples show how to make a wipe-through text selection.

1 Move the pointer to the beginning of the text you want to select and press SELECT, as shown in Figure 17-1. The window need not have an active caret. If a caret (either active or inactive) is visible in the text pane, it is reset at the pointer location while you are pressing SELECT, and the header highlights.

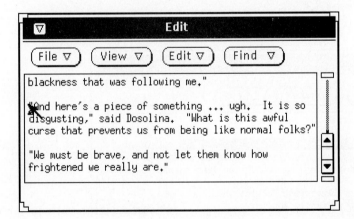

Figure 17-1   To select text by wiping through it, first press SELECT.

2 Drag the pointer to the end of the text you want to select. As you move the pointer, the highlighting is anchored at the initial insert point and moves with the pointer, as shown in Figure 17-2. The caret is not displayed while you are dragging the pointer. You can move the pointer either forward or backward in the text.

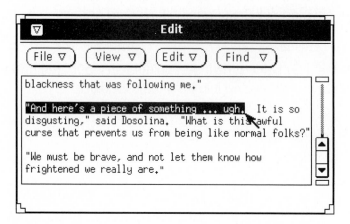

Figure 17-2   Drag the pointer to highlight selected text.

3 When the text you want to select is highlighted, release SELECT. The insert point is set at the end of the highlighted text (to the right of the highlighting if you drag the pointer forward, to the left if you drag backward), as shown in Figure 17-3.

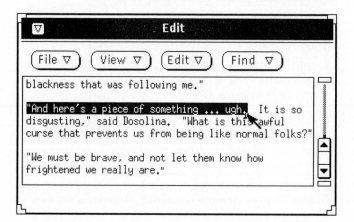

Figure 17-3   Release SELECT to end the selection.

When you make a wipe-through selection, the highlighting is anchored at the insert point. When you drag the pointer to the right and downward, the insert point marks the beginning of the selection. When you drag the pointer to the left and upward, the insert point marks the end of the selection.

You can make a wipe-through selection in the same way with ADJUST when the caret is inactive and the first mouse button you use in the text pane is ADJUST. Under those circumstances, making a wipe-through selection with ADJUST is the same as using SELECT.

When the caret is active, pressing ADJUST extends the selection to the pointer location. You can drag the pointer to adjust the highlighting and release ADJUST to complete the selection.

Selecting Text with SELECT/ADJUST

You can also select text by clicking SELECT to mark the beginning, and then clicking ADJUST to mark the end of the text that you want to select. When the caret is inactive, you can begin your selection by clicking ADJUST. Otherwise the ADJUST click extends or reduces the selection. This type of selection is shown in the following steps and examples:

1 Move the pointer to the beginning of the text you want to select and click SELECT. The header of the window highlights and the insert point is set at the pointer location, as shown in Figure 17-4.

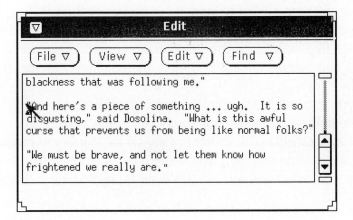

Figure 17-4   Click SELECT to mark the beginning of a text selection.

2 Move the pointer either forward or backward to the end of the text you want to select and click ADJUST. The text between the insert point and the pointer is highlighted. The active caret is displayed at the end of the selected text, as shown in Figure 17-5.

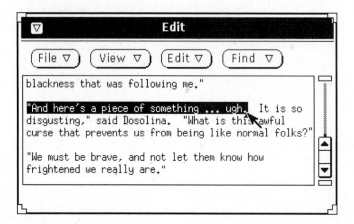

Figure 17-5 Click ADJUST to mark the end of the text selection.

Adjusting a Text Selection

To change (adjust) the end of the highlighting, move the pointer to a different place in the text, either on or off the highlighting, and click ADJUST. The active caret moves to the location of the ADJUST click.

When you click ADJUST off the highlighting, the selection is expanded in the appropriate direction. For example, clicking after the selection extends the end of the selection, and clicking before the selection extends the beginning of the selection.

When you click ADJUST on the current highlighting, the end of the selection is adjusted to the pointer location, maintaining the beginning of the selection.

When you click SELECT with the pointer on the current highlighting, the selection is cleared when you *release* SELECT without moving the pointer. If you move the pointer beyond the damping factor, the selection is moved by dragging and is not cleared.

Selecting Graphic Objects

Graphic objects are selected in the same way that windows and icons are selected. You select graphic objects in the following ways:

☐ Clicking SELECT selects an object.
☐ Clicking SELECT on a different object deselects the first object and selects the object at the pointer location.
☐ Clicking ADJUST toggles the state of the object at the pointer location, selecting it if not selected and deselecting it if selected. Other selections are not affected.
☐ When an application supports bounding box selection, pressing SELECT, dragging a bounding box, and releasing SELECT selects all objects that fall completely within the bounding box.
☐ Pressing ADJUST, dragging a bounding box, and releasing ADJUST toggles the state of all objects that fall completely within the bounding box.

A common way a graphic application indicates a selected object is by surrounding it with a rectangle with eight *grab handles*. Applications that are not object-oriented may use some other visual feedback such as highlighting to show you the selected state. Figure 17-6 summarizes these methods of selecting graphic objects using grab handles to show the selected state.

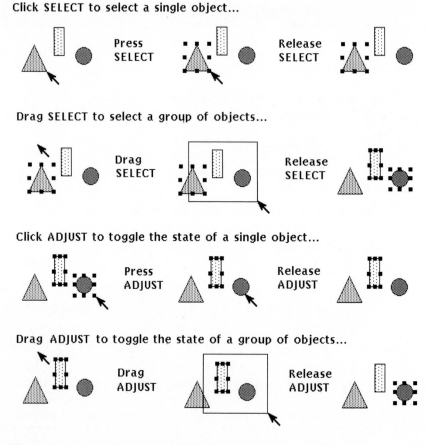

Figure 17-6   Selecting graphic objects.

Multi-Click Selecting

"Multi-click SELECT" in text or graphics means "select the next larger unit" in any application that has a hierarchical structure.

When selecting text, multi-clicking SELECT selects a unit at successive syntactic levels, but does not include any terminating end-of-line character. For example, double-clicking selects a word, triple-clicking selects a sentence or a line, and quadruple-clicking selects a paragraph or the entire document. When you use multi-clicking to select text, the active caret is positioned at the end of the highlighting.

The precise definition of what constitutes a word, a sentence, a line, or a paragraph is determined by the application when it is not specified by the OPEN LOOK UI implementation. The syntactic level of selection is also defined by the application developer.

Copying Text

An OPEN LOOK UI implementation supports the following three ways to copy text:

☐ Copying text to a clipboard and then pasting it in a window
☐ Pressing the DUPLICATE modifier key and SELECT on selected text and dragging it
☐ Using Quick Duplicate

Each method is described in this section.

Copying Text with the Clipboard

The following steps and examples show how to copy text using the clipboard:

1 Select the text to be copied, as shown in Figure 17-7.

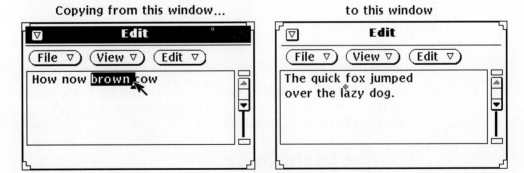

Figure 17-7   To copy text using the clipboard, first select the text.

2 Press and release the Copy key.
3 Move the pointer to the place where the text is to be inserted, and click SELECT to set the insert point, as shown in Figure 17-8.

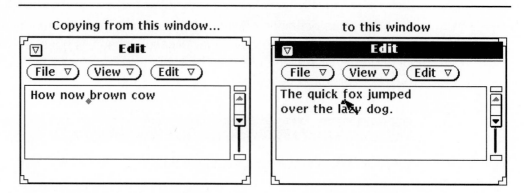

Figure 17-8 Set the insert point where you want to insert the text.

4 Press and release the Paste key. The text is copied at the caret location, as shown in Figure 17-9. The caret is repositioned at the end of the inserted text, as it is when text is typed directly at the insert point.

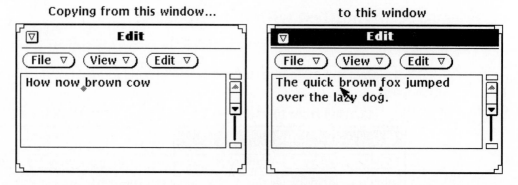

Figure 17-9 Press and release the Paste key to copy the text to the caret location.

Copying Text by Dragging

You copy text by first selecting text and then using the DUPLICATE modifier key with SELECT to initiate dragging the text. The default DUPLICATE modifier is the Shift key. You can change the DUPLICATE modifier key from the Workspace Properties window.

When the application supports it, you can constrain the direction in which you drag the selected text by pressing the CONSTRAIN key at any time during the drag operation to constrain the drag to either the x or y axis. The direction of the constraint depends on the direction in which you are dragging the pointer when you press the CONSTRAIN key. See Chapter 14 for more information about the CONSTRAIN key.

The following steps and examples show how you copy text by dragging:

1 Select some text, as shown in Figure 17-10.

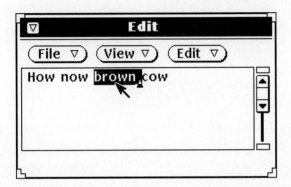

Figure 17-10   To copy text by dragging, first select some text.

2 Move the pointer onto the selected text and press both the DUPLICATE modifier key and SELECT.

3 When you move the pointer beyond the 5-pixel damping factor, the pointer changes to the text duplicate pointer, as shown in Figure 17-11. It displays at least the first three characters of the selected text within its border and adds the More arrow when the selection does not fit inside the text duplicate pointer. The text remains highlighted.

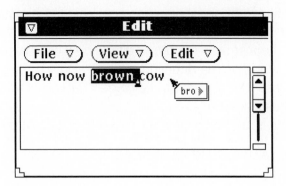

Figure 17-11 Dragging the pointer beyond the damping factor displays the text duplicate pointer.

4 Once the text duplicate pointer is displayed, you can release the DUPLICATE key.

5 Drag the text duplicate pointer to a location outside the highlighted area.

6 Release SELECT. The text is copied to the new location and remains highlighted, as shown in Figure 17-12. The highlighting is removed from the original text. If you release SELECT with the pointer inside the highlighted area, nothing happens.

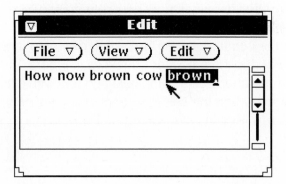

Figure 17-12 Release SELECT to copy the text at the pointer location.

Quick Duplicate

A Level 2 implementation provides a Quick Duplicate function that allows you to perform the following functions:

☐ Copy read-only text that may not be otherwise selectable.
☐ Copy text that is otherwise selectable without clearing the current selection.

Quick Duplicate operations always maintain the current selection and bypass the clipboard, preserving the current contents of the clipboard.

You can quickly copy text using the Quick Duplicate method by following these steps:

1 Set the insert point.
2 Hold down the Paste key.
3 Press and drag SELECT to highlight a temporary selection with a solid underline.
4 Release SELECT.
5 Release the Paste key.

The selected text is inserted at the insert point.
The clipboard does not keep track of Quick Duplicate selections.
As much as possible, the application developer should allow all text on the screen to respond to Quick Duplicate, including read-only text that cannot normally be selected. For example, text from a Help window or the header of an application could be selected and copied into any window. The application developer ultimately decides what text can be accessed in this way. For example, it may not be productive to program the clock so that its text can be quick duplicated.

To permit you to select text for Quick Duplicate, when the Paste key is pressed, all the usual window selection and dragging operations are suppressed so that pressing SELECT on a message area in the header or footer of a window marks the beginning of the text selection, and dragging SELECT underlines the text instead of dragging the window.

When an OPEN LOOK UI implementation provides Quick Duplicate functionality in the header and footer of a window, it allows you to use Quick Duplicate to include information that is displayed in the header or in the footer message area in other windows. For example, you might want to include such information in a mail message that you are composing.

Figure 17-13 shows an example of a window in which you have initiated a Quick Duplicate operation but have not yet released the Paste key. The word "windshield" is the active selection, and the phrase "Selection starts in line 1." is underlined.

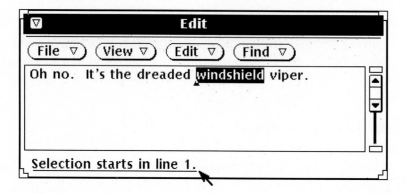

Figure 17-13 A window with both a current selection and a Quick Duplicate selection highlighted.

When you release the Paste key, the highlighted text is deleted and the underlined text is inserted at the active caret, which marks the insert point.

Copying Graphic Objects

An OPEN LOOK UI implementation supports the following ways to copy graphic objects:

☐ Copying a graphic object to a clipboard and then pasting it in a window
☐ Pressing the DUPLICATE modifier key and SELECT on a selected graphic object and dragging it

Each method works the same as it does for text.

Moving Text

An OPEN LOOK UI implementation supports moving text in the following three ways:

☐ Cutting text to the clipboard and then pasting it in a window
☐ Pressing SELECT on selected text and dragging it
☐ Using Quick Move

Each method is described in this section.

Moving Text Using the Clipboard

The following examples show how you move text using the clipboard.

1 Select the text to be moved, as shown in Figure 17-14.

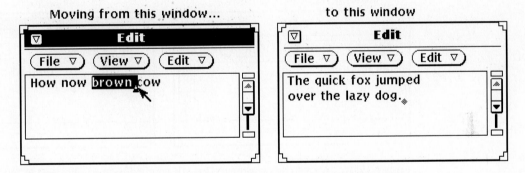

Figure 17-14   To move text using the clipboard, first select the text.

2 Press and release the Cut key to move the text from its current location onto the clipboard. The text is removed from the pane, as shown in Figure 17-15.

Figure 17-15   Press the Cut key to move the selected text from the pane onto the clipboard.

3 Move the pointer to the place where the text is to be moved, and click SELECT to set the insert point, as shown in Figure 17-16.

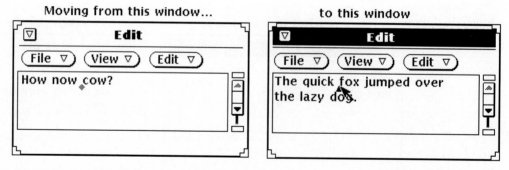

Figure 17-16   Move the pointer to the other window and click SELECT to set the insert point.

4 Press and release the Paste key. The text is inserted at the insert point, as shown in Figure 17-17.

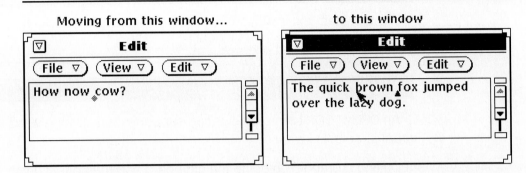

Figure 17-17   Press Paste to move the text from the clipboard to the insert point.

Moving Text by Dragging

Moving text by dragging is similar to copying text. However, you do not need to use a modifier key to initiate the dragging. Pressing SELECT on highlighted text and dragging the text move pointer to a location outside the highlighted area moves the text. The text remains highlighted at the selected location until you release SELECT.

When the application supports constrained moving, you can constrain the drag move operation to the x or y coordinate on the screen in the same way that you constrain a copy operation: Press the CONSTRAIN modifier key while you are dragging the text to be moved. See Chapter 14 for more information about the CONSTRAIN modifier key.

Quick Move

Quick Move works in the following way:

1 Click SELECT to set the insert point.
2 Hold down the Cut key.
3 Press and drag SELECT to make a temporary selection. The temporary selection is highlighted with a horizontal line striking through the center of the text.
4 Release SELECT.
5 Release the Cut key.

The selected text is moved to the caret. The clipboard does not hold Quick Move selections.

Moving Graphic Objects

An OPEN LOOK UI implementation supports the following ways to move graphic objects:

☐ Cutting a graphic object to the clipboard and then pasting it in a window
☐ Pressing SELECT on a selected graphic object and dragging it

Each method works the same as with text.

18

USING PROPERTY WINDOWS

This chapter tells you how to use property windows.

Applying Properties to a Single Selection

You make a selection and apply properties from a property window using the following steps:

1 Select an object.
2 Display the property window.
3 Change some settings in the property window.
4 Click SELECT on the Apply button to apply the properties. The changed properties are applied to the selection, and the property window is dismissed if it is not pinned to the workspace.

The following examples illustrate how to use these steps with a text selection. First, select some text in the Edit application, as shown in Figure 18-1. See Chapter 17 for more information about selecting text.

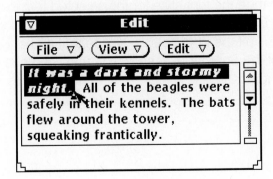

Figure 18-1 To apply properties, first select some text.

Bring up the text property window by choosing Properties from the Edit button menu or by pressing and releasing the Properties key.

The input area is changed to the property window, and the pointer jumps to the Apply button, as shown in Figure 18-2. Note that the header of the property window highlights to show that it has the active input area. The settings Sans Serif, 12, Bold, and Italic in the text property window show the attributes of the text that you selected.

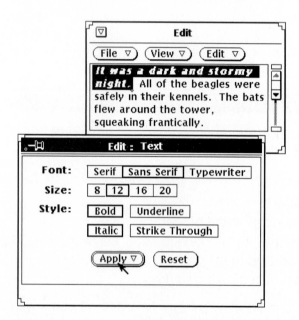

Figure 18-2   Display the text property window.

You are going to change the font style for the selected text to make it match the rest of the text. To do this, you move the pointer to the Bold setting and click SELECT. This turns off the Bold setting. Notice that a change bar is displayed to the left of the Style label to show you that you have changed the setting, as shown in Figure 18-3.

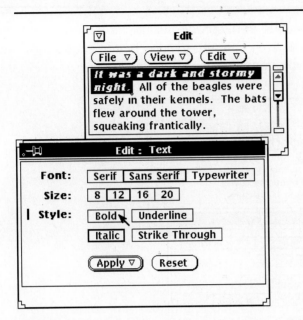

Figure 18-3 Change a nonexclusive setting in the property window.

Next move the pointer to the Italic setting and click SELECT to turn it off, as shown in Figure 18-4.

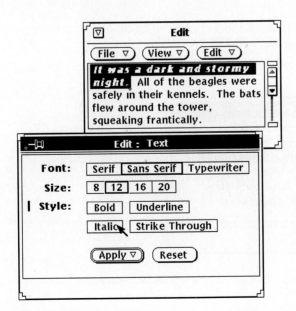

Figure 18-4 Change another nonexclusive setting in the property window.

You are now ready to apply properties. Move the pointer to the Apply menu button and click SELECT. The Apply menu button shows the standard busy pattern while the changes are being applied, as shown in Figure 18-5.

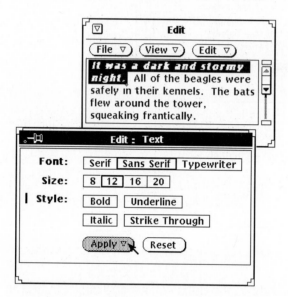

Figure 18-5   Click SELECT on the Apply menu button to apply properties.

The selected text is changed and remains selected, as shown in Figure 18-6. The active input area is restored in the text window, as shown by the highlighting in the header and the active caret. The property window is dismissed.

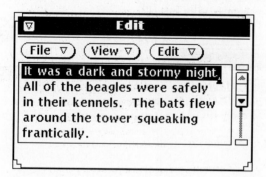

Figure 18-6   Changes are applied to the selected text.

390

If you want to apply changed properties to a sequence of selections, you can pin the property window to the workspace so that it is not dismissed when changes are applied.

Additional Selections

Property windows support two selections at the same time. When you make a new selection anywhere on the workspace, the original selection is dimmed and the property window remains active for that selection. This feature lets you perform operations anywhere on the workspace without losing the selection for the property window.

You can make text selections in the same window or in other windows, select graphic objects in the same window or in other windows, or select windows and icons. The following sections contain examples of some of these selections.

New Selections That Do Not Use the Property Window

The following examples show an original property window selection with new selections that do not use the property window. These examples illustrate where the selections are made and show the changes in header highlighting and pointer location. They are not intended to show changes in the caret or give functional information about how to use the selections. See Chapters 16 and 17 for detailed information about using selections.

Figure 18-7 shows Application A with the original selection, the pinned Properties window, and the configuration of other windows on the workspace that are used in the following examples.

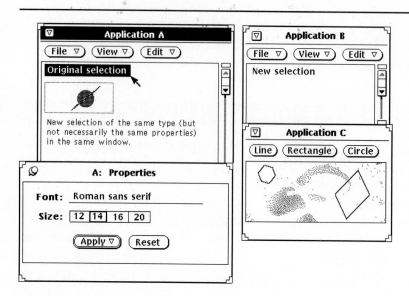

Figure 18-7 Original selection.

Suppose you want to change the information in the text field of the Properties window for Application A. You can select text in the Properties window without losing your original selection. Move the pointer to the text field and highlight the words "Roman sans serif." The new selection is highlighted in the usual way, and the original selection is dimmed, as shown in Figure 18-8. The Properties window is still active, and you can apply changes to the original selection at any time by clicking SELECT on the Apply menu button.

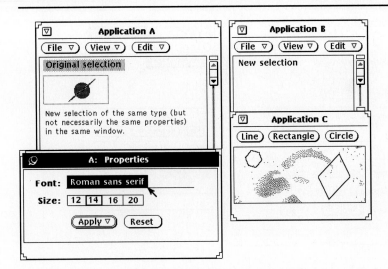

Figure 18-8   The original selection is dimmed when you make a new selection.

You do not have to limit your selections to the Properties window. You can make selections of the same or a different kind in another application. Suppose you then want to select and operate on text in a different application, and leave the Properties window displayed while retaining the original selection. To do this, move the pointer to Application B and select some text.

The active input area changes to Application B, and the original selection remains unchanged, as shown in Figure 18-9. The selection in the Properties window of Application A is cleared.

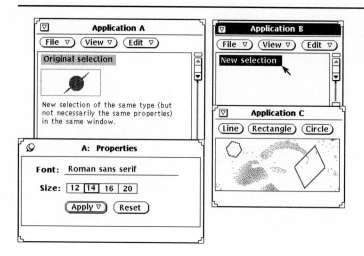

Figure 18-9   The original selection is preserved when you make selections in other windows.

You do not have to limit your selections to objects within an application. You can select a window or an icon, perform operations on it, and still maintain the original selection for the Properties window.

In Figure 18-10, a selection of a different type is made in the same application. The circle is selected.

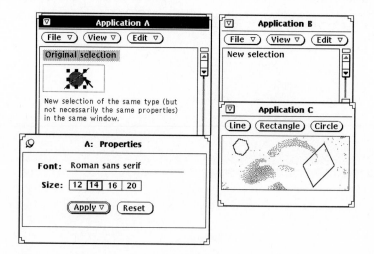

Figure 18-10   A new selection of a different kind in the same application window.

New Selections That Use the Property Window

When you make new selections in the same application that are the same kind of object as the original selection, and the application supports it, you can use the same Properties window to apply changes to either selection. The following examples show you how to apply properties to the new selection from the Properties window of Application A.

In Figure 18-11, the text beneath the graphic objects is selected. The original selection is dimmed, and the new selection is highlighted.

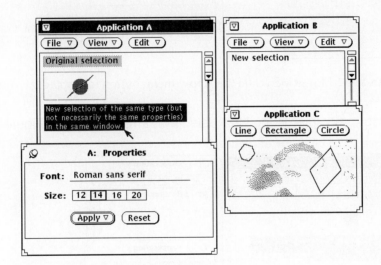

Figure 18-11 Making a new selection of the same kind in the same window activates the New Selection item on the Apply menu.

The New Selection item on the Apply button menu is activated. Note that the properties in the Properties window still reflect the text attributes of the original selection. To apply the settings from the original selection to the new selection, move the pointer to the Apply menu button and press MENU. The Apply menu is displayed as shown in Figure 18-12.

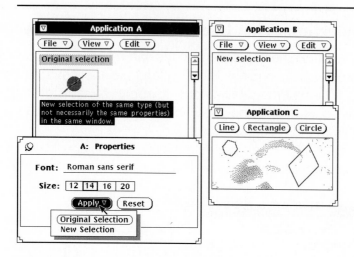

Figure 18-12   Press MENU on the Apply menu button to display the Apply menu.

Drag the pointer to the New Selection item, as shown in Figure 18-13.

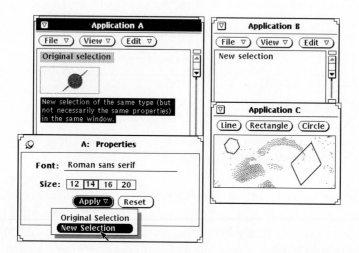

Figure 18-13   Drag the pointer to highlight the New Selection item in the Apply menu.

Release MENU to apply the properties to the new selection and dismiss the Apply menu.

If you apply properties using the Original Selection item on the Apply menu, the original selection accepts those properties and retains the dimmed highlighting. To remove the dimmed highlighting, you must dismiss the Properties window.

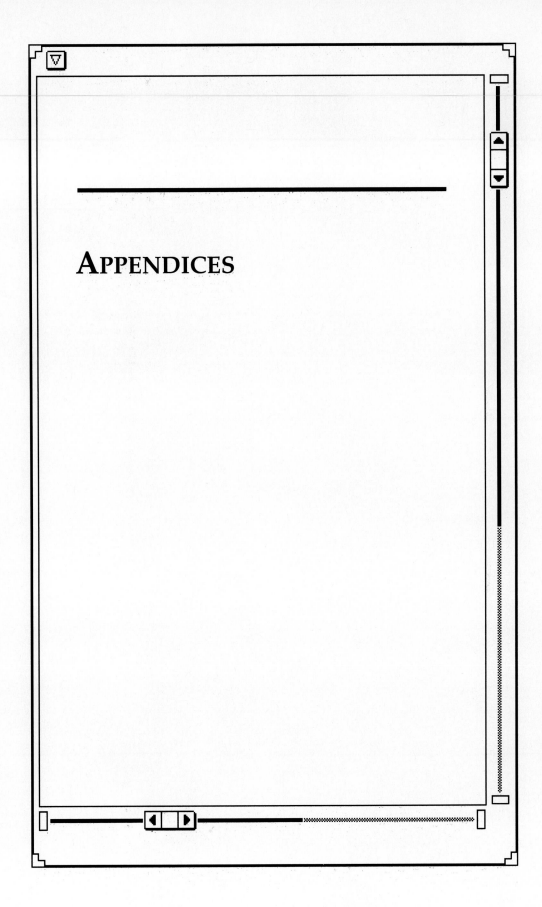

APPENDICES

Appendix A

CERTIFICATION

The right to use the OPEN LOOK trademark is subject to a certification procedure. For detailed information about the certification procedure, see the *OPEN LOOK Graphical User Interface Trademark Guide*, available from AT&T. The address is AT&T OPEN LOOK GUI Trademark Quality Control Manager, 60 Columbia Turnpike, Room 129B-A208, Morristown, NJ 07962, phone (201) 829-8996.

To facilitate implementation, the functionality of the OPEN LOOK User Interface is divided into three levels:

☐ Level 1 is a complete user interface, containing all the essential features. This is the minimum feature set required for a toolkit to be certified as Level 1 compliant.

☐ Level 2 is a superset of Level 1. It is anticipated that this level will be the most common level of compliance. The complete set of Level 2 features must be provided for an implementation to be certified as Level 2 compliant.

☐ Level 3 is a superset of Level 2. This level is provided for more specialized features and to provide a mechanism for extending the functionality of the OPEN LOOK UI.

Alphabetized lists of the main features in each level follow.

Level 1

Basic window types: base, command, property, Help, and Notice windows

Control areas with:

☐ Button controls
☐ Abbreviated menu buttons

☐ Exclusive and nonexclusive settings
☐ Text fields (scrollable)

☐ Basic horizontal sliders
☐ Check boxes

Icons

Menus

☐ Both press-drag-release and stay-up modes
☐ Controls of the same kind: items, exclusive or nonexclusive settings
☐ Optional pushpins

Mouse/keyboard:

☐ Mouse buttons: SELECT, ADJUST, MENU
☐ Mouse modifiers: DUPLICATE, PAN, CONSTRAIN, SETMENUDEFAULT
☐ Core functions: COPY, CUT, HELP, PASTE, PROPERTIES, UNDO
☐ Pop-up accelerators: DEFAULTACTION, CANCEL
☐ Text Field Navigation: NEXTFIELD, PREVFIELD

Pointer jumping (with preference to disable)

Pointers

☐ Basic pointer
☐ Busy pointer
☐ Duplicate pointer

☐ Move pointer
☐ Question mark pointer

☐ Text duplicate pointer
☐ Text move pointer

Scrollbars

☐ Basic scrollbar
☐ Scrollbar without cable
☐ Abbreviated scrollbar

☐ View need not be updated while elevator is dragged

☐ Vertical or horizontal
☐ Scrollbar menus

Scrolling lists

☐ Basic ☐ Support text only

Window management

☐ Windows and icons are selectable
☐ Selected windows/ icons are moved as a group

Window menus (base and pop-up)

Window properties

☐ Initial location
☐ Initial state (icon or window)
☐ Initial size
☐ Record current base window state

Workspace properties

☐ Color
　▫ Workspace
　▫ Windows
　▫ Selection
☐ Icons
　▫ Location
☐ Keyboard core functions
　▫ COPY
　▫ CUT
　▫ HELP
　▫ PASTE
　▫ PROPERTIES
　▫ UNDO

☐ Keyboard miscellaneous functions
　▫ CANCEL
　▫ DEFAULTACTION
　▫ NEXTFIELD
　▫ PREVFIELD
☐ Menus
　▫ Drag-right distance
☐ Miscellaneous
　▫ System beeping
☐ Mouse modifiers
　▫ SELECT
　▫ ADJUST
　▫ MENU

　▫ NONE
　▫ DUPLICATE
　▫ PAN
　▫ CONSTRAIN
　▫ SETMENUDEFAULT
☐ Mouse settings
　▫ Enable/disable scrollbar pointer jumping
　▫ Enable/disable pop-up pointer jumping
☐ Programs submenu
　▫ Editable scrolling list

Level 2

Abbreviated buttons

Basic window types: nonstandard

Blocking pop-up windows

Borderless icon setting for color implementations

Change bars in property windows

Clipboard

☐ Clipboard item on Workspace Utilities menu

☐ Ability to append to the clipboard

Color

Controls

☐ Multi-line text areas
☐ Edit menu for text fields

☐ Numeric text fields with increment/decre-ment buttons

☐ Read-only gauges

File Manager

Menus containing more than one type of control

Mouse/keyboard:

☐ Core functions
  ▫ STOP
☐ Accelerators and modifiers
  ▫ ADJUST
  ▫ CHARBAK
  ▫ CHARFWD
  ▫ DELCHARBAK
  ▫ DELCHARFWD

▫ DELLINEBAK
▫ DELLINE
▫ DELLINEFWD
▫ DELWORDBAK
▫ DELWORDFWD
▫ DOCEND
▫ DOCSTART
▫ LINEEND
▫ LINESTART

▫ MENU
▫ NEXTWINDOW
▫ PAGE
▫ PANEEND
▫ PANESTART
▫ POINTERDOWN
▫ POINTERLEFT
▫ POINTERRIGHT
▫ POINTERUP

- PREVWINDOW
- ROWDOWN
- ROWUP
- SCROLLBOTTOM
- SCROLLDOWN
- SCROLLLEFT
- SCROLLLEFTEDGE

- SCROLLRIGHT
- SCROLLRIGHTEDGE
- SCROLLTOP
- SCROLLUP
- SELECT
- SELCHARFWD
- SELLINEFWD

- SELWORDFWD
- TOGGLEINPUT
- UNSELCHARBAK
- UNSELINEBAK
- WORDFWD
- WORDBAK

Panes

- ☐ Resizable
- ☐ Selectable
- ☐ Splittable

Pointers

- ☐ Panning pointer
- ☐ Target pointer

Scrollbars

- ☐ Minimum scrollbar
- ☐ View must be updated while elevator is dragged
- ☐ Page-oriented option
- ☐ Split View and Join Views items on Scrollbar menu

Scrolling

- ☐ Automatic scrolling
- ☐ Panning

Scrolling lists

- ☐ Glyphs in scrolling lists
- ☐ Hierarchical

Sliders

- ☐ End boxes
- ☐ Tick marks
- ☐ Vertical sliders

Soft function keys

Text

- ☐ Dragging text to move/copy
- ☐ Quick Move and Quick Duplicate on text

Window manager

☐ Constrained move/ resize of windows/ icons

☐ Pop-up control panel for operating on selected windows/icons

Window properties

☐ Base window scale
☐ Pop-up window scale
☐ Manage Windows settings

☐ Record Current State buttons for base window, pop-up window, and menus

Workspace properties

☐ Icons
  ◻ Border
  ◻ Align to grid
  ◻ Grid origin
  ◻ Grid spacing
☐ Keyboard core functions
  ◻ STOP

☐ Menu
  ◻ MENU mouse click
☐ Miscellaneous
  ◻ Scale at startup
  ◻ Set input area
  ◻ SELECT always brings window forward

☐ Workspace menu replaces the Programs Submenu category. A hierarchical scrolling list permits editing of all levels of the Workspace menu.

Level 3

Process Manager

Appendix B

DETAILS OF DESIGN ELEMENTS

This appendix provides the following detailed information about the design elements of the OPEN LOOK UI:

- ☐ Bitmap drawings specified in pixels
  - ▫ Required pointers
  - ▫ Workspace pattern
  - ▫ 75 percent menu drop shadow
  - ▫ Icon borders
- ☐ Detailed engineering drawings for the visual elements of the OPEN LOOK UI specified in points for 10, 12, 14, and 19 point scaling sizes
  - ▫ Window elements, including headers, footers, Window menu buttons, pushpins, and panes
  - ▫ Scrollbars
  - ▫ Controls including buttons, menu buttons, abbreviated menu buttons, text field scrolling buttons, settings, check boxes, sliders, and gauges
  - ▫ Menus
  - ▫ Scrolling lists
  - ▫ Help windows
  - ▫ Notices

The engineering drawings have been optimized for a screen resolution of approximately 72 pixels per inch. However, the visual integrity of the designs can be maintained on other resolution screens when the screen pixels are generally square. These drawings are not to scale. Do not attempt to measure features of the elements if they are not dimensioned.

Use the engineering drawings only for screen resolutions above 120 dots per inch. Where the resolution is less, use bitmap specifications for 10, 12, 14, and 19 point sizes. These bitmaps have refinements and adjustments to optimize the look for lower resolution images. The Bitmap Specifications can be ordered by calling 1-800-821-4643 or 1-800-821-4642 (California).

Pointers

The figures in this section show the bitmaps in pixels for the recommended default pointers.

Basic pointer

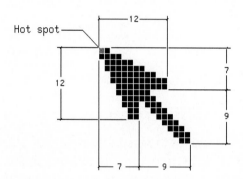

Figure B-1 The basic pointer.

Move pointer

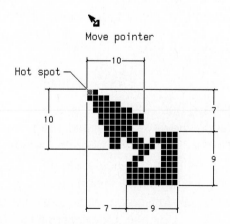

Figure B-2 The move pointer.

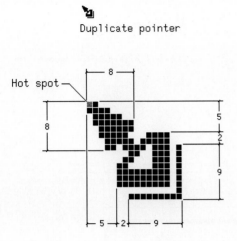

Figure B-3   The duplicate pointer.

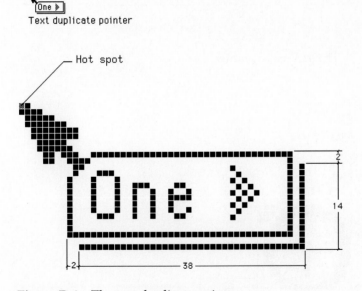

Figure B-3   The duplicate pointer.

Figure B-4   The text duplicate pointer.

Text move pointer

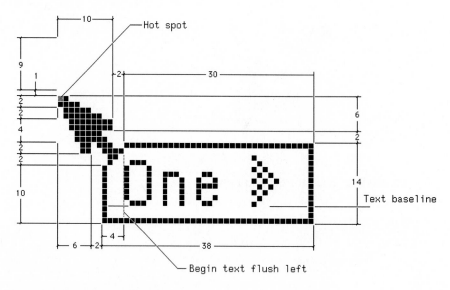

Figure B-5 The text move pointer.

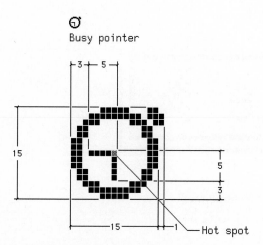
Busy pointer

Figure B-6 The busy pointer.

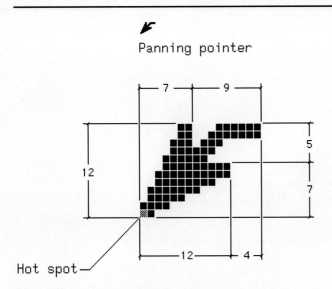

Panning pointer

Figure B-7   The panning pointer.

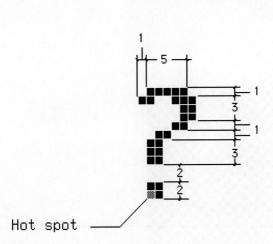

Question mark pointer

Figure B-8   The question mark pointer.

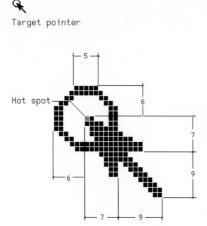

Figure B-9   The target pointer.

Workspace Pattern

Figure B-10 shows the bitmap for the 50 percent workspace pattern.

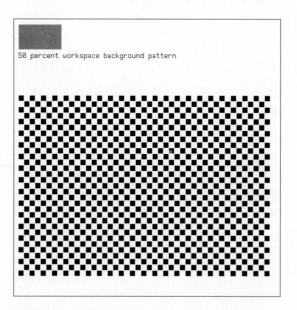

Figure B-10   The 50 percent workspace pattern.

Menu Drop Shadow Pattern

Figure B-11 shows the bitmap for the 75 percent pattern of menu drop shadows.

75 percent pattern for menu shadows

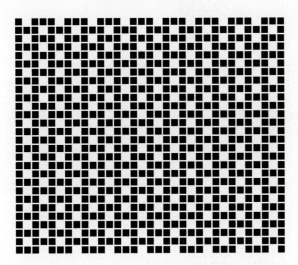

Figure B-11   The 75 percent menu drop shadow.

Icons

The figures in this section show bitmaps in pixels for icons for two different scaling sizes:

☐ 47-point for use on low-resolution systems
☐ 65-point for use on medium- and high-resolution systems

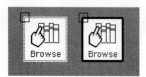

Normal and selected details for 65-point monochrome icons

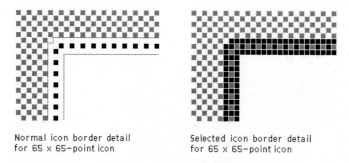

Normal icon border detail
for 65 x 65-point icon

Selected icon border detail
for 65 x 65-point icon

Figure B-12   65-point monochrome icons.

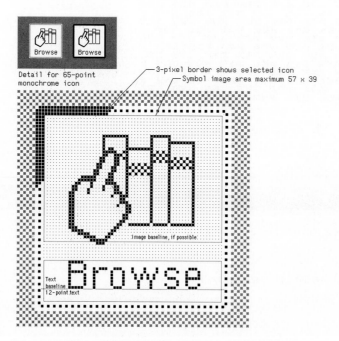

Detail for 65-point
monochrome icon

3-pixel border shows selected icon
Symbol image area maximum 57 x 39

Image baseline, if possible

Text
baseline
12-point text

Figure B-13   65-point monochrome icon detail.

414

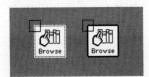

Normal and selected details for 47-point monochrome icons

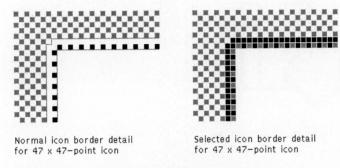

Normal icon border detail
for 47 x 47-point icon

Selected icon border detail
for 47 x 47-point icon

Figure B-14   47-point monochrome icons.

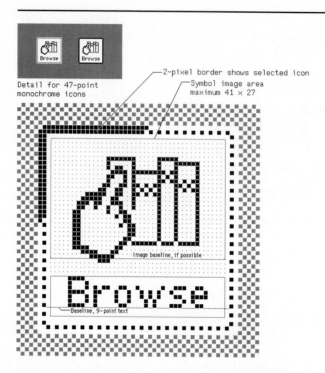

Figure B-15   47-point monochrome icon detail.

Window Elements

The figures and tables in this section are engineering drawings showing details of the following window elements:

☐ Headers
☐ Footers
☐ Window menu buttons
☐ Pushpins
☐ Panes

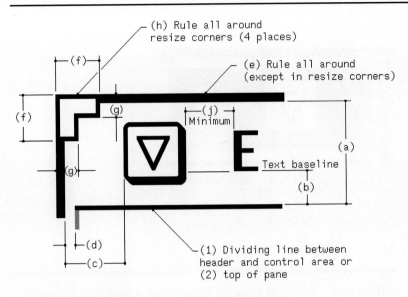

Figure B-16   Header (left side) and resize corners.

Table B-1   Dimensions for header and resize corner (points)

	10 pt	12 pt	14 pt	19 pt
(a)	20	22	26	32
(b)	7	7	8	11
(c)	10	12	14	19
(d)	1.6	2	2.4	3.2
(e)	1.6	2	2.4	3.2
(f)	10	11	12	14
(g)	5	5	6	6
(h)	.8	1	1.2	1.6
(j)	8	9	10	14

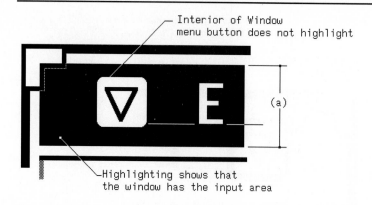

Figure B-17   Header with input area.

Table B-2   Dimensions for header highlighting (points)

	10 pt	12 pt	14 pt	19 pt
(a)	16	18	22	26

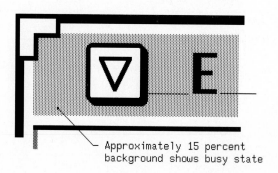

Figure B-18   Headers with busy pattern.

418

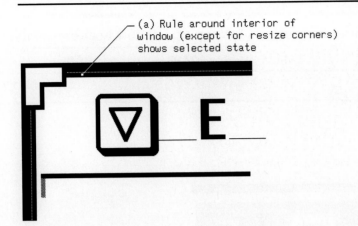

Figure B-19 Headers for selected window.

Table B-3   Dimensions for selected header (points)

	10 pt	12 pt	14 pt	19 pt
(a)	.8	1	1.2	1.6

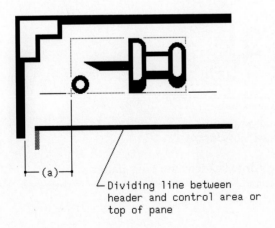

Figure B-20 Pop-up window header with pushpin.

Table B-4   Dimensions for pop-up window header (points)

	10 pt	12 pt	14 pt	19 pt
(b)	10	12	14	19

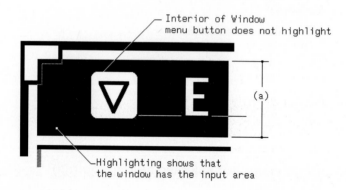

Figure B-21   Pop-up window header with input area.

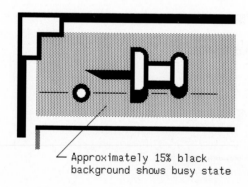

Figure B-22   Pop-up window header with busy pattern.

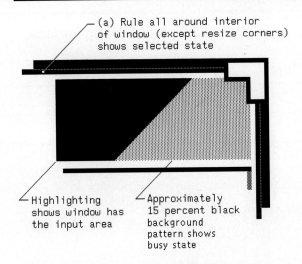

Figure B-23 Header with busy pattern, selection, and highlighting.

Table B-5   Dimensions for selected header (points)

	10 pt	12 pt	14 pt	19 pt
(a)	.8	1	1.2	1.6

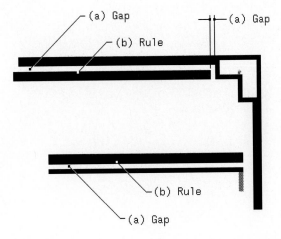

Figure B-24 Header highlighting for Move Pointer option.

Table B-6   Dimensions for header highlighting for Move Pointer option (points)

	10 pt	12 pt	14 pt	19 pt
(a)	.8	1	1.2	1.6
(b)	1.6	2	2.4	3.2

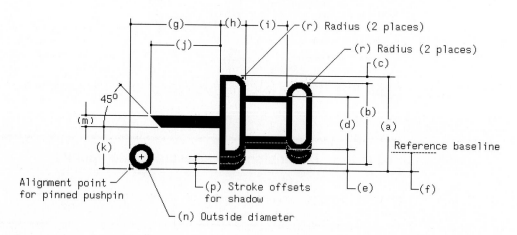

Figure B-25   Unpinned pushpin.

Table B-7   Dimensions for unpinned pushpin (points)

	10 pt	12 pt	14 pt	19 pt
(a)	9.6	12	14.4	19.2
(b)	8	10	12	16
(c)	.8	1	1.2	1.6
(d)	4.8	6	7.2	9.6
(e)	2.4	3	3.6	4.8
(f)	2.4	3	3.6	4.8
(g)	10.4	13	15.6	20.8
(h)	3.2	4	4.8	6.4
(i)	4	5	6	8
(j)	7.2	9	10.8	14.4
(k)	4	5	6	8
(m)	1.6	2	2.4	3.2
(n)	3.2	4	4.8	6.4
(p)	.8	1	1.2	1.6
(r)	1.6	2	2.4	3.2

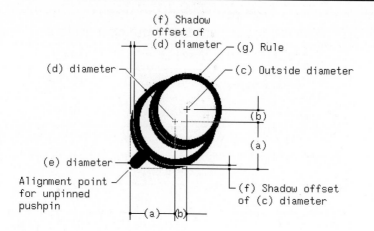

Figure B-26   Pinned pushpin.

Table B-8   **Dimensions for pinned pushpin (points)**

	10 pt	12 pt	14 pt	19 pt
(a)	4.8	6	7.2	9.6
(b)	1.6	2	2.4	3.2
(c)	7.2	9	10.8	14.4
(d)	8.8	11	13.2	17.6
(e)	1.6	2	2.4	3.2
(f)	.4	.5	.6	.8
(g)	.8	1	1.2	1.6

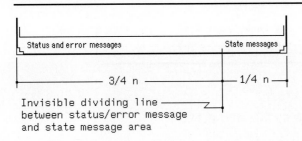

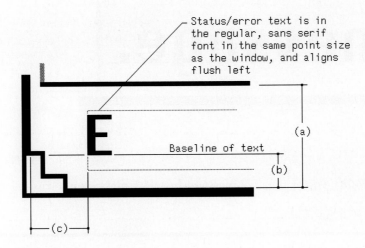

Figure B-27 Footer (left side).

Table B-9 Dimensions for footer (points)

	10 pt	12 pt	14 pt	19 pt
(a)	20	22	24	32
(b)	7	7	8	11
(c)	10	12	14	19

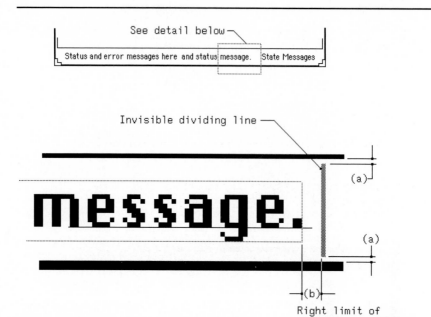

Figure B-28   Footer, detail of message area with message not truncated.

Table B-10   Dimensions for footer with text not truncated (points)

	10 pt	12 pt	14 pt	19 pt
(a)	.8	1	1.2	1.6
(b)	4	4	5	7

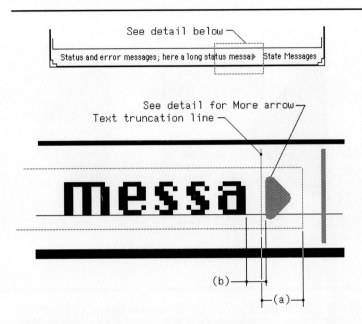

Figure B-29 Footer with More arrow showing truncated status and error message.

Table B-11 Dimensions for footers with truncated text (points)

	10 pt	12 pt	14 pt	19 pt
(a)	9	9	10	13
(b)	4	4	5	7

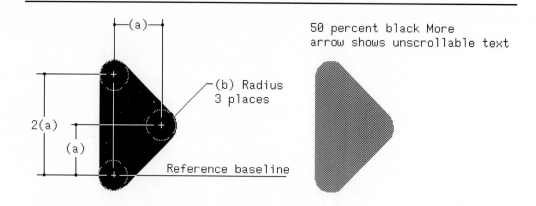

Figure B-30   More arrow.

Table B-12   Dimensions for More arrow detail (points)

	10 pt	12 pt	14 pt	19 pt
(a)	2.4	3	3.6	4.8
(b)	.8	1	1.2	1.6

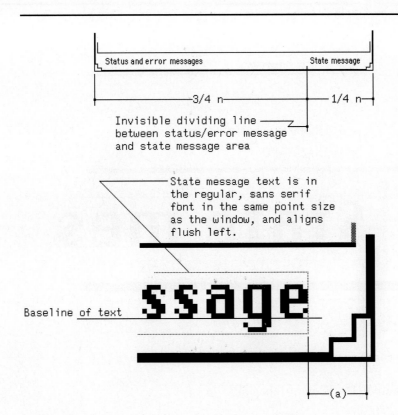

Figure B-31   Footer (right side) state message area.

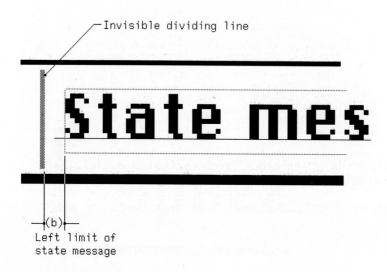

Figure B-32   Footer (right side).

Table B-13   Dimensions for footer state message placement (points)

	10 pt	12 pt	14 pt	19 pt
(a)	4	4	5	7

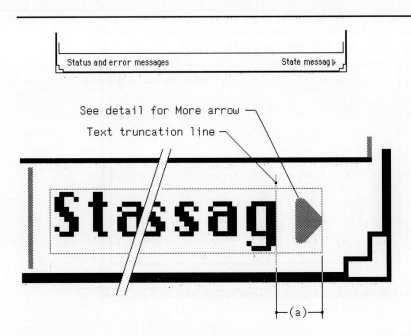

Figure B-33   Footer (right side) with More arrow.

Table B-14   Dimensions for state message More arrow placement (points)

	10 pt	12 pt	14 pt	19 pt
(a)	.8	1	1.2	1.6

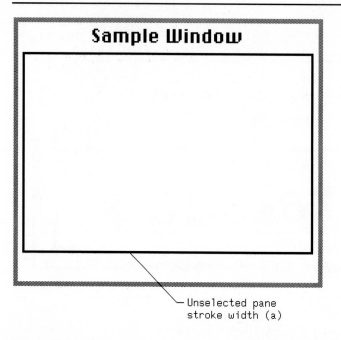

Figure B-34   Pane.

Table B-15   Dimensions for unselected pane borders (points)

	10 pt	12 pt	14 pt	19 pt
(a)	9	9	10	13

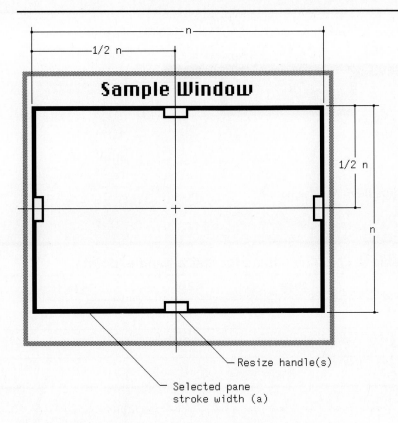

Figure B-35   Selected pane with resize handles.

Table B-16   Dimensions for selected pane border (points)

	10 pt	12 pt	14 pt	19 pt
(a)	1.6	2	2.4	3.2

(n) is the application-specific dimension of the pane.

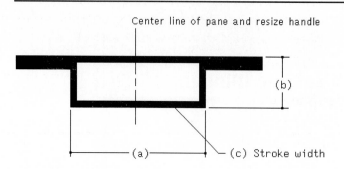

Figure B-36 Resize handle.

Table B-17   Dimensions for resize handle (points)

	10 pt	12 pt	14 pt	19 pt
(a)	13	15	17	22
(b)	5	6	7	9
(c)	.8	1	1.2	1.6

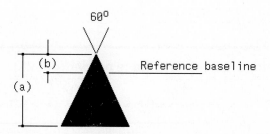

Figure B-37 Active caret.

Table B-18   Dimensions for active caret (points)

	10 pt	12 pt	14 pt	19 pt
(a)	5	6	7	9
(b)	2	2	2	3

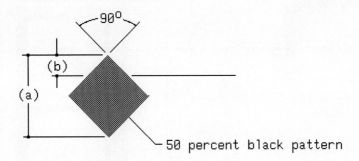

Figure B-38   Inactive caret.

Table B-19   Dimensions for inactive caret (points)

	10 pt	12 pt	14 pt	19 pt
(a)	5	6	7	9
(b)	2	2	2	3

Scrollbars

The figures and tables in this section show details for standard, abbreviated, minimum, and page-oriented scrollbars.

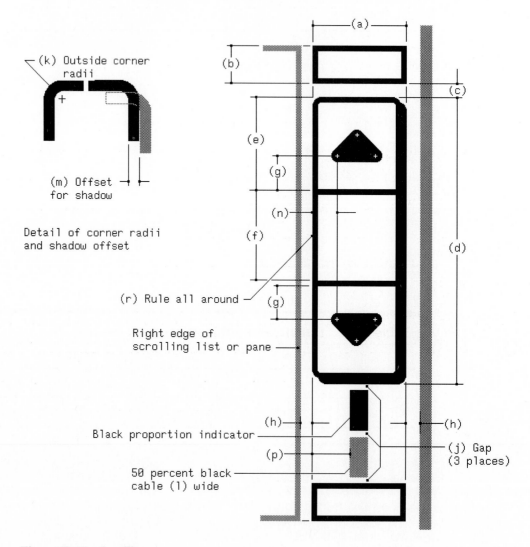

Figure B-39 Scrollbar.

Table B-20 Dimensions for scrollbar (points)

	10 pt	12 pt	14 pt	19 pt
(a)	13	15	17	22
(b)	5	6	7	9
(c)	1.6	2	2.4	3.2
(d)	40.6	47	53.4	69.2
(e)	13	15	17	22
(f)	13	15	17	22
(g)	4.9	5.5	6.1	7.8
(h)	1.6	2	2.4	3.6
(i)	2.4	3	3.6	4.8
(j)	.8	1	1.2	1.6
(k)	1.2	1.5	1.8	2.4
(m)	.8	1	1.2	1.6
(n)	3.7	4	4.3	5.4
(p)	5.3	6	6.7	8.6
(r)	.8	1	1.2	1.6

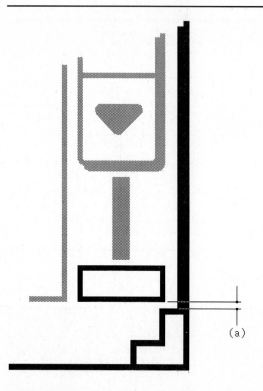

Figure B-40   Spacing for a window with a scrollbar, resize corners, and no footer (lower left corner).

Table B-21   Dimensions for scrollbar and resize corner spacing (points)

	10 pt	12 pt	14 pt	19 pt
(a)	.8	1	1.2	1.6

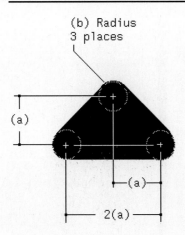

Figure B-41 Scrolling arrow.

Table B-22   Dimensions for scrolling arrow detail (points)

	10 pt	12 pt	14 pt	19 pt
(a)	2.4	3	3.6	4.8
(b)	.8	1	1.2	1.6

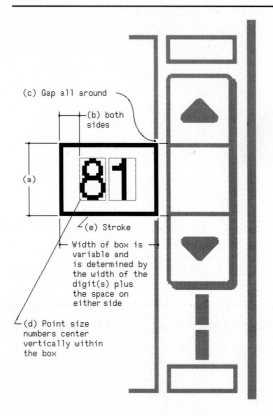

Figure B-42   Page-oriented scrollbar.

Table B-23   Dimensions for page-oriented scrollbar (points)

	10 pt	12 pt	14 pt	19 pt
(a)	13.8	16	18.2	23.6
(b)	5	6	7	9
(c)	.8	1	1.2	1.6
(d)	10	12	14	19
(e)	.8	1	1.2	1.6

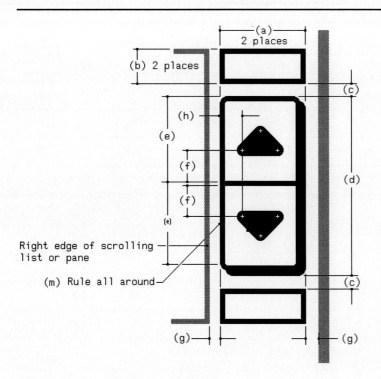

Figure B-43   Abbreviated scrollbar.

Table B-24   Dimensions for abbreviated scrollbar (points)

	10 pt	12 pt	14 pt	19 pt
(a)	13	15	17	22
(b)	5	6	7	9
(c)	1.6	2	2.4	3.2
(d)	27.6	32	36.4	47.2
(e)	13	15	17	22
(f)	4.9	5.5	6.1	7.8
(g)	1.6	2	2.4	3.6
(h)	3.7	4	4.3	5.4
(j)	1.2	1.5	1.8	2.4
(k)	.8	1	1.2	1.6
(m)	.8	1	1.2	1.6

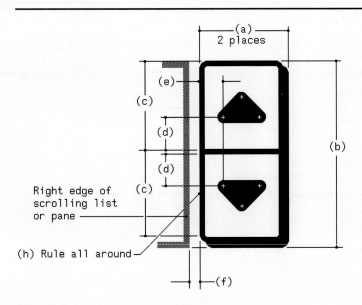

Figure B-44   Minimum scrollbar.

Table B-25   Dimensions for minimum scrollbar (points)

	10 pt	12 pt	14 pt	19 pt
(a)	13	15	17	22
(b)	27.6	32	36.4	47.2
(c)	13	15	17	22
(d)	4.9	5.5	6.1	7.8
(e)	3.7	4	4.3	5.4
(f)	1.6	2	2.4	3.6
(g)	1.2	1.5	1.8	2.4
(h)	.8	1	1.2	1.6
(j)	.8	1	1.2	1.6

Controls

The figures and tables in this section show details of the following OPEN LOOK UI controls:

☐ Buttons
☐ Menu buttons
☐ Abbreviated menu buttons
☐ Text field scrolling buttons
☐ Settings (exclusive and nonexclusive)
☐ Check boxes
☐ Sliders
☐ Gauges

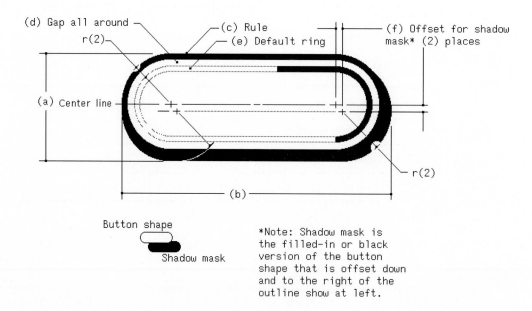

*Note: Shadow mask is the filled-in or black version of the button shape that is offset down and to the right of the outline show at left.

Figure B-45 Command button and default ring.

Table B-26 Dimensions for button (points)

	10 pt	12 pt	14 pt	19 pt
(a)	18	20	22	28
(b)	8n	10n	12n	16n
(c)	.8	1	1.2	1.6
(d)	.8	1	1.2	1.6
(e)	.8	1	1.2	1.6
(f)	.8	1	1.2	1.6

(n) is the application-specified button width.

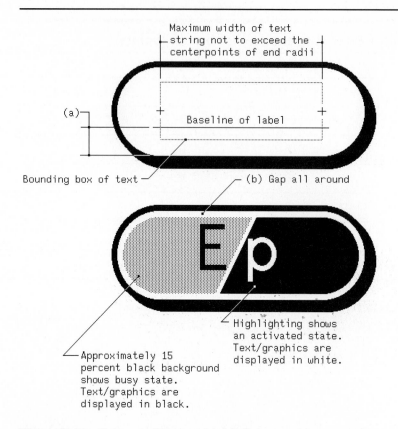

Figure B-46   Command button, highlighting, and busy pattern.

Table B-27   Dimensions for command button (points)

	10 pt	12 pt	14 pt	19 pt
(a)	4	5	5.5	7
(b)	.8	1	1.2	1.6

Note: All text is sans serif, in the regular font, and centered within the bounding box. Text size corresponds to button size (for example, 10 point text in 10 point buttons).

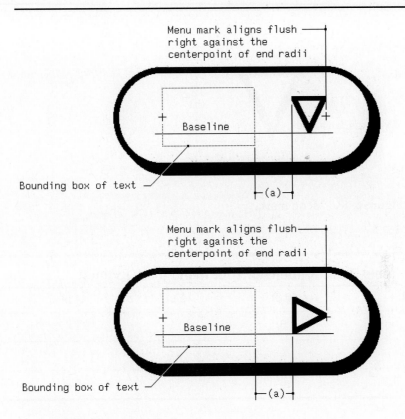

Figure B-47 Menu button.

Table B-28   Dimensions for menu button (points)

	10 pt	12 pt	14 pt	19 pt
(a)	7	8	10	12

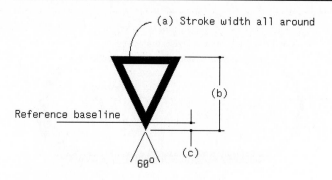

Figure B-48   Menu mark.

Table B-29   Dimensions for menu mark (points)

	10 pt	12 pt	14 pt	19 pt
(a)	.8	1	1.2	1.6
(b)	7	8	9	11
(c)	.8	1	1.2	1.6

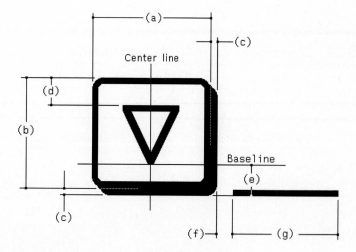

Figure B-49   Abbreviated menu button.

Table B-30   Dimensions for abbreviated menu button (points)

	10 pt	12 pt	14 pt	19 pt
(a)	14	16	18	24
(b)	13	15	17	23
(c)	.8	1	1.2	1.6
(d)	2.8	3.4	4.2	5.9
(e)	3	3	4	5
(f)	2	2	2	3
(g)	8n	10n	12n	16n

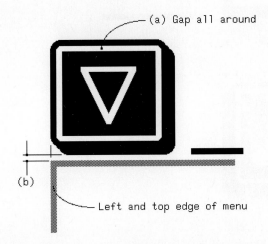

Figure B-50   Highlighted abbreviated menu button and menu position.

Table B-31   Dimensions for abbreviated menu button (points)

	10 pt	12 pt	14 pt	19 pt
(a)	.8	1	1.2	1.6
(b)	.8	1	1.2	1.6

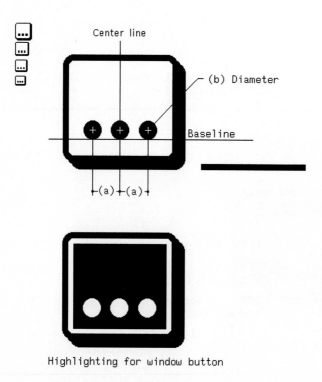

Highlighting for window button

Figure B-51   Abbreviated window button.

Table B-32   Dimensions for abbreviated window button (points)

	10 pt	12 pt	14 pt	19 pt
(a)	3	3.5	4	5
(b)	1.6	2	2.4	3

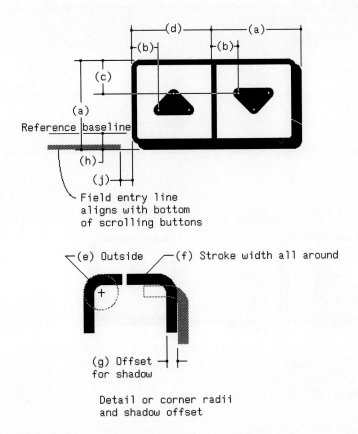

Figure B-52   Increment/decrement buttons for a numeric field.

Table B-33   Dimensions for numeric field scrolling buttons (points)

	10 pt	12 pt	14 pt	19 pt
(a)	13	15	18	25
(b)	3.7	4	4.8	6.9
(c)	4.9	5.5	6.6	9.3
(d)	11.4	13	15.6	21.8
(e)	1.2	1.5	1.8	2.4
(f)	.8	1	1.2	1.6
(g)	.8	1	1.2	1.6
(h)	2.8	3	3.6	4.8
(j)	1.6	2	2.4	3.2

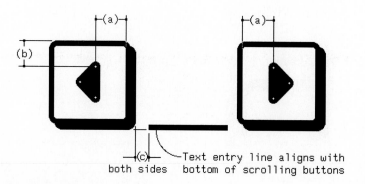

Figure B-53   Text field scrolling buttons.

Table B-34   Dimensions for text field scrolling buttons (points)

	10 pt	12 pt	14 pt	19 pt
(a)	4.9	5.5	6.6	9.3
(b)	3.7	4	4.8	6.9
(c)	1.6	2	2.4	3.2

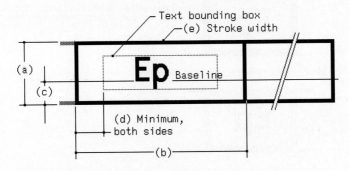

Figure B-54   Exclusive setting.

Table B-35   Dimensions for exclusive setting (points)

	10 pt	12 pt	14 pt	19 pt
(a)	18	20	22	27
(b)	8n	10n	12n	16n
(c)	6	6	7	8
(d)	5	6	8	10
(e)	.8	1	1.2	1.6

(n) is the application-specified length of each setting.

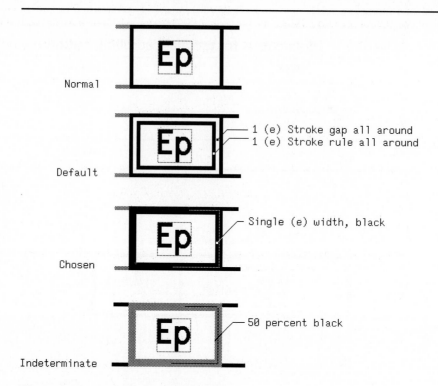

Figure B-55   Exclusive setting states.

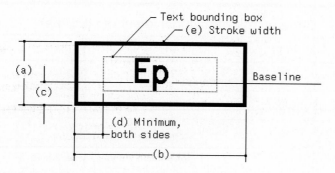

Figure B-56   Nonexclusive setting.

Table B-36 Dimensions for nonexclusive setting (points)

	10 pt	12 pt	14 pt	19 pt
(a)	18	20	22	27
(b)	8n	10n	12n	16n
(c)	6	7	7	8
(d)	5	6	8	10
(e)	.8	1	1.2	1.6

(n) is the application-specified width of each setting.

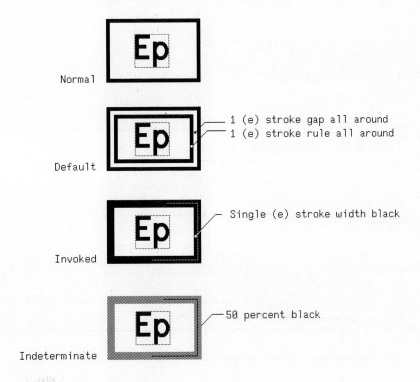

Figure B-57 Nonexclusive setting states.

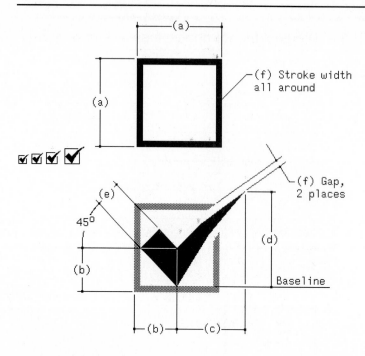

Figure B-58 Check box.

Table B-37 Dimensions for check box (points)

	10 pt	12 pt	14 pt	19 pt
(a)	11	13	15	20
(b)	5.5	6.5	7.5	10
(c)	7	9	11	16
(d)	11	13	16	21
(e)	3	3.6	4.2	5.5
(f)	.8	1	1.2	1.6

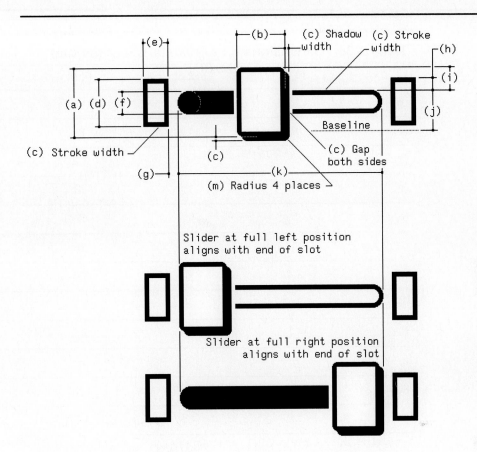

Figure B-59   Horizontal slider.

Table B-38   Dimensions for horizontal slider (points)

	10 pt	12 pt	14 pt	19 pt
(a)	13	15	17	21
(b)	9	10	11	14
(c)	.8	1	1.2	1.6
(d)	9	11	13	17
(e)	5	6	7	9
(f)	4	5	6	8
(g)	2.4	3	3.6	4.8
(h)	2.5	3	3.5	4.5
(i)	4.5	5	5.5	6.5
(j)	6	7	8	10.5
(k)	8n	10n	12n	16n
(m)	1.2	1.5	1.8	2.4

(n) is the application-specified length of the slider.

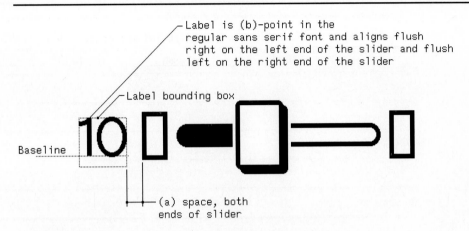

Figure B-60   Horizontal slider with labels and end boxes.

Table B-39   Dimensions for slider with labels and end boxes (points)

	10 pt	12 pt	14 pt	19 pt
(a)	5	6	7	9
(b)	10	12	14	19

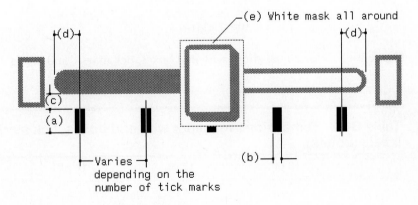

Figure B-61   Horizontal slider with tick marks.

459

Table B-40   Dimensions for horizontal slider with tick marks (points)

	10 pt	12 pt	14 pt	19 pt
(a)	5	6	7	9
(b)	1.6	2	2.4	3.2
(c)	2.4	3	3.6	4.8
(d)	4.5	5	5.5	7
(e)	.8	1	1.2	1.6

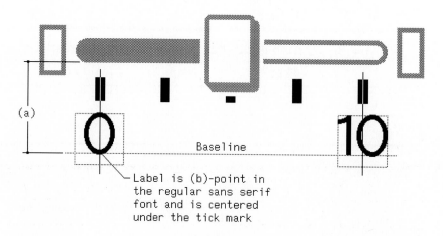

Figure B-62   Horizontal slider with end boxes, tick marks, and labels.

Table B-41   Dimensions for slider with end boxes, tick marks, and labels (points)

	10 pt	12 pt	14 pt	19 pt
(a)	18	21	24	31
(b)	10	12	14	19

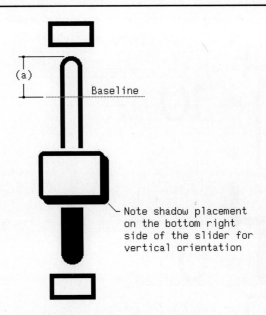

Baseline

(a)

Note shadow placement
on the bottom right
side of the slider for
vertical orientation

Note: All dimensions for vertical sliders are
the same as those for horizontal sliders
except for the location and orientation of the
baseline.

Figure B-63   Vertical slider.

Table B-42   Dimensions for vertical slider (points)

	10 pt	12 pt	14 pt	19 pt
(a)	9	10	11	14

461

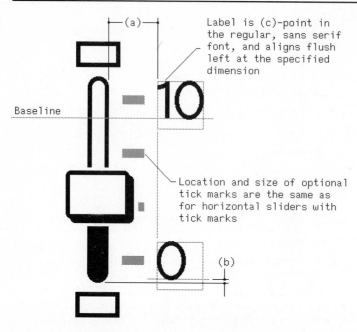

```
                    ┌─(a)─┐        Label is (c)-point in
                                   the regular, sans serif
                                   font, and aligns flush
                                   left at the specified
                                   dimension

Baseline

                                  Location and size of optional
                                  tick marks are the same as
                                  for horizontal sliders with
                                  tick marks

                                            (b)
```

```
Note: All dimensions for vertical sliders
with labels are the same as those for
horizontal sliders, except for the
location and orientation of the labels and
their respective baselines.
```

Figure B-64   Vertical slider with end boxes, tick marks, and labels.

Table B-43   Dimensions for vertical sliders with end boxes, tick marks, and labels (points)

	10 pt	12 pt	14 pt	19 pt
(a)	10	12	14	18
(b)	.8	1	1.2	1.6
(c)	10	12	14	19

462

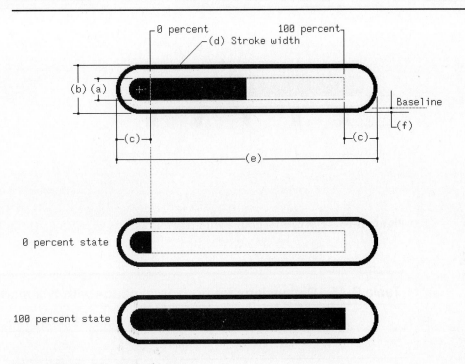

Figure B-65   Horizontal gauge.

Table B-44   Dimensions for horizontal gauge (points)

	10 pt	12 pt	14 pt	19 pt
(a)	4	5	6	8
(b)	10	11	13.2	17.6
(c)	7	8	9.6	12.8
(d)	.8	1	1.2	1.6
(e)	8n	10n	12n	16n
(f)	2	2	2.6	3.8

(n) is the application-specified length of the gauge.

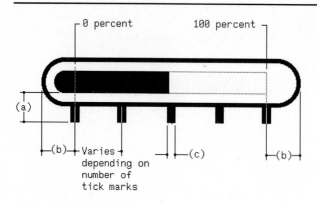

Figure B-66   Horizontal gauge with tick marks.

Table B-45   Dimensions for horizontal gauge with tick marks (points)

	10 pt	12 pt	14 pt	19 pt
(a)	7.4	9	10.6	13.8
(b)	7	8	9.6	12.8
(c)	1.6	2	2.4	3.2

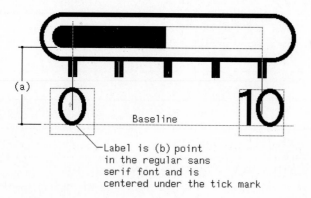

Figure B-67   Horizontal gauge with tick marks and labels.

Table B-46 Dimensions for horizontal gauge with tick marks and labels (points)

	10 pt	12 pt	14 pt	19 pt
(a)	18	21	24	31
(b)	10	12	14	19

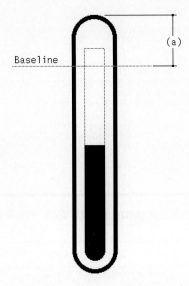

Baseline

(a)

Note: All dimensions for vertical gauges with labels and tick marks are the same as those for horizontal gauges except for the location and orientation of the reference baseline.

Figure B-68   Vertical gauge.

Table B-47 Dimensions for vertical gauge (points)

	10 pt	12 pt	14 pt	19 pt
(a)	11	12.5	14.6	19.3

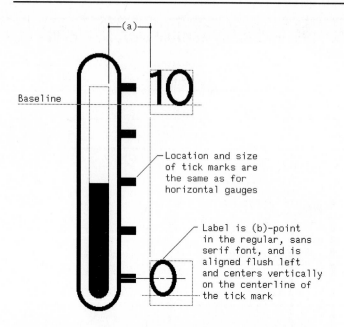

Figure B-69   Vertical gauge with tick marks and labels.

Table B-48   Dimensions for vertical gauge with tick marks and labels (points)

	10 pt	12 pt	14 pt	19 pt
(a)	10	12	14	18
(b)	10	12	14	19

Menus

The figures and tables in this section show details of text items on menus, menu marks, pinned and unpinned menus, submenus, and pop-up menus.

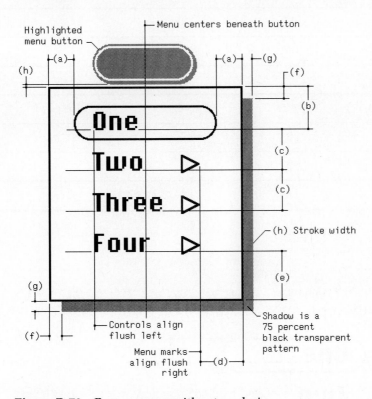

Figure B-70 Button menu without pushpin.

Table B-49 Dimensions for button menu (points)

	10 pt	12 pt	14 pt	19 pt
(a)	8	9	10	14
(b)	17	19	21	25
(c)	17	19	21	25
(d)	17	19	21	29
(e)	12	14	16	20
(f)	6	7	8	10
(g)	5	6	7	9
(h)	.8	1	1.2	1.6

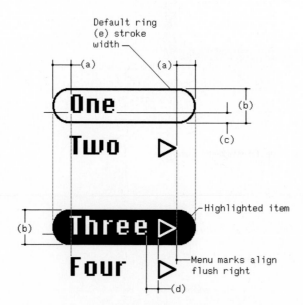

Figure B-71 Menu item with default ring and highlighting.

Table B-50 Dimensions for menu item (points)

	10 pt	12 pt	14 pt	19 pt
(a)	8	9	10	14
(b)	16	18	20	23
(c)	4	5	5.5	7
(d)	8	9	10	14
(e)	.8	1	1.2	1.6

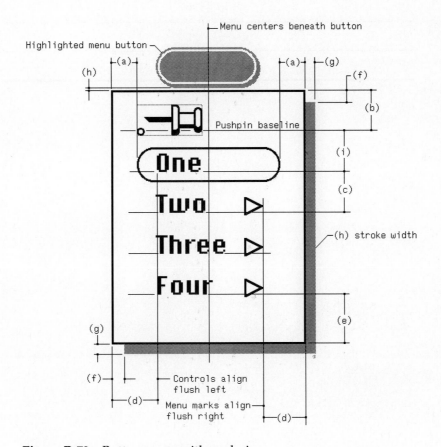

Figure B-72 Button menu with pushpin.

Table B-51   Dimensions for button menu (points)

	10 pt	12 pt	14 pt	19 pt
(a)	8	9	10	14
(b)	14	16	17	22
(c)	17	19	21	25
(d)	17	19	21	29
(e)	12	14	16	20
(f)	6	7	8	10
(g)	5	6	7	9
(h)	.8	1	1.2	1.6
(i)	25	27	32	37

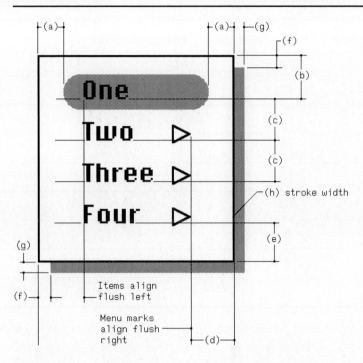

Figure B-73 Submenu.

Table B-52   Dimensions for submenu (points)

	10 pt	12 pt	14 pt	19 pt
(a)	8	9	10	14
(b)	17	19	21	25
(c)	17	19	21	25
(d)	17	19	21	29
(e)	12	14	16	20
(f)	6	7	8	10
(g)	5	6	7	9
(h)	.8	1	1.2	1.6

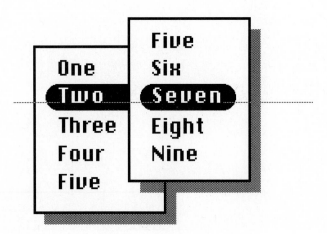

Figure B-74   Submenu horizontal alignment.

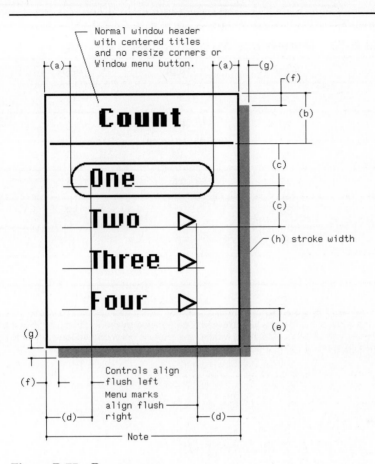

Figure B-75   Pop-up menu.

Table B-53   Dimensions for pop-up menu (points)

	10 pt	12 pt	14 pt	19 pt
(a)	8	9	10	14
(b)	22	24	30	34
(c)	17	19	21	25
(d)	17	19	21	29
(e)	12	14	16	20
(f)	6	7	8	10
(g)	5	6	7	9
(h)	.8	1	1.2	1.6

Note: The width of the menu is variable and is determined by the width of the longest label plus the specified space on either side. If the width of the menu is not wide enough to display the entire menu title, then the menu is made wide enough to accommodate the width of the title.

Scrolling Lists

The figures and tables in this section show details of basic, editable, and multi-level scrolling lists.

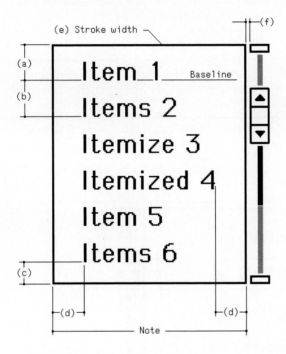

Figure B-76   Basic scrolling list.

Table B-54   Dimensions for basic scrolling lists (points)

	10 pt	12 pt	14 pt	19 pt
(a)	17	19	21	25
(b)	17	19	21	25
(c)	12	14	16	20
(d)	16	18	20	25
(e)	.8	1	1.2	1.6

Note: Width of scrolling list is determined by the longest item in the scrolling list plus 2(d).

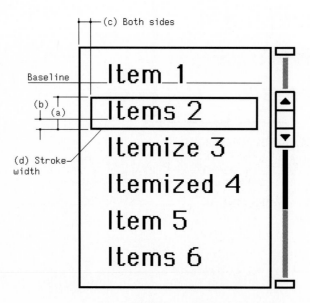

Figure B-77   Basic scrolling list with current item.

Table B-55   Dimensions for scrolling list with a current item (points)

	10 pt	12 pt	14 pt	19 pt
(a)	17	19	21	25
(b)	17	19	21	25
(c)	12	14	16	20
(d)	.8	1	1.2	1.6

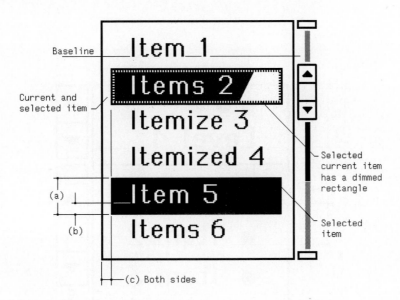

Figure B-78   Selectable scrolling list with highlighting.

Table B-56 Dimensions for selectable scrolling list (points)

	10 pt	12 pt	14 pt	19 pt
(a)	16	18	20	23
(b)	5	5	5.5	7
(c)	8	9	10	14

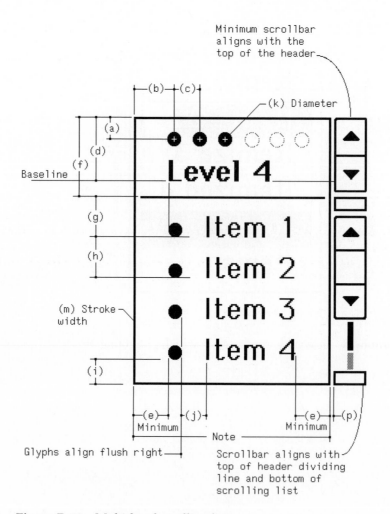

Figure B-79 Multi-level scrolling list.

Table B-57   Dimensions for multi-level scrolling list (points)

	10 pt	12 pt	14 pt	19 pt
(a)	8	9	11	13
(b)	17	19.5	22	28
(c)	8	10	12	16
(d)	23	27	31	39
(e)	16	18	20	25
(f)	30	34	39	50
(g)	17	19	21	25
(h)	17	19	21	25
(i)	11	13	15	20
(j)	8	9	10	12
(k)	4	5	6	8
(m)	.8	1	1.2	1.6
(p)	1.6	2	2.4	3.6

Note: Width of scrolling list is determined by the longest item in the scrolling list plus (j), 2(e) and width of the default glyph.

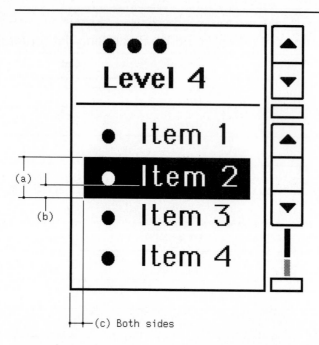

Figure B-80   Multi-level scrolling list with selection highlighted.

Table B-58   Dimensions for multi-level scrolling list (points)

	10 pt	12 pt	14 pt	19 pt
(a)	16	18	20	25
(b)	4.8	5	6.2	7.6
(c)	4.2	4	4.8	5.4

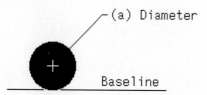

Figure B-81   Multi-level scrolling list default glyph

480

Table B-59   Dimensions for multi-level scrolling list default glyph (points)

	10 pt	12 pt	14 pt	19 pt
(a)	4	5	6	8

Help Windows

The figures and tables in this section show details of elements for Help windows.

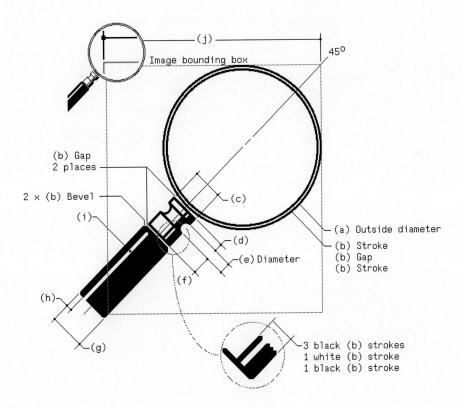

Figure B-82   Help window magnifying glass.

Table B-60   Dimensions for Help window magnifying glass (points)

	10 pt	12 pt	14 pt	19 pt
(a)	66	80	94	126
(b)	.8	1	1.2	1.6
(c)	12	14	16	22
(d)	5	6	7	9
(e)	6	8	10	13
(f)	8	10	12	16
(g)	14	16	18	25
(h)	2.4	3	3.6	4.8
(i)	2	2.4	2.8	4
(j)	94	112	130	176

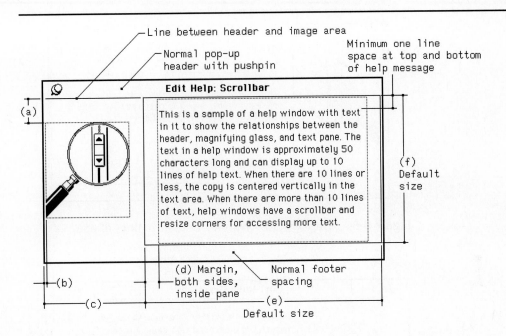

Figure B-83   Help window.

Table B-61   Dimensions for default Help window (points)

	10 pt	12 pt	14 pt	19 pt
(a)	24	30	36	48
(b)	1.6	2	2.4	3.6
(c)	110	132	154	208
(d)	16	20	24	32
(e)	332	390	448	596
(f)	142	170	198	254

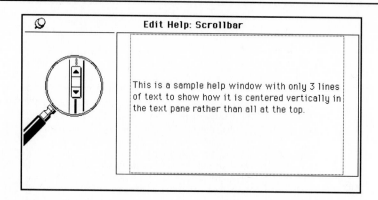

Figure B-84   Help window with fewer than 10 lines of text.

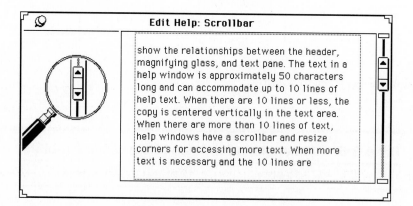

Figure B-85   Help window with scrollbar and resize corners.

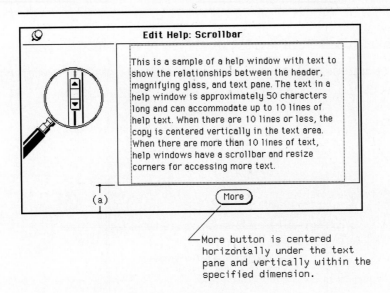

Figure B-86   Help window with More button.

Table B-62   Dimensions for Help window with More button (points)

	10 pt	12 pt	14 pt	19 pt
(a)	32	36	40	48

Notices

The figures and tables in this section show details of design elements for Notices.

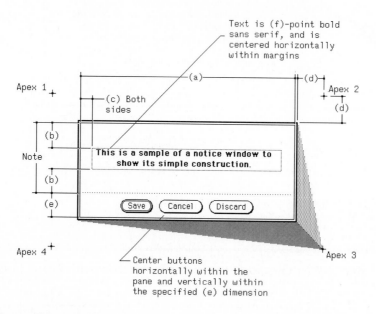

Figure B-87   Notice.

Table B-63   Dimensions for Notice (points)

	10 pt	12 pt	14 pt	19 pt
(a)	332	390	448	596
(b)	30	36	42	54
(c)	16	20	24	32
(d)	36	42	50	64
(e)	32	36	40	48
(f)	10	12	14	19

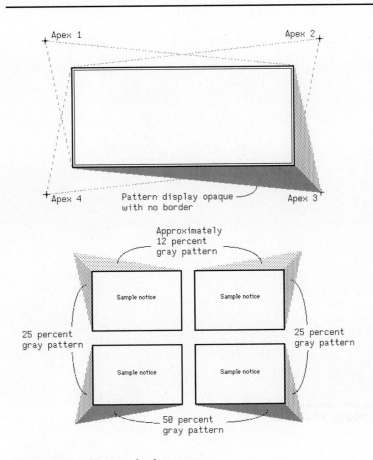

Figure B-88   Notice shadow patterns.

Appendix C

OPEN LOOK UI HELP TEXT

This appendix contains help text for the basic required visual elements and menus of the OPEN LOOK User Interface.

The first-level heads in this appendix correspond to titles displayed in the header of the Help window of the OPEN LOOK UI implementation. The object under the pointer is displayed in the magnifying glass, and the help text for that object is displayed in the pane of the Help window.

The help text of the OPEN LOOK UI is organized by logical groupings, from the general to the specific. For example, when the pointer is on the workspace and you press the HELP key, the OPEN LOOK UI implementation provides a general description of how to use the mouse and access windows from the workspace. When the pointer is on the background of a menu, you see a description of the general functions for a menu and how to choose from it. When the pointer is on an item, you see a description of what that control does and information about how to use it.

It is recommended that implementations follow the paragraph formatting presented here so that users can easily distinguish between explanatory material and detailed instructions. It is also recommended that application help text follow these guidelines.

Workspace

The workspace is the whole screen. Windows and icons are displayed on the workspace. Windows are application work areas. Icons are windows that are displayed in a compressed form to keep them readily available but out of the way.

Using the Mouse

You use the mouse pointer to control windows and icons and to choose activities from menus. You use the pointer by moving it with the mouse to a specific place on the screen and then pressing or clicking a mouse button to perform an action. You can perform the following actions with the mouse:

☐ *Press* a mouse button down and hold it.
☐ *Release* a mouse button to initiate the action.
☐ *Click* a mouse button by pressing and releasing it without moving the pointer.
☐ *Double-click* a mouse button by clicking twice within a short time period.
☐ *Move* the pointer by sliding the mouse with no buttons pressed.
☐ *Drag* the pointer by sliding the mouse with one or more buttons pressed.

To maintain consistency, each mouse button is assigned a specific function. The three basic mouse functions are:

☐ SELECT to select objects or manipulate controls
☐ ADJUST to add or take away from a group of selected objects
☐ MENU to display and choose from menus

Starting Applications

You start applications by moving the pointer anywhere on the background of the workspace and pressing MENU to display the Workspace menu. Drag the pointer to the right in the Programs item to display a submenu with a list of applications. Drag the pointer to an item in the submenu, and release MENU to start the application and dismiss the menu group.

Using Menus

Each region on the workspace, the window background, or in an application pane that is not a control has a pop-up menu associated with it. Each menu button has a button menu associated with it. Menus contain items or settings. You can view and choose from any OPEN LOOK UI menu in two ways using the MENU mouse button:

☐ Press-drag-release
☐ Click-move-click

490

To use press-drag release, press MENU. The menu appropriate for the pointer location is displayed. When the pointer is not on a control in the menu, the default ring is displayed. When you drag the pointer onto a control, it highlights. When you drag the pointer from control to control, the highlighting follows the pointer. When the pointer is on the control you want, release MENU. The control is activated and the menu is dismissed.

When an item has a menu mark (an open triangle), that item has a submenu with additional items. Releasing MENU when an item with a menu mark is highlighted activates the default from the submenu. To display a submenu for an item that has a menu mark, drag the pointer to the right. Drag the pointer to the left to dismiss the submenu while leaving the originating menu displayed.

If you do not want to choose an item from a menu or submenu, move the pointer off the menu and release the MENU mouse button.

To use click-move-click, click MENU. The menu appropriate for the pointer location is displayed and stays on the screen. You do not need to keep pressing the MENU button. Move the pointer to the control you want to choose. Click SELECT or MENU to activate the control. The control is executed and the menu is dismissed. If you do not want to choose a control, move the pointer off the menu and click SELECT or MENU to dismiss the menu. Clicking SELECT on an item that has a menu mark executes the default from the submenu. Clicking MENU on an item that has a menu mark displays the submenu.

Selecting and Moving Windows and Icons

You can move windows and icons on the workspace individually or in groups by selecting and then dragging them. You select a window by moving the pointer to the top or bottom of a window and clicking SELECT. You select an icon by moving the pointer onto the icon and clicking SELECT. To move a window or icon, press SELECT and drag the pointer. Depending on the implementation, a bounding box is displayed showing the outline of the window or icon. When the bounding box is at the place where you want to move the window or icon, release SELECT.

Moving groups of windows and icons works in the same way once they are selected. To select more than one window or icon, click SELECT to select the first window or icon, and then click ADJUST to select additional windows or icons. Clicking ADJUST on any selected window or icon deselects it, without affecting the other selected objects.

Window Basics

This section provides help text for the basic OPEN LOOK UI window elements: Window menu button, window and pane borders, resize corners, scrollbar elements, and resize handles.

Window Menu Buttons

Use the Window menu button to activate the default item from the Window menu without displaying the menu. For example, when Close is the default item on the Window menu, moving the pointer to the Window menu button and clicking SELECT closes the window to an icon.

Window Borders

The window border thickens to show that you have selected the window. Select a window for the following reasons:

☐ To set the input area to that window, a process that activates an inactive caret and brings the window to the front of the screen
☐ To move it by dragging with SELECT

To select a window, move the pointer onto the window background (header, footer, or border edge without a scrollbar) and click SELECT.

Select groups of windows or icons when you want to do the same operation on all of them, such as moving by dragging or quitting all selected items. To select additional windows or icons, or toggle the state of the window or icon, move the pointer onto the window background and click ADJUST.

To operate on groups of selected windows and icons, choose Window Commands from the Workspace Utilities submenu. When the Window Commands pop-up window is displayed, select the windows and icons you want to operate on and then click SELECT on the appropriate button in the Window Commands pop-up.

Pane Borders

When you can perform an operation on a pane such as setting properties, resizing, or deleting, you select the pane by moving the pointer onto the border of the pane. When the pane can be selected, the target pointer is displayed. Click SELECT. The border thickens to show that it is selected.

When a pane can be resized, resize handles are displayed on the sides of the pane that can be adjusted.

To delete a selected pane, move the pointer to one of the cable anchors, press SELECT, and drag the cable anchor until it overlaps the other cable anchor for that pane. Release SELECT to delete the pane.

Resize Handles

Resize handles are displayed only when a pane is selected. To select a pane, move the pointer to the border of the pane until the target pointer is displayed and click SELECT. A resize handle is displayed on the side or sides of a pane that can be adjusted.

Move the pointer to the resize handle, press SELECT, and drag the pointer to adjust the area of the selected and the adjacent panes. The resize handle highlights, and a bounding line is displayed to show you where the new pane border will be. Release SELECT to resize the panes.

More Arrow

When you resize a window so that it is too small to display all the text in the header or footer, a nonscrollable arrow is displayed at the end of the text that is truncated to show you that there is more text. If you want to view all the text, use the resize corners to increase the size of the window.

Resize Corners

Use the resize corners to expand or contract the area of a window. Move the pointer to any resize corner, press SELECT, and drag the pointer. The resize corner highlights and a bounding box is displayed to show you the location of the new window border. Release SELECT. The window is redisplayed in the new size, and the contents adjust to fit within the borders of the window.

If you want to constrain the move to horizontal or vertical, press the CONSTRAIN modifier and SELECT. The movement is constrained to the direction in which you first drag the resize corner.

Scrollbars

This section provides help text for the scrollbar elements.

Cable Anchors

Use the cable anchors to move quickly to the beginning or end of the data by moving the pointer to the cable anchor and clicking SELECT.

When a pane can be split into multiple views, you do this by moving the pointer to one of the cable anchors of that pane. Press SELECT and drag the cable anchor. The cable anchor highlights, and a bounding line is displayed to show you where the pane will split. Release SELECT to split the pane. You have created two separate views into the same pane.

To resize a split pane, move the pointer onto the pane border and click SELECT. A resize handle is displayed on the side or sides of a pane that can be resized. Move the pointer to the resize handle, press SELECT, and drag the pointer to adjust the sizes of the adjacent panes. The resize handle highlights, and a bounding line is displayed to show you where the new pane border will be. Release SELECT to resize the panes.

To delete a split pane, move the pointer to one of the cable anchors for the pane, press SELECT, and drag the cable anchor until it overlaps the other cable anchor for that pane. Release SELECT to delete the pane. The split pane is removed and the remaining panes readjust to fill the available space.

You can also create or remove splits from the Scrollbar menu. Move the pointer to any part of the scrollbar and press or click MENU to display the scrollbar menu.

Arrow Buttons

Use the arrow buttons on the scrollbar elevator to change the view on the data that is displayed in the pane. When an arrow in the arrow button is dimmed, the elevator is at the beginning or the end of the data. Move the pointer to an arrow button and click SELECT to scroll the contents of the pane one unit at a time. Press SELECT to repeatedly scroll the contents of the pane.

Move the pointer to any part of the scrollbar and press or click MENU to display the scrollbar menu.

Drag Area

Use the drag area of the scrollbar elevator to move to an arbitrary location in the data. Move the pointer to the drag area and press SELECT. The drag area highlights. Drag the pointer to move the view in the pane forward or backward in the application data. The pointer can be moved anywhere, but remains constrained to the drag area until you release SELECT.

Move the pointer to any part of the scrollbar and press or click MENU to display the scrollbar menu.

Cable

The length of the scrollbar cable represents the total size of the data from the application that can be viewed incrementally in the pane. The position of the elevator on the cable shows the location of the pane contents in the total data. Move the pointer to the cable above the elevator and click SELECT to move backward in the data one pane. Move the pointer to the cable below the elevator and click SELECT to move forward in the data one pane.

The dark area of the scrollbar cable shows the portion of the total application data that is visible in the pane. If the cable is mostly dark, most of the file is visible. If the dark area of the cable is small, the file is large relative to the size of the pane. The proportion indicator does not affect scrolling operations when you click SELECT on the cable to move the view on the data forward or backward one pane.

Move the pointer to any part of the scrollbar and press or click MENU to display the scrollbar menu.

Menu Background

You can view and choose from any menu in three ways using the MENU mouse button:

☐ Press-drag-release
☐ Click-move-click
☐ Pin the menu

Using Press-Drag-Release

To use press-drag-release, press MENU, drag the pointer to the control you want, and release MENU. If you do not want to choose an item, move the pointer off the menu and release the mouse button.

Using Click-Move-Click

To use click-move-click, click MENU. The menu is displayed and stays on the screen. Move the pointer to the control you want and click SELECT or MENU. The control is executed and the menu is dismissed. If you do not want to choose a control, move the pointer off the menu and click SELECT or MENU to dismiss the menu.

Using the Pushpin

To pin up any menu that has a pushpin, press MENU, and drag the pointer to the pushpin. When the pin pops into the hole, release MENU. The menu becomes a pop-up window, and you choose from it in the same way that you use controls in the control area of a window: Click SELECT to choose a control. The pinned menu remains on the screen until you dismiss it. To dismiss a pinned menu, move the pointer to the pushpin and click SELECT.

Changing the Default Setting

Each menu in a menu group has a default setting. The menu default is displayed when the pointer is off the menu and when you press the DEFAULT modifier key. You can change the default setting for any menu using the steps below:

1 Press MENU to display the menu. To change the default for a submenu, drag the pointer into the submenu.
2 Press the DEFAULT modifier key.
3 Drag the pointer from control to control. The default ring follows the pointer.
4 When the default ring is on the control you want to use as the default, release MENU and then release the modifier key.

You can press and release the DEFAULT modifier key at any time, either before or after you press MENU. If you release the DEFAULT modifier key first and then release MENU, in addition to setting the default, the command is executed.

Pop-Up Windows

This section provides help text for the pushpin, and for common elements of Help and property windows.

Pushpin

Use the pushpin to pin up a pop-up window for continued access. Move the pointer to an unpinned pushpin and click SELECT to push the pin in the hole. Click SELECT on a pinned pushpin to pop it out of the hole and dismiss the pop-up window.

When the pop-up window is displayed in an unpinned state, the pop-up window is automatically dismissed the next time you click SELECT on an action button in that window. If you want to dismiss the window without issuing a command, click SELECT on the pushpin to pin the window, and then click SELECT to dismiss the window.

Help Window

The Help window for each application displays help for the object under the pointer. To see more help text for the same application without dismissing the Help window, move the pointer to another object in the same application and press the HELP key again. The view in the magnifying glass changes, and appropriate help text is displayed in the pane of the same Help window.

If you move the pointer to a different application window and press the HELP key without dismissing the original Help window, a second Help window is displayed.

You dismiss a Help window by moving the pointer to the pushpin and clicking SELECT. Alternatively, you can move the pointer to the header of the Help window, press MENU, move the pointer onto the Dismiss item, and release MENU.

Magnifying Glass

The view in the magnifying glass shows the object at the pointer position when you pressed the HELP key. To change the view in the magnifying glass and display help text in the pane for the new object, move the pointer to another object in the same application and press the HELP key again.

Property Windows Settings

This section provides help text for the following elements of property windows:

☐ Apply, Reset, and Set Defaults buttons
☐ Settings menu items

Apply Buttons

Use the Apply button to apply properties that you have changed to the selection.

Move the pointer to the Apply button and click SELECT. If the pushpin is out, the changes are applied and the property window is dismissed. If the pushpin is in, the changes are applied and the property window remains displayed until you dismiss it.

When the original selection is dimmed, you can still apply changes to it in the usual way with the Apply button.

New Selection Item

Use the New Selection item on the Apply menu to apply properties that you have changed to the highlighted selection without changing the original selection.

Drag the pointer to the New Selection item and release MENU. The changes are applied and the property window remains displayed until you dismiss it or click SELECT on the Apply button.

Original Selection Item

Use the Original Selection item on the Apply menu to apply properties that you have changed to the original selection.

Drag the pointer to the Original Selection item and release MENU. The changes are applied and the property window remains displayed until you dismiss it or click SELECT on the Apply button.

Reset Button

Use the Reset button to change the settings in the property window so that they reflect the settings for the original selection.

Move the pointer to the Reset button and click SELECT. The property window remains displayed until you dismiss it or click SELECT on the Apply button.

Set Default Button

Use the Set Default button to record the settings in the property window so that they are the default.

Change the settings in the property window to those you want to use as the default. Then move the pointer to the Set Default button and click SELECT. The property window remains displayed until you dismiss it or click SELECT on the Apply button.

Apply Item

Use the Apply item to apply changes made in property window settings to the original selection.

Drag MENU onto the Apply item then release MENU to apply the changes to the original selection. When the property window is not pinned, it is dismissed after the changes are applied.

Apply to New Selection Item

Use the Apply to New Selection item to apply changes made in property window settings to a new selection. When there is not a new selection, the item is not available.

Drag MENU onto the Apply to New Selection item, and then release MENU to apply the changes to the new selection. The property window remains displayed until you dismiss it or click SELECT on the Apply button.

Reset Item

Use the Reset item to reset the property window settings to reflect the values for the original selection.

Drag MENU onto the Reset item, and then release MENU to reset the values to reflect the current setting for the original selection. The property window remains displayed until you dismiss it or click SELECT on the Apply button.

Set Default

Use the Set Default item to change the default settings for the property window to the current settings. First change the settings in the property window to reflect the values you want to use as the defaults.

Then display the Settings menu, drag the pointer onto the Set Default item, and release MENU to set the defaults. The property window remains displayed until you dismiss it or click SELECT on the Apply button.

Icon

An icon is a window that has been closed. To open an icon, move the pointer onto the icon and double-click SELECT, or press or click MENU to display the Window menu and choose Open.

To move an icon, move the pointer onto the icon, press SELECT, drag the pointer to a new location, and release SELECT.

Clicking ADJUST toggles the state of the icon between being selected and not selected.

Active Caret

The active caret shows the place in the window where characters that you type are displayed. To set an active caret in a text area, move the pointer to the place at which you want to type characters and click SELECT or ADJUST.

The header of a window that has the active input area is highlighted.

Inactive Caret

The inactive caret shows the place in the window that had the last active input area. To activate an inactive caret, click SELECT on the window background. To set a new active caret, move the pointer to the place at which you want to type characters and click SELECT or ADJUST.

Workspace Menu

Use the Menu Background help text when the pointer is on the background of the Workspace menu. The following sections provide help text for each item on the Workspace menu.

Programs

The Programs item has a menu mark. The Programs submenu has a list of programs that you can run on the workspace. You can choose the default setting from the submenu without displaying it by moving the pointer onto the Programs item and releasing MENU. To display the Programs submenu, drag the pointer to the right. To choose an item from the Programs submenu, drag the pointer onto an item and release MENU.

You can edit the Programs submenu from the Workspace Properties window to add new programs or remove old ones from the menu.

Utilities

The Utilities submenu has items representing utilities that you can use on the workspace.

Drag MENU onto the Utilities menu item and release MENU to choose the default from the Utilities submenu. To display the Utilities submenu, drag MENU to the right of the Utilities item. To choose an item from the Utilities submenu, drag the pointer onto an item on the submenu, and then release MENU.

Refresh

Use the Refresh item to redisplay all the objects on the workspace.

Drag the pointer onto the item, and then release MENU to refresh the workspace.

Clipboard

The clipboard is for cut/copy/paste operations. Use the Clipboard item to display the contents of the clipboard.

Drag MENU onto the item and release MENU to display the clipboard window.

Window Controls

Window Controls are for operating on groups of selected windows and/or icons. Use the Window Controls item to display the Window Controls pop-up window.

Drag MENU onto the item and release MENU to display the Window Controls pop-up window.

Properties

Use the Properties item to display the Workspace Properties window. Use the Workspace Properties window to set global workspace properties. The Categories menu of the Properties window offers the following choices:

☐ Color
☐ Icons
☐ Keyboard Core Functions
☐ Keyboard Miscellaneous Functions
☐ Menus
☐ Miscellaneous
☐ Mouse Modifiers
☐ Mouse Settings
☐ Programs Submenu

To display the Workspace Properties window, drag MENU onto the Properties item, and release MENU.

Exit

Use the Exit item to quit all applications on the workspace, leave the workspace, and return to your system prompt.

Drag MENU onto the item and release MENU to exit the workspace.

Window Menu

Use the Menu Background help text when the pointer is on the background of the Window menu. The following sections provide help text for each item of the Window menu.

Open

Use the Open item to open the icon at the pointer location. When an application is started up as an icon, the first time you open it the application base window is displayed in a location specified by the application. Subsequently, each time you open an icon, it is displayed in the same location and state that it had when you closed it to an icon.

You can open an icon without displaying the Window menu by moving the pointer onto an icon and double-clicking SELECT.

Close

Use the Close item to change the visual representation of the base window at the pointer location to an icon. When an application base window is closed, its associated pop-up windows are also closed whether or not the pop-up windows are selected.

Drag MENU onto the item and release MENU to close the window.

Full Size

Use the Full Size item to expand the dimensions of the window or icon at the pointer location to a larger format (specified by the application). An icon is opened and displayed in the full-size format when you choose Full Size from the icon Window menu.

Drag MENU onto the item and release MENU to increase the size of the window or icon at the pointer location.

You can use the Full Size command without displaying the Window menu by moving the pointer onto the window background and double-clicking SELECT.

Restore Size

Use the Restore Size item to return the dimensions of the window at the pointer location to the default window size. The Restore Size command does not return windows to an iconic state.

Drag MENU onto the item and release MENU to restore the size of the window at the pointer location to the default size.

You can use the Restore Size command without displaying the Window menu by moving the pointer onto the window background and double-clicking SELECT.

Properties

Use the Properties item to display the application property window. You can set the following properties from this window:

☐ Window color
☐ Initial location
☐ Initial state
☐ Initial size
☐ Base window scale
☐ Pop-up window scale
☐ Manage windows
☐ Record current state

To display the Properties window, drag MENU onto the Properties item, and release MENU.

Window Color Category

Use this setting to change the default background color for the application window and its pop-up windows. The area to the right of the menu button shows the color that you chose from the Color button menu.

To return to the default color setting, move the pointer to the menu button and click SELECT. To choose a different color setting, move the pointer to the menu button, press MENU to display the Color menu, move the pointer to the color you want to set, and release MENU.

To apply the color setting to the application, click SELECT on the Apply button.

Current Color Setting

When the property window is displayed, this area shows the color setting that is used for the application window background. When you make another choice from the Window Color button menu, that color is shown in this area and is applied to the application windows when you click SELECT on the Apply button.

Color Menu Button

Use the menu under this menu button to view the palette of colors from which you can choose the window background of an application.

Color Menu

You use the Color menu to change the default window background color setting.

To choose a color from the palette, move the pointer to the menu button, press MENU, drag the pointer onto a color, and release MENU.

To apply the color setting to the application, click SELECT on the Apply button.

Initial Location Category

Use the Initial Location category to specify the location of the upper left corner of the application window on an x-y grid in which x = 0, y = 0 at the upper left corner of the workspace.

Default Setting

Click SELECT on the Default setting to return the settings to the application-specified initial location for the upper left corner of the base window. When you choose Default, the numeric text fields are not displayed.

Specified Setting

Click SELECT on the Specified setting to display the numeric fields for the x and y coordinates. Enter numbers into the numeric fields, and then click SELECT on the Apply button.

X Numeric Field

The number displayed in this field shows the x coordinate for the upper left corner of the application base window. You can type a new number in this field to change the x coordinate.

Click SELECT in the numeric field to set the active caret and highlight the default number. Type a new number.

To apply the setting, click SELECT on the Apply button.

Y Numeric Field

The number displayed in this field shows the y coordinate for the upper left corner of the application base window. You can type a new number in this field to change the y coordinate.

Click SELECT in the numeric field to set the active caret and highlight the default number. Type a new number.

To apply the setting, click SELECT on the Apply button.

Initial State Category

Use the Initial State category to set how the application window is displayed when you choose it from the Workspace menu. When you choose Window, the application is displayed as an opened window. When you choose Icon, the application is displayed as an icon.

Move the pointer to the Window or Icon setting and click SELECT. To apply the setting, click SELECT on the Apply button.

Initial Size Category

Use the Initial Size category to determine the total area of the base window for the application in units of rows and columns. When the property window is displayed, the current numbers of rows and columns are displayed in the numeric fields.

Rows Setting

Use the Rows numeric field to choose the number of rows for the base window of the application.

Move the pointer to the numeric field and click SELECT to set the active caret and highlight the default number. Type a new number.

Alternatively, you can click SELECT on the up or down arrows at the end of the numeric field to increment or decrement the number that is displayed in the field.

To apply the setting, click SELECT on the Apply button.

Columns Setting

Use the Columns numeric field to choose the number of columns for the base window of the application.

Move the pointer to the numeric field and click SELECT to set the active caret and highlight the default number. Type a new number.

Alternatively, you can click SELECT on the up or down arrow at the end of the numeric field to increment or decrement the number that is displayed in the field.

To apply the setting, click SELECT on the Apply button.

Increment/Decrement Buttons

Use the increment/decrement buttons to change the number in the numeric field. Click SELECT on the up arrow to display a smaller number. Click SELECT on the down arrow to display a larger number.

Record Current State

Use the Record Current State category to save the current configuration of an application's base windows, pop-up windows, and menu states and default settings. Clicking SELECT on the Base Window button enters the current location and size in the numeric fields of the property window.

To apply these settings, click SELECT on the Apply button.

Manage Windows

Use the Manage Windows category to determine whether the application base window and its pop-up windows are moved individually or as a group to the front or the back of the workspace when you click SELECT on the window background of a base window or when you choose Back from the base Window menu.

The Group Windows setting also determines whether or not the pop-up windows are moved with the base window when you change its location by dragging.

To apply the setting, click SELECT on the Apply button.

Base Window Scale

Use the Base Window Scale setting to choose the scaling size for the base window of the application.

Move the pointer to the drag area of the slider, press SELECT, and drag the pointer to the left to choose a smaller scaling size or to the right to choose a larger scaling size. Release SELECT. To apply the setting to the application base window, click SELECT on the Apply button.

Pop-up Window Scale

Use the Pop-up Window Scale setting to choose the scaling size for all the pop-up windows of the application. You cannot scale pop-up windows individually.

Move the pointer to the drag area of the slider, press SELECT, and drag the pointer to the left to choose a smaller scaling size or to the right to choose a larger scaling size. Release SELECT. To apply the setting to the pop-up windows, click SELECT on the Apply button.

Back

Use the Back item to move the window or icon at the pointer location to the back of the workspace and tuck it behind any overlapping windows and icons.

Drag MENU onto the item and release MENU to move the window or icon at the pointer location to the back of the workspace.

You can bring a window or icon to the front of the screen by selecting it. To select a window, move the pointer to the window background and click SELECT. To select an icon, move the pointer onto an icon and click SELECT.

Refresh

Use the Refresh item to redisplay the window or icon at the pointer location. Drag MENU onto the item and release MENU to refresh the window or icon.

Quit

Use the Quit item to exit the application and remove the window or icon from the workspace. If you have made changes to the application that have not been saved, a Notice is displayed asking you if you want to save the changes.

Drag MENU onto the item and release MENU to quit the application.

Pop-Up Window Menu

Use the Menu Background help text when the pointer is on the background of the pop-up Window menu. The following sections provide help text for each item of the pop-up Window menu.

Dismiss

When you remove pop-up windows from the workspace, they do not close to an icon. The label on the top menu item of the pop-up Window menu is Dismiss to show this distinction.

The Dismiss submenu has two choices:

☐ This Window
☐ All Pop-ups

When you use This Window, the pop-up window at the pointer location is dismissed.

When you use All Pop-ups, all the pop-up windows for the application are dismissed.

You can choose the default setting from the Dismiss submenu without displaying it by dragging MENU onto the Dismiss item and releasing MENU. To display the Dismiss submenu, drag MENU to the right in the Dismiss item. To choose an item from the Dismiss submenu, drag the pointer onto an item and release MENU.

Cancel

When you have made changes to a property window but have not applied those changes, the label on the top menu item of the pop-up window menu is Cancel to show you that the changes to the property window will be discarded when you dismiss it.

The Cancel submenu has two choices:

☐ This Window
☐ All Pop-ups

When you use This Window, the property window at the pointer location is dismissed.

When you use All Pop-ups, the property window and the rest of the pop-up windows for the application are dismissed.

You can choose the default setting from the Cancel submenu without displaying it by dragging MENU onto the Cancel item and releasing MENU. To display the Cancel submenu, drag MENU to the right in the Cancel item. To choose an item from the Cancel submenu, drag the pointer onto an item and release MENU.

This Window

Use This Window to dismiss the pop-up window at the pointer location.
Drag MENU onto the item and release MENU to dismiss selected windows.

All Pop-ups

Use All Pop-ups to dismiss all the pop-up windows for the application that are open on the workspace.

Drag MENU onto the item and release MENU to dismiss all pop-up windows for the application.

Back

Use the Back item to move the window at the pointer location to the back of the workspace, tucking it behind any overlapping windows and icons.

Drag MENU onto the item and release MENU to move selected windows and icons to the back of the workspace.

You can bring a window or icon to the front of the screen by selecting it. To select a window, move the pointer to the window background and click SELECT. To select an icon, move the pointer onto an icon and click SELECT.

Refresh

Use the Refresh item to redisplay the pop-up window at the pointer location. Drag MENU onto the item and release MENU to refresh selected windows.

Owner?

Use the Owner? item to identify the base window that originated the pop-up window. The title bar of the originating base window flashes and comes to the front of the screen.

Drag MENU onto the item and release MENU to locate the owner of the pop-up window at the pointer location.

Scrollbar Menu

Use the Menu Background help text when the pointer is on the background of the Scrollbar menu. The following sections provide help text for each item of the Scrollbar menu.

Here to Top

Use the Here to Top item to scroll the line at the pointer location to the top of the pane. Drag MENU onto the item and release MENU.

Here to Left

Use the Here to Left item to scroll the line at the pointer location to the left of the pane. Drag MENU onto the item and release MENU.

Top to Here

Use the Top to Here item to scroll the line at the top of the pane to the pointer location. Drag MENU onto the item and release MENU.

Left to Here

Use the Left to Here item to scroll the line at the left of the pane to the pointer location. Drag MENU onto the item and release MENU.

Previous

Use the Previous item to undo the last scrolling action and restore the view in the pane to its condition before the last scrolling action. Drag MENU onto the item and release MENU.

Split View

Use the Split View item to split a pane. Move the pointer into the scrollbar area and position it next to the place where you want to split the pane. Press MENU, drag the pointer onto the Split View item, and release MENU.

Join Views

Use the Join Views item to remove a pane that you created by splitting a pane. Move the pointer into the scrollbar area next to the pane you want to remove, press MENU, drag the pointer onto the Join Views item, and release MENU.

Appendix D

INTERNATIONAL CONSIDERATIONS FOR THE OPEN LOOK USER INTERFACE

The OPEN LOOK User Interface encourages international implementations to make it easy to localize the environment and applications.

The following sections describe fundamental issues to be considered in designing a system for multinational use. It is not intended to be a comprehensive list.

The most important functions needed to develop an international product are summarized here:

☐ Appropriate character sets
☐ Multiple orientation and direction of text
☐ A way to translate all visible text
☐ A way to localize dates, units, formats, colors, and symbols

Programmatic Interface

This section discusses the following categories that relate to developing an international OPEN LOOK UI programmatic interface:

☐ Character sets and fonts
☐ Text strings
☐ Text direction
☐ Formats, including interapplication exchange
☐ Layout
☐ Physical devices

Character Sets and Fonts

To support multinational functionality, it is very important for the programmatic interface to provide support for a suitable collection of character sets. The collection of character sets depends on the intended market and may be tailored to local needs. Most of the European languages can be supported by adding a small number of characters such as nonspacing accents to the ASCII (American Standard Code for Information Interchange) character set or by using ISO character sets.

International requirements differ for different markets. For example, a product designed primarily for the European market is unlikely to include a capability to display Asian character sets.

All software must handle characters from all supported sets in the collection. In particular, you must be able to type, display, edit, delete, and print all characters. When applications validate text, it must validate characters from all available character sets.

When considering fonts, remember that some character sets such as Asian languages support specific font heights, do not support text attributes such as bold, and do not have serifs.

The Virtual Keyboard that is defined as a Level 2 requirement for the OPEN LOOK UI provides a specified mechanism that you can use to view the current keyboard mapping and change between specified character sets.

Text Strings

All text that an application displays must be translatable. This includes text such as window titles, button and setting labels, menu items, error messages, and text that is displayed in Notices and help windows.

It is recommended that the programmatic interface provide a mechanism such as "message" or "resource" files to separate text strings from the program code. It may also be necessary for the programmatic interface to externalize the format of the strings as well as the text, since the order of arguments provided by the application may differ among languages.

Text Directions

The programmatic interface must support different directions of text flow, as specified below:

☐ Left to right for languages such as English
☐ Right to left for languages such as Arabic and Hebrew
☐ Vertical for some Asian languages

Multiple directions must also be supported. This is required so that an application can mix languages with different directions on the same screen. These are also required because certain languages, such as Japanese, require both horizontal and vertical typesetting. Other languages, such as Arabic, read characters from right to left and numbers from left to right.

Formats

In general, the programmatic interface must permit both users and translators to specify choices of formats, units, and sort sequences, and for applications to reflect the specified choices.

Consider the following when designing an international implementation:

☐ Languages have different punctuation types and rules.
☐ A word is defined differently in different languages. Japanese, for example, does not have spaces between "words." The language's definition of a word affects white space and word delimiter definitions.
☐ Formats and rules for numbers differ.
☐ Formats and rules for dates differ.
☐ Formats for calendars differ. For example, some countries define a week as Monday through Sunday, while others define it as Sunday through Saturday.
☐ Decimal and thousands separators differ. This issue also affects decimal-aligned tab formats.
☐ Standard page sizes differ, at both the workstation and the printer.
☐ Monetary units and rules differ.
☐ Units of measurement and rules differ.
☐ Sort orders and collating sequences vary or are inappropriate.
☐ Certain languages have specific requirements for placement of characters and prohibit some characters from displaying at the beginning of a line. Asian languages have many restrictions for character placement.
☐ When windows are resized, care must be taken to truncate text strings in a sensible way.
☐ Word wrapping must keep a nonspacing accented character with its associated character, treating it as a single unit.

Layout

The sizes of OPEN LOOK UI elements that contain text strings must not be hard-coded. Most text strings expand when translated from English to another language.

The programmatic interface should provide a facility that the application developer can use to measure the length of text strings and adjust the elements that contain the strings accordingly. Window placement and size should also use these measurements. Positions and layout of elements should be relative to one another to prevent overlapping elements or unneeded white space between elements when translation increases or decreases the length of the text strings.

When the application sizes windows dynamically using this measurement facility, it is possible that the contents may not fit on the screen at the required size and place. It is strongly recommended that all windows have resize handles and scrollbars.

Physical Devices

Consider the variety of physical keyboards and pointing devices that may be used with your implementation. A virtual input mechanism that allows these devices to be mapped is extremely useful.

Consider international standards for communications protocols when designing a programmatic interface.

OPEN LOOK UI Elements

This section addresses the issues of font size, direction of text flow, and localization for OPEN LOOK UI elements.

Font Size

This specification defines elements relative to the size of the characters in the default system font. Some languages require a larger minimum point size than that for English. When larger characters such as accented or Asian characters are part of the default system font, the implementation should scale all the elements to accommodate the height and width of the font characters. The window shown in Figure D-1 is an example of a base window in a Japanese implementation.

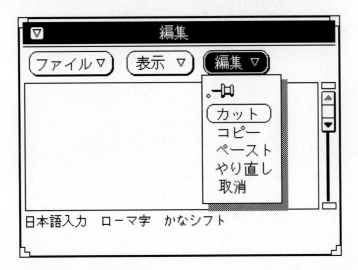

Figure D-1   A base window for a Japanese implementation.

The application developer must consider the following additional factors:

☐ The icon label area may be too small to accommodate the default system font.
☐ The definition of text baseline may change depending on the font. The text baseline for Kanji, for example, is different from that of English.
☐ Windows, including help and property windows, must have resize corners, and panes must have scrollbars, since larger fonts may make the windows too large.

Direction of Text Flow

The direction in which text flows in the local language affects the orientation of OPEN LOOK UI elements. Window header and scrollbar placement, control orientation, menu group displays, and pointer orientation are all linked to the primary text direction in the native language. For example, in a language that reads vertically and from right to left, the following changes might be appropriate:

☐ The header is displayed at the right side of the window.

☐ The horizontal scrollbar is the primary scrollbar. The top of the scrollbar is to the right, and the elevator is, therefore, initially positioned on the right.

☐ Controls in the control area are arrayed vertically, top to bottom, and right to left.

☐ The basic pointer points to the upper right corner of the screen, opposite to the direction of text flow.

☐ The light source for shadows is the upper right corner of the screen.

Localization

Other elements of the OPEN LOOK UI that should be considered for localization are:

☐ Color has special local meaning. Some colors are taboo in certain cultures. The concept of background and foreground may be reversed.

☐ Symbols often need to be localized. For example, the pushpin may be an unfamiliar glyph, and a check mark has an opposite connotation in some cultures.

☐ Characters from languages with large character sets and inflection distinctions such as Kanji or Chinese require careful consideration to present unambiguous information.

When developing a toolkit for international markets, consider the issues discussed in this appendix as a preliminary checklist. The languages and character sets to be supported determine the scope of development work required and the issues to be considered.

GLOSSARY

Abbreviated button

A button can be displayed as a small square with a glyph inside the border. Abbreviated buttons function just like buttons.

Abbreviated menu button

A menu button can be displayed as a small square with a hollow triangle inside the border. The triangle points downward when the menu is displayed below the menu button, and to the right when the menu is displayed to the right. The current setting is usually displayed to the right of the abbreviated menu button. Abbreviated menu buttons function just like menu buttons.

Abbreviated scrollbar

When a split pane is too small to display a complete scrollbar or a scrollbar without a cable, an abbreviated scrollbar is displayed. The abbreviated scrollbar has cable anchors and up and down arrows.

Accelerator

A key or sequence of keys on the keyboard or multiple clicks of mouse buttons that quickly perform specific menu or application functions without using a menu.

ADJUST mouse button

The mouse button that is used to adjust (extend or reduce) selections.

Arrow button

An abbreviated button with a solid triangular glyph inside the border that is used for scrolling. An arrow button is a specific kind of abbreviated button.

ASCII	American Standard Code for Information Interchange.
Automatic scrolling	When not all of a file is visible in a window, the view in a pane automatically shifts to follow the movement of the pointer as you press SELECT and wipe through the data.
Back	An item on the Window menu that is used to move the window or icon to the back of the screen.
Base window	The primary window for an application.
Basic pointer	An arrow pointing northeast that shows the mouse position on the workspace.
Binding	Logically connecting data files, icons, and images to File Manager functionality.
Bottom cable anchor	The button at the bottom of a scrollbar cable.
Bounding box	A rectangle that is displayed on the screen to define a region for selection.
Busy pattern	A standard pattern displayed in the header of a window or in the border of a button to show that the application is temporarily performing a function and cannot accept input.
Busy pointer	A stopwatch is displayed by the system when an application is busy and cannot accept input.
Button	A one-choice element of a control area or a menu. Buttons are used to execute commands (command button), display pop-up windows (window button), or to display menus (menu button).
Button menu	A menu that is displayed when the pointer is on a menu button and you press MENU.

Cable	The scrollbar cable represents the total size of the data that you can view in the pane. The elevator moves up and down the cable to show the position of the view into the data.
Cable anchor	The buttons at the ends of the scrollbar cable.
Cancel	To remove a property window from the screen when it has settings that have been modified but not applied.
CANCEL	A Level 1 pop-up window accelerator that you use to dismiss the pop-up window without choosing an action.
Caret	Windows that accept keyboard input display a caret to show the insert point. An active caret is a solid triangle that may blink. An inactive caret is a dimmed diamond.
Categories	Groups of like settings in a property window.
Change bars	Solid vertical lines on the left side of property window panes that show that a setting has been modified but not applied.
Character encoding	A mapping of codes, usually binary, to each character in a corresponding character set.
Character set	Any collection of characters for display on the screen or printer. These include alphabet, digit, punctuation, and special characters. Sets are usually named and ordered so that codes may be associated with each member. The character set is independent of font, which defines the exact appearance of each character in the set.
CHARBAK	A Level 2 text caret motion function that you use to move the insert point backward one character.

CHARFWD	A Level 2 text caret motion function that you use to move the insert point forward one character.
Check boxes ☑ ☐	A nonexclusive setting that shows a check mark in a square box when the setting is chosen.
Click	To press a mouse button once and release it without moving the pointer beyond the damping factor.
Click-to-type	You set the insert point by clicking SELECT in an area of the screen that accepts keyboard input.
Clipboard	The clipboard keeps track of data that are cut or copied. The Paste key is used to insert information from the clipboard into a pane. The contents of the clipboard are viewed in a window that is accessed from the Workspace menu. An item on the Workspace Utilities submenu displays a window that shows the contents of the clipboard.
Close	A choice on the base Window menu that is used to change the visual representation from a window to an icon. When Close is chosen, only the visual representation of the window is changed, and the item name toggles to Open. See also "Open."
COLUMNBAK	A Level 2 text caret movement function that you use to move the insert point up one line in the current column (or to the end of the line if the column is past the end of the previous line).
COLUMNFWD	A Level 2 text caret movement function that you use to move the insert point down one line in the current column (or to the end of the line if the column is past the end of the previous line).
Command window	A pop-up window that is used to execute application commands or set parameters.

Command button	A button that you use to execute application commands.
Command item	An item on a menu that you use to execute application commands.
CONSTRAIN	A Level 1 mouse modifier function that you use to constrain the direction of a dragging operation to only the x or y coordinate, depending on the direction in which you move the pointer to initiate dragging.
Control area	An unbordered region of a window where controls such as buttons, settings, and text fields are displayed.
Controls	Objects in a control area, a pane, or on a menu that are used to perform an action. Controls include buttons, items on menus, exclusive and nonexclusive settings, sliders, gauges, text fields, and check boxes.
Copy	Duplicating text or graphics. The Copy key is used to copy selected text or graphics to the clipboard.
COPY	A Level 1 core function that you use to put a copy of the selected object onto the clipboard and then delete the object from the workspace. This key can also be used as a mouse modifier for Quick Move operations.
Core functions	Essential functions that are always available from the keyboard. These functions can also be provided on buttons in control areas or on menus.
Current item	An active item in a scrolling list.
Cut	To remove selected text or graphics from a window and store them on the clipboard.

CUT	A Level 1 core function that you use to put a copy of the selected object onto a clipboard and then delete the object from the workspace. This key can also be used as a mouse modifier for Quick Move operations.
Cut/copy/paste	Functions that are provided from keys on the keyboard and that use the clipboard to store and transfer text and graphics.
Damping factor	The number of pixels you can move the pointer before a drag is initiated.
Default ring	The default button in a pop-up window has a ring displayed inside the button border. The default item on a menu or submenu has a 1-point ring around the item when an item is not highlighted.

Default icon region	The side of the screen (top, bottom, left, or right) the icon moves to the first time it is displayed.
DEFAULTACTION	A Level 1 pop-up window accelerator that you use to execute the default button action and dismiss the pop-up window.
DELCHARBAK	A Level 2 text caret motion function that you use to delete the character to the left of the insert point.
DELCHARFWD	A Level 2 text caret motion function that you use to delete the character to the right of the insert point.
DELLINEBAK	A Level 2 text caret motion function that you use to delete from the insert point to the beginning of the line.
DELLINE	A Level 2 text caret motion function that you use to delete the entire current line.
DELLINEFWD	A Level 2 text caret motion function that you use to delete from the insert point to the end of the line.
DELWORDBAK	A Level 2 text caret motion function that you use to delete the word to the left of the insert point.

524

DELWORDFWD	A Level 2 text caret motion function that you use to delete the word to the right of the insert point.
Dimmed controls	An inactive control is dimmed. It cannot accept input from the mouse or the keyboard.
Direct manipulation	To move or copy a selected object by dragging it.
Dismiss	To remove a menu or a pop-up window from the screen. Also, an item on the pop-up Window menu. Since pop-up windows do not have an iconic form and closing a window, by definition, means changing its visual representation to an icon, "dismiss" is used instead.
DOCEND	A Level 2 text caret movement function that you use to move the insert point after the last printable character of the document. When the insert point is already there, there is no action.
DOCSTART	A Level 2 text caret movement function that you use to move the insert point before the first character of the document. When the insert point is already there, the caret is not moved.
Double-click	Clicking twice on a mouse button is an accelerator that performs a specific function without using a menu.
DUPLICATE	A Level 1 mouse modifier function that you use to copy the selected object by dragging.
Duplicate pointer	The duplicate pointer is displayed when you copy an object by dragging.
Drag	To press and hold down any mouse button while moving the pointer—and the object under the pointer—on the screen.

Drag area	The area in the middle of the scrollbar elevator or slider.
Drop shadow	The 75 percent gray pattern to the right and below the border of a menu.
Elevator	The part of the scrollbar that has up and down arrows and a drag area. The elevator rides the scrollbar cable and shows the position of the view in the pane relative to the total data available.
Embedded objects	Objects that are nested in other containers, typically frames, either of the same or a different type.
Exclusive setting	A control that is used for mutually exclusive settings and is shown by touching rectangles. The chosen setting is shown with a bold border around it.
File Manager	The file management application used in an OPEN LOOK UI implementation to load, store, and browse through files from the workspace and from within an application.
Font	A complete set of characters in one typeface and size.
Footer	The bottom area of a window. The footer is used by an application for information and error messages.
Full Size	To increase the size of a window to its maximum. The specifications are determined by the application. Full Size is an item on the Window menu that allows you to perform that function. After you make a window full size, the label in the item toggles to Restore Size.

526

Gauge	A read-only control that shows the percent of use or the portion of an action that has been completed.

Glyph	A picture or graphic representation of an object.
Grab handles	The small squares that are displayed at the corners and midpoints of the region that defines a selected graphic object.
Halation	The effect of screen elements "glowing" and giving off light.
Header	The band across the top of every window. Each header has a centered title. Base windows have a Window menu button on the left. Pop-up windows have a pushpin on the left.
Help	An OPEN LOOK UI implementation provides on-screen help for each element in a window. The application provides help for application functions and elements. The Help function must be available from the keyboard.
HELP	A Level 1 core function that you use to display a Help window for the object under the pointer.
Highlighting	A visual indication that an object is in a special state. In monochrome implementations the visual indication is reverse video. In color implementations, the user can set the selection highlighting color. Button highlighting is shown by a pseudo three-dimensional effect.
Hot spot	The place on the pointer that determines the exact spot on the screen where an action is performed.
Icon	A small pictorial representation of a base window. Displaying objects as icons conserves screen real estate while keeping the window available for easy access.

Important message	A message from the operating system or an application that provides information that is essential to continued operation.
Inactive controls	An inactive control is dimmed. It cannot accept input from the mouse or the keyboard.
Indeterminate state	When the application cannot clearly show all the attributes of a selected object, the borders for settings that are indeterminate are dimmed. The label and setting names are not dimmed.
Input area	The place on the screen that accepts keyboard input. Click SELECT to set the insert point in the input area (click-to-type).
Insert point	The specific location in the input area where keyboard input is displayed. When you set the insert point, an active caret is displayed.
Internationalization	A way of writing applications that facilitates translation to other languages. Generally, key names, prompts, messages, and warnings are grouped in separate files that are not part of the application code.
Keyboard accelerator	A key or sequence of keys on the keyboard or multiple clicks of mouse buttons that quickly perform specific menu or application functions without using a menu.
Keyboard equivalent	Keyboards and mice are not the same from system to system. An OPEN LOOK UI implementation provides specific default key sequences to provide uniform functionality when specific keys or mouse buttons are not available on a system. You can change the default keyboard equivalents from the Workspace Properties window.
Keyboard input	To type alphanumeric characters from the keyboard at the insert point, a place on the screen that accepts text.

Label	The title of a button, item, or setting that describes it function.
Layer	Windows and icons that overlap one another on the workspace.
Levels	Different parts of a hierarchical structure that can be accessed in a scrolling list.
Menu	A rectangle containing a group of controls. Menus are displayed in two ways: from a menu button with choices appropriate to the menu button label (button menu) and from any place on the screen that is not a control (pop-up menu). The pop-up menu displays choices appropriate to the pointer location.
Menu button (**Menu Button** ▽)	A multiple-choice element of a control area. A menu button always has a menu mark and is used to display a menu.
Menu items **Command Item** **Window Item...** **Menu Item** ▷	A menu contains items that you can use to execute commands, display a pop-up window, or display a submenu.
Menu mark ▽ ▷	A hollow triangle in the border of a button or following a menu item that has a submenu attached to it. The triangle points to where the menu or submenu is displayed.
MENU mouse button	The mouse button that is used to display menus.
Menu group	A menu and its associated submenus.
Message	Information generated by an application that informs you about the status of a process.
More arrow ≫	A small, nonscrollable triangle that is displayed at the end of text in the header or footer of a window that has been truncated during a resize operation.

More button	A button an application can add to its Help window to allow you to access other types of on-line help such as on-line documentation.
Mouse	An electronic or mechanical device that you use to select and manipulate information on a computer screen.
Move pointer	When you move an object by dragging, the move pointer is displayed.
Multi-click	Clicking a mouse button rapidly a specific number of times. Multi-clicking is usually an accelerator for functions that can be accessed in other ways.
NEXTFIELD	A Level 1 text field navigation function that you use to move the caret to the next input area in the pane and select the contents of the field. When the caret is in the last input area, the caret moves to the first input area.
NEXTWINDOW	A Level 2 input area navigation accelerator that you use to cycle the active input area to the next window (least recently used).
Nonexclusive setting **Bold** Italic	A list of nonexclusive choices indicated by separated rectangles. The chosen settings are surrounded by a bold border.
Normal message	A message that is displayed in the footer of a window to inform you about the status of a requested operation.
Normalization	Moving scrolled objects in discrete units so that a defined unit is always visible in the pane. For example, normalized text scrolls line by line. Characters in a line are never chopped in half.

Notice	When an application generates warning and error messages that require an action before you can proceed, a Notice is displayed that blocks input to the application until you click on one of the buttons in the Notice pop-up window.
Open	An item on the window menu that is used to open an icon to a window. When the icon is opened, the title on the item toggles to Close. See also "Close."
OPEN LOOK™	A registered trademark of AT&T.
PAGE	A Level 2 scrolling accelerator. Page scrolling operations are defined by application-specific accelerators. These accelerators are usually mapped to PAGEUP, PAGEDOWN, HOME, and END on a keyboard.
Page-oriented scrollbar	A scrollbar with a box that shows the current page number when you press SELECT on the drag area of the elevator. The box expands and contracts to the left to accommodate different numbers of digits.
Palette	A set of coordinated colors provided for defining the color of the workspace, window background, selection, and caret.
PAN	A Level 1 mouse modifier function that you use to scroll the contents of a pane by panning.
Pane	A bordered rectangle in a window where the application displays its data.
Panning	A method of scrolling in which you directly drag the contents of the pane instead of using the scrollbar.
Panning pointer	When you initiate panning, the pointer bends down to hold the image to it while it is being dragged. The point of the arrow is the hot spot.

Paste	To insert data from the clipboard into a window. Selected data are placed on the clipboard with the Copy or Cut key.
PASTE	A Level 1 core function that you use to insert a copy of the data on a clipboard at the insert point. This key can also be used as a mouse modifier for Quick Move operations.
Picture frame corners	See "Resize corners."
Pinned menu	A menu that has its pushpin pushed in. A pinned menu is a pop-up window and remains on the workspace until you dismiss it.
Pixel	An abbreviation for picture element; the smallest unit of display on a video screen.
Point	The standard typographical unit of measurement, equal to approximately 1/72 of an inch (0.352 millimeters).
Pointer	Any graphic representation of the location of the mouse on the screen. See also "Basic pointer," "Busy pointer," "Duplicate pointer," "Move pointer," "Panning pointer," "Text duplicate pointer," and "Text move pointer."
Pointer jumping	When the pointer automatically moves to a specific location, such as to a Notice or a pop-up window.
POINTERDOWN	A Level 2 pointer movement function that you use to move the pointer down one pixel (repeats and accelerates).
POINTERLEFT	A Level 2 pointer movement function that you use to move the pointer left one pixel (repeats and accelerates).

POINTERRIGHT	A Level 2 pointer movement function that you use to move the pointer right one pixel (repeats and accelerates).
POINTERUP	A Level 2 pointer movement function that you use to move the pointer up one pixel (repeats and accelerates).
Pop-up menu	A menu that you access by pressing MENU on any area of the workspace that is not a control. The menu that is displayed depends on the location of the mouse pointer.
Pop-up window	A window that pops up to perform a specific function and is then dismissed. Command windows, property windows, Help windows and Notices are all pop-up windows.
Pop-up Window menu	The Window menu that is displayed when you press MENU on the background of a pop-up window.
Press	To push and hold a mouse button.
PREVFIELD	A Level 1 text field navigation function that you use to move the caret to the previous input area in the pane and select the contents of the field. When the caret is in the first input area, moves the caret to the last input area.
PREVWINDOW	A Level 2 input area navigation accelerator that you use to cycle the active input area to the previous (most recently used) window.
Programs	An item on the Workspace menu that displays a submenu with a list of application programs that can be accessed from the workspace.
Properties	Characteristics of an object that you can set, such as the color of a window.
PROPERTIES	A Level 1 core function that you use to display a property window for the selected object.

Property window	A pop-up window that is used to set properties associated with an object, an application, or a window.
Proportion indicator	The dark area of the scrollbar cable shows the proportion of data that is currently viewed in the pane, relative to the total length of the cable, which represents the total size.
Pushpin	A glyph that can be used to keep a menu, property window, or command window displayed on the screen.
Question mark pointer	The pointer that is displayed when you click or press a mouse button and the window manager cannot perform an action. This pointer is also displayed if you drag an object to an inappropriate destination.
Quick Duplicate	A means of copying text without changing the existing text selection.
Quick Move	A means of moving text without changing the existing text selection.
Quit	To exit an application. Quit is an item on both the Window menu (quit the window) and the Workspace menu (quit the workspace).
Refresh	An item on the Window menu that redisplays an icon or the contents of the window. Also an item on the Workspace menu that is used to redisplay all the windows and icons on the workspace.
Release	To stop pressing a mouse button.
Reserved area	An area of the screen that is reserved for the display of icons and a certain class of applications. See also "Virtual edge."

Resize corner	Windows that can be resized have a resize area in each corner. These areas provide unconstrained resizing of the boundaries of the window without changing the scale of the contents of the window.
Resize handles	When you select a pane that can be resized, resize handles are displayed on the sides of the pane that can be adjusted.
Restore Size	To return a window to its size before it was displayed at full size. Also, an item on the Window menu that allows you to perform that function. After you restore the size of a window, the label in the item toggles to Full Size.
Sans serif	Type styles that do not have serifs, small cross-strokes or ornaments at the ends of the main strokes making up a character.
Scale	To make everything in the window bigger or smaller while keeping all elements of the window proportional to one another, and the contents anchored at the upper left corner. You choose the scale for base or pop-up windows from the application property window.
Scrollbar	The scrollbar is used to move the view of the data displayed in the pane.
Scrollbar menu	Each scrollbar has a pop-up menu that is used to reposition the data in the pane.
SCROLLBOTTOM	A Level 2 scrolling accelerator that you use to scroll the view to the bottom of the pane (same as clicking SELECT on the bottom cable anchor).
SCROLLDOWN	A Level 2 scrolling accelerator that you use to scroll the view down one screen (same as moving the pointer to the cable below the elevator of a vertical scrollbar and clicking SELECT).

Scrolling	Moving through data that cannot be viewed entirely in a pane.
Scrolling button	An abbreviated button with a solid triangular arrowhead inside the border that is used for scrolling.
Scrolling list	A pane containing a list of text fields. The list can be read-only or it can be editable.
SCROLLLEFT	A Level 2 scrolling accelerator that you use to scroll the view left one screen (same as moving the pointer to the cable left of the elevator of a horizontal scrollbar and clicking SELECT).
SCROLLLEFTEDGE	A Level 2 scrolling accelerator that you use to scroll the view to the left edge of the pane (same as clicking SELECT on the left cable anchor).
SCROLLRIGHT	A Level 2 scrolling accelerator that you use to scroll the view right one screen (same as moving the pointer to the cable right of the elevator of a horizontal scrollbar and clicking SELECT).
SCROLLRIGHTEDGE	A Level 2 scrolling accelerator that you use to scroll the view to the right edge of the pane (same as clicking SELECT on the right cable anchor).
SCROLLTOP	A Level 2 scrolling accelerator that you use to scroll the view to the top of the pane (same as clicking SELECT on the top cable anchor).
SCROLLUP	A Level 2 scrolling accelerator that you use to scroll the view up one screen (same as moving the pointer to the cable above the elevator of a vertical scrollbar and clicking SELECT).
Select	To distinguish an object or objects on the screen so that they can be operated on.
SELECT mouse button	The mouse button that is used to select objects, set the insert point, manipulate controls, and drag objects.

Select-then-operate paradigm	You select an object and then choose an operation from a menu (or the keyboard) to perform on the selected object. The object (or objects) for selection can be text or graphics within an application, or a pane, a window, or an icon.
SELCHARFWD	A Level 2 text selection function that you use to adjust the selection one character forward.
SELLINEFWD	A Level 2 text selection function that you use to adjust the selection to the end of the current line, then lines forward.
SELWORDFWD	A Level 2 text selection function that you use to adjust the selection to the end of the current word, then words forward.
SETMENUDEFAULT	A Level 1 mouse modifier function that you use display menu defaults and to set the current item in the menu as the default.
Shrink	To resize a window so that its area is reduced.
Slider	Sliders are used to set a numeric value and give a visual indication of the setting.
Split	To divide a pane into parts, using the cable anchors of the scrollbar.
Stay-up menus	Menus stay up on the screen when you click MENU. They remain on the screen until you choose an item or dismiss them.
STOP	A Level 2 core function that you use to cancel pending operations in the window under the pointer.
Submenu	A menu that displays additional choices under a menu item on a menu.
Table	A display of data in rows and columns.

Target pointer	The halo that is displayed around the hot spot of the basic pointer when the pointer is on the border of a narrow or small object.
Text duplicate pointer	The pointer that is displayed when you are copying text directly by dragging.
Text move pointer	The pointer that is displayed when you are moving text directly by dragging.
Text field	An area in a window into which you type text from the keyboard.
Tiling	Panes that are laid out separately in a window so that they do not overlap.
Title	The name of the application or function that is displayed at the top of a window or a pop-up menu.
TOGGLEINPUT	A Level 2 text caret movement function that you use to toggle the input area to the most recently used window.
Toolkit	A set of programming components used to build applications.
Top cable anchor	The button at the top of a scrollbar.
Transitory window	Another way of referring to a pop-up window.
Unbind	Logically disconnecting data files, icons, and images from File Manager functionality.
Undo	To return an object to its state before you performed the last operation. Levels of undo are determined by the application.
UNDO	A Level 1 core function that you use to undo the last operation. If the last operation is an undo, it restores the last operation.

Unpinned menu	A menu with a pushpin that is not pinned to the workspace. When you make a choice from an unpinned menu, the action is performed and the menu is dismissed.
Up-down encoded	A keyboard that can discriminate between pressing a key down and releasing it.
Validate	To have the application verify that the contents of a text field are appropriate to the function.
Virtual edge	A Workspace Properties setting that permits you to define an artificial edge of the screen. The area between the virtual edge and the actual edge of the screen is reserved for the display of icons and certain specified application windows. See also Reserved Area.
Virtual keyboard	An image of the keyboard that is displayed in a window and that you can use to change the mapping of keys, specify international character sets, and bind accelerators.
Window background	The area outside any panes, including the header, footer, and sides of the window.
Window button	A button that you use to display a window containing additional controls.
Window item	An item on a menu that you use to display a window containing additional controls.
Window mark	The three dots (...) that are displayed following the button label on window buttons, and following a window item on a menu.
Window menu	The menu that is accessed from the background of a window. Pop-up windows have a window menu with slightly different choices from those of the base window menu.

Window menu button ▽	The abbreviated menu button that is always displayed at the left of the header that you can use to execute the default setting on the Window menu (by clicking SELECT) and to display the Window menu (by pressing MENU).
Wipe-through selection	Pressing SELECT and moving the pointer through objects to be selected (text or graphics).
WORDFWD	Level 2 text caret movement function that you use to move the insert point after the last printable character of the next word, not including any end-of-line character when the word is at the end of a line (or the current word if the insert point is within a word).
Workspace	The background screen area on which windows and icons are displayed.
Workspace menu	The menu that controls global functions.
Workspace Properties window	The property window accessed from the Workspace menu that allows you to customize your workspace environment.

INDEX

A

541

default, 72, 137
dimmed, 329
help, 496
help window, 88
menu, 142, 150, 317, 326, 469
menu default, 150, 334
pinned, 424
    dimensions, 424
pop-up window, help, 497
pop-up window header, 419
states, 72, 74
unpinned, 422
    dimensions, 423

Q

quadruple-click selection, 376
question mark pointer, 38, 96, 411
quick duplicate, 369, 381
    read-only messages, 381
quick move, 369, 385
quit, 14
Quit button, 224
Quit item, 228
    help, 509
quitting, multiple base windows, 57

R

read-only gauge, 117
read-only messages, 17, 124
    quick duplicate, 381
    summary table, 125
rearranging, removed panes, 364
record current, 83
record current state, 85, 86, 507
reference keyboard, 308
Refresh item, 222, 223, 228, 230

help, 501, 508, 511
region
    application, 201
    default icon, 47
    interface, 201
related panes, resizing, 363
release, 10
removing
    dimmed highlighting, 397
    multiple splits, 364
    split pane, 169, 171, 364
Replace function, 52
replacing, text, 371
required elements
    command window, 71
    property window, 75
required menus, 221
    adding choices to, 20
    Edit menu for text fields, 19, 119, 221
    pop-up Window menu, 19, 221
    Scrollbar menu, 19, 221
    Scrolling List menus, 19, 181, 221
    Settings menu, 19, 77
    Window menu, 19, 221
    Workspace menu, 19, 221
reserved areas, 36, 47, 223
Reset button, 75
    help, 498
Reset item, 231
    help, 499
resize corners, 13, 26, 52, 53, 353, 417
    command window, 72
    dimensions, 417
    help, 493
    Help window, 484
    Window Controls pop-up, 224
resize handles, 358, 433–34
    help, 493
    using, 358, 359
resizing, 26
    border box, 354

File Manager base window, 269
pane contents, 354
panes, 56
pop-up window, 56
window behavior, 54
Restore Size item, 227
    help, 504
restoring, insert point, 71
restraint, color, 201
Return, scan code, 310
Return key, 310
ring, default, 96
ROWDOWN, 299
Rows setting, help, 506
ROWUP, 299

S

sans serif font, 5
save configuration, window properties, 74
scale, 27
    at startup, 257
    base window, 30, 85
    pop-up window, 30
    sizes, 87
    windows, 87
scan codes, 310
screen edge
    bumping, 352
    submenu placement, 337
screen resolution, engineering drawings, 407
scrollable text pane, 55
scrollbar, 13, 52, 55, 155, 436
    abbreviated, 157, 441
    abbreviated dimensions, 442
    area, 157
    cable, 18, 158
        help, 495
        proportion indicator, 159
    cable anchors, 162